People

in Projects

People
in Projects

Project Management Institute

Library of Congress Cataloging-in-Publication Data

People in projects.
     p.   cm.
Includes bibliographical references and index.
   ISBN: 1-880410-72-9 (alk. paper)
   1. Project management. 2. Personnel management. I. Project Management Institute.

HD69.P75 P463 2001
658.3--dc21
                                    2001041870
                                          CIP

ISBN: 1-880410-72-9

Published by: Project Management Institute, Inc.
               Four Campus Boulevard
               Newtown Square, Pennsylvania 19073-3299 USA
               Phone +610-356-4600 or visit our website: www.pmi.org

10 9 8 7 6 5 4 3 2 1

Contents

SECTION 8—WORLDWIDE TEAMS AND CULTURAL ISSUES

SECTION 9—MANAGING CHANGE

Foreword

Jeffrey K. Pinto, Ph.D.,
Samuel A. and Elizabeth B. Breene Fellow and
Professor of Management, Penn State-Erie

One of the most common snares people fall into when beginning to engage in project-based work is to assume that because there are well-defined tools and techniques already extant (PERT/CPM, earned value, duration estimation, and so on), project management is somehow more "objective" than other innovative practices or management disciplines. That is, the easy lure lies in assuming that project management has somehow solved its "people" problems and progressed to the point when all activities become technique driven. For those with even minimal project management experience, we know that nothing could be further from the truth. Project management is fortunate in possessing a rich and growing body of tools and metrics that aid in helping us to more effectively run our projects, but that is all they are: tools and metrics. Project management is no less prone to the problems inherent in managing people than any other discipline. In fact, a strong argument could be made that project management offers far more people problems than other forms of corporate activities.

The reasons become obvious when we think of the project challenge as a simple cooking exercise. Take one disparate group of individuals with (most likely) dual loyalties; add problems with motivation, team building, and leadership; stir in time pressures, shrinking budgets, and other constraints; add unrealistic upper-management expectations; and finally blend in only rudimentary levels of project management training and experience (in most organizations). Every reader can see that we have created a recipe for disaster. And yet ... it is also the recipe for sometimes dramatic successes, measured in terms of market share and profits, technical achievements, and enduring customer/contractor relationships. The key, I am convinced, lies in how we manage these problems—hence the "people challenge" of project management.

This book is a collection of some of the most important writing relating to the people side of project management that the Project Management Institute has ever produced. The topics are far ranging, and the authors are acknowledged experts in their fields. Section One (Key Management Skills and Duties) sets the stage for the balance of the book by first addressing the leadership challenge in project management. In previous writings I have long maintained that project management is one of the most "leader-intensive" undertakings within organizations today. Section One develops this theme throughout a series of articles by noted experts in the area. Section Two (Organizational Planning) expands the readers' horizons to move beyond the core skills of the project manager to understanding the nature of networking and relationship building, both with the project team and with other key stakeholders. Section Three (Human Resource Theory) asks project managers to get involved: with staff development and stakeholder planning. Effective projects are not run solely by the team leader but are an extension of a dedicated and motivated team all rowing in the same direction. Section Four (Staff Acquisition and Kickoff) shows us how to set the stage correctly, both by finding the best people for the project team and by creating an initial positive environment from which downstream success can more easily flow.

Section Five (Team Development) is one of the most powerful parts of the book. Project managers feeling frustration from their perceived inability to get team buy-in and positive development will find this a welcome set of articles that addresses the heart of the project leadership challenge. The next section (Resolving Conflict) is also an important component of this book. Anyone who has tried to create a high-functioning project team has had to deal with a great deal of residual conflict. Conflict is not a poor reflection on the project manager's efforts—far from it. Conflict is the natural side effect of any effort made toward enhancing cooperation. The key for successful project management lies not in eliminating conflict but, once it has arisen, in acting most appropriately to minimize its negative effects. Section Seven (Closeout and Evaluation) is another gem that focuses on what has rightly been called the "forgotten phase" of the project. Properly handled, project closeout sows the seeds for future team motivation and success. Done poorly, closeout becomes another source of burnout and team member cynicism. Section Eight (Worldwide Teams and Cultural Issues) reflects a rapidly growing trend in project management toward geographically dispersed project organizations. I have held a number of conversations over the past several years with project managers who complain that the difficulties in making a project work when everyone is around are hard enough. How are they to pull this off when their "team" consists of seven people in six different time zones? The challenges of multi-location project teams are not likely to wane in the short term; indeed, they will continue to grow. Finally, the concluding section on Managing Change puts the burden squarely on all readers to anticipate the likely future trends in project management. We are getting a sense of where we are. Anticipating where we are going, on the other hand, offers an entirely new sort of challenge.

One thing we do know: the challenge of managing people within the unique context of project-based work continues to confound and frustrate us. We want our projects to run smoothly, somehow conveniently, forgetting along the way that the only "smooth" projects are those that are characterized by high-performing project leaders and their teams. It is with this very challenge squarely in mind that the Project Management Institute and the PMI Publishing Division created this book. Its chapters are diverse but share an important common feature: experts who know whereof they speak have written them. No marginally useful theory here—this is the real deal. As a result, any project manager, whether a seasoned professional or newly minted beginner, will find a wealth of information on every page. I wish you all good reading and good future project practice!

Introduction

Galadriel LaVere

This book was the beginning of a project for me. A project to create a book focusing on one of the nine knowledge areas of *A Guide to the Project Management Body of Knowledge (PMBOK® Guide)*. As a beginner with this project and with project management, I didn't know what to expect, what steps I would take, the problems I would encounter, or the outcome.

I started at the logical place: the *PMBOK® Guide*. Reading through the knowledge areas, I have to admit that one word came to mind: stuffy. Being a book-editor intern from Western Carolina University, I did not have a specific interest in project management and—not to stereotype—but as an English major, the technical side of project management did not interest me.

Seeing it as my only chance for interest, I decided to go with human resource (HR) management. Honestly, I was still expecting stuffiness. But I found out very quickly that there is another side to project management. And, contrary to some beliefs, it is a very important side. The stuffiness I expected was replaced by the human side of project management.

After reading this wealth of knowledge, ideas, and advice by the enclosed authors I hope you can truly see how important the people are on your teams. Not for their technical expertise or for the money they bring to your corporation, but for their personalities, their individuality, and their own creativity and for what these traits bring to the workplace. Learning to deal with these differences and cultivate their rewards will bring great things to your projects. The way to do this is with HR skills.

Can you imagine a project succeeding without proper leadership qualities? I'm sure that there is the rare example of team members that take all the initiative upon themselves and manage to succeed, but, as I said, that's a "rare" example. What about a project team without the proper training or mentoring? How far will an international team with no training in cultural differences and sensitivity get? How can a project be successful if there is strife between the team members, a lack of shared vision, or confusion because of conflicting ideas that have never been discussed?

It is part of the job of being project manager to evoke and contain the qualities necessary to put together the best, most effective project team. While this does include the skills necessary to carry out risk analysis, evaluate cost, and procure resources, all of these can be ineffective if the project team is unable to work together in a productive manner.

On a basic level, the people skills are the most important. As Greg Hutchins states in one of the articles in this book, "The project manager is a role player." All of the roles that Hutchins mentions are intertwined with HR skills. If a team cannot work together effectively on a project, how successful will it be in reaching the completion of a project? And if it does reach completion, what quality will the end product be?

People are the building blocks of all projects; I would say that they are the foundation. Focusing on HR skills can only build stronger teams, techniques, and end products. Reading this book will help you focus.

Section 1

Key Management Skills and Duties

Project Leadership Means Role Playing

Greg Hutchins, PE

PM Network 30 (April 2000)

Great project leaders are chameleons. Don't get me wrong; they are genuine and authentic, but they are also resilient and manage as circumstances dictate.

In my experience, the truly successful and effective project leaders are the ones who can adapt successfully to changing project circumstances. The project leader assumes many roles depending on the situation, results required, stakeholders involved, and expediency.

Leader. Leadership is often an art. Depending on customer requirements, organizational culture, and project member abilities, leadership may involve anything from command and control elements to coaching and mentoring. Sensitivity to circumstances and flexibility are key. A project leader may suggest and demonstrate as opposed to command and control.

Role Model. The effective project leader models appropriate behaviors such as integrity and honoring commitments. Personal integrity is a key moral principle to guide personal performance and instill project trust.

Change Agent. A project leader often is a change agent. This person must move the project team in new directions. Old ways of business may no longer be sufficient. A project team may have to change from a purely technical- to a customer-focused mindset.

Champion. If there's no corporate champion, the project leader must always remind the organization of the importance of the project. The true project champion knows the political game to keep the project visible and funded.

Coach. Project leader as coach is also changing. The coach is nominally in charge, decides who's on the team and who plays. But the coach is not responsible for the big play or series of downs. Professional, competent, and committed team members win games and complete projects.

Mentor. One of the soft project disciplines, mentoring project members may be as simple as explaining organizational and project protocols to new employees, or may entail providing long-term career development to a team member.

Enabler. The project leader is also an enabler, assisting project team members with establishing and meeting personal and project goals. This may mean reviewing plans, assessing project processes, and training that supports team members. The enabler does not control or punish, but assists and counsels team members to do the right things right.

Cheerleader. Can-do project leaders have a higher hit ratio than sour project managers. Project cheerleaders are infectious self-starters and generate enthusiasm in others with encouragement or simply giving thanks.

Ombudsperson. Great term! The project leader may become an ombudsperson to resolve project, customer, stakeholder, and team member conflicts.

Delegator. Delegation means being able to let go, establish trust, and share a common project vision. Smart project leaders want to establish clear project protocols and eventually be able to manage by exception or variance.

Entrepreneur. Project entrepreneurs may have a leadership or team-member role or even rotate these roles as circumstances dictate. High-performance project teams are self-directed, with each project member being self-managed. Each person becomes responsible for seeking and taking advantage of project opportunities as they arise.

Translator. Projects have their own protocols and methodologies. Look at *A Guide to the Project Management Body of Knowledge (PMBOK® Guide)*, full of suggested project management principles and practices. The project leader may have to explain, even translate, project language to the rest of the organization.

System Architect. The project leader may have to lead, support, or explain organizational transformations. This may entail adopting new methodologies, deploying virtual teams, or heading up an organizational change initiative.

Manager/Administrator. This is the traditional project manager role: planner, organizer, controller, and staffer of the project.

Organizer. The project leader also organizes resources, people, and information, often electronically rather than on paper.

Compliance Officer. Probably the most onerous job of a project leader is communicating accepted behaviors, correcting unacceptable behaviors, and disciplining if necessary. The project leader is responsible for ensuring compliance to workplace regulations, to technical requirements, and to sexual harassment, equal opportunity, and disability laws.

Look at all the roles a project leader assumes. How many are technical? How many are soft and people driven?

Attributes of the Successful Project Leader

Neal Whitten, PMP

PM Network 29 (June 1996)

Why are some project leaders more successful than others? Are there common traits that characterize successful project leaders, traits that set them apart from less successful, less effective leaders?

Like many, I have long had an interest in understanding why some leaders are more successful than others. Over the years, I have observed that the most successful leaders seem to do things and work with people in certain ways. I have converged on a set of common attributes that the most successful leaders seem to possess. These leadership attributes have worked for me, and I have seen them work for others. Being a leader carries a lot of responsibility, and it also can be a lonely, stressful job if you allow the role to control you, rather than taking charge of your own emotions. These attributes serve to help you stay in control. Before discussing these attributes, let's consider some definitions of a leader. A leader:

- Is the principal player on a team, the human "glue" that holds the team together.
- Inspires and guides a team toward a common goal.
- Exhibits integrity.
- Is a continual source of energy.
- Encourages desired behavior from others.
- Sets an example for others.
- Is accountable.
- Achieves results.

While not an exhaustive list of what being a leader is all about, this definition is sufficiently complete to point out the importance of a leader in creating and nurturing a successful organization. In fact, regardless of the skills and talents of the people that make up an organization, if the organization lacks an effective project leader, its potential greatness is considerably reduced.

One last point before launching into the attributes: Drawing from your own experiences, identify those leaders you believe are the most successful. Then decide whether the attributes shared by these leaders are included in the list presented here. You might even ask yourself how your project leader, manager, or your manager's manager stacks up against these attributes. More importantly, however, how do you stack up against these attributes?

The Ability to Create and Nurture a Vision

As a leader, it is important to create and nurture a vision—a far-reaching purpose—that you can share with your entire team and that the team can think about all day long, all week long, all project long. This vision will translate into the team purpose. Having a purpose has a powerful effect on the positive outcome of the team's mission. Not only does a purpose channel the energies of the team into a single focus, it helps to ensure that the tradeoffs and compromises made along the way fully support the vision.

Note, however, that creating a vision requires you to know where you want to go. This is essential if you plan to lead others to that destination. Only then can you be sure that the journey followed will be a successful one. Great accomplishments are made possible by great visions.

The Ability to Not Fear Failure

We all fail at things—all the time. It's natural and expected; it is the way we learn. You couldn't walk the first time you tried. When we were very young, we simply got up, dusted ourselves off, and tried again until we mastered our goal. But something happened to some of us as we "matured." We began to fear failing and therefore shunned opportunities that we believed increased our chances of failing.

> Failure is, in a sense, the highway to success, inasmuch as every discovery of what is false leads us to seek earnestly after what is true.
>
> John Keats

You see, life is full of paradoxes. The person who is no stranger to failure is often the person who is *most likely to succeed*. Every failure offers a lesson and from every lesson comes strength. If you learn from each failure, you get a little stronger. And after a while, you will even amaze yourself at the progress you have made.

Of course, all this is made more possible if you don't fear failure. Fear perpetuates failure and encourages you to "quit." Think of those around you who fear failure. Most likely they are not leaders, are content with complacency, and seek so-called "safety" by maintaining the status quo wherever they may be. They literally withdraw from many of life's opportunities.

Now look at those whose failures seem to be visible, yet from each fall they rise to prepare for the next challenge. If failure means growth and opportunity, then it should never be feared. The only real failures are the experiences from which we don't learn. The most successful leaders have learned to view failures as the positive force they are—necessary steps that enable us to grow and achieve those things that are important to us.

The Ability to Expect and Accept Criticism

If you expect criticism, you will seldom be disappointed. However, there are two types of criticism: *constructive* and *destructive*. Of course, you should welcome constructive criticism, which is well-meaning and useful feedback. Constructive criticism should leave you feeling that you have been helped. This type of feedback can help you to learn about yourself and the impact you are having as a result of your actions. It is information you can use to make choices for yourself and to grow in the direction of your personal goals.

Destructive criticism might be maliciously rooted. It offers little, if any, real value for your learning and growth. However, often what appears to be destructive criticism is, in fact, just an unfortunate and ineffective attempt to offer some useful information by a person who doesn't know how best to communicate the information. Be aware that some well-intentioned criticism might come your way awkwardly masked in destructive garb.

> Criticism is something we can avoid easily—by saying nothing, doing nothing, and being nothing.
>
> Aristotle

You will always find those who disapprove of your behavior or your decisions. Even the people you love, and who love you, will, at times, disapprove of your actions. When people criticize you, remember it is only their opinion. If you allow the absence of their approval to immobilize you, then you are allowing others to control you. You are, in effect, saying that what other people think about you is more important than what you think about yourself. Instead, you should ask yourself if there is something to be learned from the criticism. If there is, then, by all means, learn! If there is nothing to be learned, then forget the experience and go about fulfilling your dreams.

The Ability to Take Risks

Risk—that simple yet mighty four-letter word. The willingness to take risks is what changed the perception of a flat world to round and gave humans wings to fly. It gives people the ability to understand their own capabilities. If you want to achieve the extraordinary, you *must* take risks. Risk-taking can occur on a small scale, such as driving a new route home from work, speaking out when you disagree with an issue, or volunteering to take on an additional assignment. If you practice becoming comfortable with smaller risks, you will find yourself much more prepared to recognize a larger risk and much more willing to take it on.

> Great deeds are usually wrought at great risks.
>
> Herodotus

If you increasingly take on more risk, you will find an unexpected benefit—the recognition that your level of energy and enthusiasm grow in proportion to the risk that you pursue. Often, assignments that are the riskiest are later viewed as the assignments that were the most enjoyable, memorable, and career-building. There is nothing wrong with gradually expanding your risk-taking abilities. Only you can decide what your limitations are and what level of risk is suitable for you. The leaders of tomorrow are taking risks today.

The Ability to Empower Others

New leaders commonly resist giving up some of their "power" by empowering others—giving them full responsibility and accountability for key tasks. Their reasons include the belief that they can do the job better or faster themselves or the fear of giving others too much work. Another reason: They allow society's work ethic—being independent and self-reliant—to interfere with their duties as a leader of others. Resist these attitudes and transfer some of your tasks, your key tasks.

> No man will make a great leader who wants to do it all himself, or to get all the credit for doing it.
>
> Andrew Carnegie

A successful leader knows that he achieves goals through the dedication, skill, and efforts of others. You must learn to trust and work with others in ways that allow them to grow and achieve their dreams. After all, you appreciated the opportunities that others gave *you* to learn. Give others their chance as well. It is good for you and good for your team members. It frees you to lead and frees them to learn. Everybody will win.

The Ability to Be Decisive

Your organization reacts to your actions. When you delay making crucial decisions, you also delay the time that will be needed to implement those decisions. Many organizations have the capacity to increase their productivity and effectiveness. By putting off decision-making, you are not driving your organization efficiently. If you delay your own decision-making, you are also preventing the next tier of decisions from being made. This *decision queue* can build to a point where progress within the organization is seriously impacted. The result is an uncontrollable sluggishness that spreads throughout the organization and that only the project leader can correct.

> Once the WHAT is decided, the HOW always follows. We must not make the HOW an excuse for not facing and accepting the WHAT.
>
> Pearl S. Buck

It's better to make decisions early—when their pain and cost to the organization are relatively minor, yet when their long-term impact can have a major positive effect. Some decisions will, in hindsight, prove to be less than the best. However, if you wait until absolutely no risk remains before taking a position on a problem, then you will lose all competitiveness.

The Ability to Persevere

Perseverance is a universal characteristic of successful leaders. This attribute can propel a so-called "common" person to achieve uncommon feats. Perseverance pushes a chemist to try that $10,000^{th}$ mixture that finally succeeds, an athlete to achieve an Olympic-class victory, an artist to create a masterpiece, and the medical biologist to locate a disease-causing gene. Perhaps, however, the most inspiring effect of perseverance can be seen in a person who overcomes a major physical handicap and goes on to accomplish a feat that would be difficult for even a fully functioning person to achieve.

> Great works are performed not by strength, but by perseverance.
>
> Dr. Samuel Johnson

Intellectual and physical capabilities vary widely among people. However, it is encouraging to know that we all have the innate ability to exercise perseverance and determination in achieving goals that are important to us. Being persistent can make all the difference between dreaming and seeing the dream blossom into reality. Act like it is impossible for you to fail. You can achieve nearly anything you set out to make happen if you are persistent in following your dreams.

The Ability to Be Happy

Be happy. Feel good about yourself. Being happy is the cornerstone of your continued effectiveness. Don't *strive* to be happy. Don't set goals and then tell yourself that once those goals are reached you will be happy. Putting off happiness until some external event occurs will guarantee that your happiness will continue to be elusive.

> Everything you need to be totally fulfilled you already have.
>
> Dr. Wayne Dyer

You have everything you need today to be happy. You don't need a promotion, an award, a new car, a vacation, or retirement to be happy. Happiness is an attitude, an acceptance of what is. It comes from within—not from external events or things, and, therefore, no one can take away it from you. You can lose all your material possessions and still be happy.

This doesn't mean you should stop working for self-improvement or improvement to your family, job, company, world, or anything else that is important to you. It means that you must not allow external forces to control you to the point at which your actual happiness is no longer within your own control. How ever you define success for yourself, you will improve your likelihood of attaining your goals significantly if you recognize and exercise your ability to be and remain happy.

The Ability to Laugh

A meeting has just been called to settle a dispute between two parties. As people assemble in the meeting room, an uncomfortable silence is felt. Everyone has arrived, and the meeting is about to start. There's instability in the air, a feeling of tension, and one wrong word or action could ignite into an emotional explosion. The first words are spoken and strike everyone in the meeting with the same response—a round of uncontrollable laughter fills the room.

> It is my belief, you cannot deal with the most serious things in the world unless you understand the most amusing.
>
> Sir Winston Churchill

Can you relate to this scenario? Most of us can. That well-timed bit of humor was sorely needed. All too often we take the moment much too seriously. We fail to loosen up and find the humor in our situation and ourselves. How terribly depressing for an organization to resist expressing the lighter side of the daily problems we face. As a leader, support a healthy dose of humor in the organization. Displaying a sense of humor also helps you to remain cool under pressure and to keep problems in perspective.

Caution: Don't use sarcasm in your humor. While many people may view your comment to be amusing, it may leave others feeling uncomfortable and unsettled. Sarcasm also can hurt the trust you have developed with others. People appreciate benevolent humor better than sarcastic humor. If you have a hard time initiating this welcomed variety of humor, then at least show appreciation when others are amusing. While humor has been shown to preserve the health of people, it also adds value to the health of the total organization.

The Ability to Leave Your Ego Behind

We all have an ego. For some, the ego can cause paralysis, inhibiting their quest for growth and opportunity. Here is another paradox: Often the person who insists on attention is the one least likely to receive the type or amount of attention desired. An overactive ego does not help win the recognition, admiration, and approval that the egotist seeks. Instead, it has a repelling effect that encourages others to want to limit their association with the egotist. Furthermore, it leads others to question the real value and substance that exist behind all the verbal arm-waving.

An oversized ego can also interfere with recognizing others for their contributions. And it can bias decisions being made, favoring *who* is right rather than *what* is right. You have probably seen leaders with large egos. Having an exaggerated ego doesn't mean you will never get to be a leader. It means that fewer people will trust you or want to work for and with you. It means that you will make your job harder and less effective than it needs to be. An unbridled ego is a haunting liability. The less approval you demand from others, the more you are likely to receive.

The Ability to Think Before Acting

Resist the temptation to criticize hastily. When you suspect poor work, ask questions and carefully listen to the answers. Once a wrong or regrettable word is spoken, it cannot be taken back. After you understand the reason behind a problem, attack the problem, not the person.

Give others the same courtesy that you would like for yourself. Take this opportunity to not only help someone resolve a problem, but also to help him benefit from the experience. Also, work at increasing the bond and trust between you and the project member. If you demonstrate constructive behavior and resist attacking the person, you may find yourself with a more loyal and dedicated project member.

The Ability to Meet Commitments

When you make a commitment, it is a personal statement about yourself. It says that you can be depended on, that you will do everything within your abilities to honor the pledge that you have made.

The success of any organization depends on its ability to meet its commitments. As the saying goes, a chain is only as strong as its weakest link. The project structure, represented as a chain, can break quickly when one or more commitments are broken.

Make no commitments lightly. Commit only to that which you believe you can achieve. To commit unconditionally to more is to be distrustful, for if your commitment is weak, so too are those commitments that depend on you. Pull your own weight, and do as you say you will.

When you meet your commitments you will be recognized as a greater value to the organization. You also may find that you will be given the option to assume greater responsibilities as well as to be exposed to increased opportunities. People will prefer to have you on their teams or will want to be on your team. You will also find that you will be given greater freedom to manage your activities as you choose.

The Ability to Coach Your Team—Be a Role Model

We all learn the easiest and fastest by observing others—by having an example to mimic. As a leader, others look to you—and rightly so—for that example. They look to you for strength, wisdom, caring, and attention. They also look to you for honesty about your human frailties. For example, the integrity that you demonstrate when you make a mistake, admit it, recover, and continue on can have a profound positive impact on those around you.

Teach what you have learned. Impart your knowledge and experience. Prepare others to take on more responsibility. You know what you want from your leaders; work to provide the same to your subordinates and peers, and even to your leaders. Work continuously to build a stronger organization this month than the one that existed last month. When you come across a problem, fix the problem—and then fix the process that caused the problem. The greatest leader leads by example. Practice what you expect from others. Show you care, offer your support, and be there to make it happen.

The Ability to Maintain a Winning Attitude

Attitude is the disposition, manner, or approach that you bring to everything you do. One of the most admired traits you can have is a good, or positive, attitude. A positive attitude can actually bring pleasure to the performance of a tedious or difficult task. A positive attitude can make a long day seem short and even improve the productivity and quality of the work being performed. People who consistently maintain positive attitudes tend to have higher energy levels than those who are less positive. These people look for something positive—and they find it—in every chore they tackle. You have probably observed situations in which two people were being considered for the same assignment and the person chosen appears to have somewhat less experience or knowledge. Usually this person was chosen because of her positive attitude.

> The quality of work is affected as much by one's attitude as by one's skill.
>
> Anonymous

As a revealing anonymous quote states, "A pessimist finds difficulty in every opportunity; an optimist finds opportunity in every difficulty." People can take great liberties in choosing how to think. A glass of water can be half filled or half empty. How a person thinks does not change the fact that the glass has 50 percent of its capacity used up by water. But how a person chooses to think does have an affect on the efficiency with which a task is completed and on the enjoyment the person derives from accomplishing that task.

As a leader, you want the people whom you are leading to demonstrate good attitudes in every endeavor that you assign them. People who exhibit these upbeat attitudes are considerably easier to manage and more enjoyable to be around than less positive people. In order for a winning attitude to permeate your team, you must demonstrate and encourage that characteristic. As a leader, the manner in which you approach your work is also the manner most likely to be adopted by those who work under, alongside, and above you. Adopt a winning attitude in the tasks that you undertake and you also create winning people and winning products in the process.

The Ability to Believe in Yourself

The most successful leaders have learned *to believe* in their ability to make something happen—to follow their dreams and transform those dreams into reality. They draw from an inner strength that they have chosen to acknowledge. An inner strength that no one can take away—unless they allow it. You *must* believe in yourself if you expect to become and remain a successful leader, and if you expect others to believe in you. In fact, the belief in one's own capabilities magnifies the contribution from all the other attributes that we have discussed.

> Always bear in mind that your own resolution to succeed is more important than any one thing.
>
> Abraham Lincoln

If you believe you can—you will. If you believe you can't—you won't. These pearls of wisdom have been around at least as long as recorded history. And the great news is that no one has a monopoly on these words. They apply to you as much as they do to anyone.

You deserve to be what you choose to be and work at becoming—regardless of your age, race, sex, religion, or current wealth. You are what you perceive yourself to be. Your vision of yourself becomes your reality. As a leader, you must believe in your ability to get the job done, to achieve the desired results. If people took on only those jobs where they knew all the answers and had no chance for conflict or failure, there would be no leaders. A successful leader knows that no one person holds the answer to every problem, but with the proper balance of time, energy, and talent, no problem escapes unsolved.

It's almost always true that our greatest obstacle to becoming what we truly want is ourselves. If it is truly important to you, then never give up. As Henry David Thoreau said, "If one advances confidently in the direction of his dreams and endeavors to live the life he has imagined, he will meet with a success unexpected in common hours."

I believe that everyone has the capability to be a successful project leader. Everyone! There is room for many more leaders, millions more. Although some are more effective than others, or rise to greater heights, this does not diminish the great opportunities of turning your visions into realities. All the attributes can be learned if you choose to learn them.

Portions of this article are excerpted from *Managing Software Development Projects, Second Edition,* by Neal Whitten. Copyright 1995, John Wiley and Sons, Inc. Reprinted by permission of the publisher, John Wiley and Sons, Inc.

Are You a Project Manager/Leader or Just Managing Projects?

C. J. Walker, PMP, and Allan S. Peterson

Proceedings of the 30th Annual Project Management Institute
1999 Seminars & Symposium

Project management is a diverse profession that transcends all industries. The essential concepts of project management application are consistent across the board. Given the trend toward a globalized and projectized environment, the role of the project leader takes on increased importance in corporate success. Therefore, it is important to recognize and understand what makes an excellent project leader. A true project leader *will* be someone who has a drive for excellence and a commitment to the professionalism of project management.

Many people can follow the tools and techniques used in project management. However, we must determine if we are willing to settle for an average project manager (either by design—meaning that an individual was placed in a position without having the right character traits, skills, or training to perform the job successfully, or by consequence—meaning that the individual is just an average performer in any position but has acceded to this position of leadership). Or would we rather develop exceptional project leaders who have insight into enhancing the process, an ability to leverage experiences, and a great leadership style?

> Managers initiate, administer, and maintain; leaders originate, innovate, and take great risks at high speed. The good manager keeps an eye on the bottom line and knows the cost of everything; the good leader keeps an eye on the vision and knows the value of everything. The manager improves the efficiency

of the status quo, asking how and when; the leader challenges the status quo, asking why. One characteristic in particular is required of today's leaders: they must thrive on change (Moravec and Manley 1995).

Although understanding the concepts, tools, and techniques is important for everyone (all project participants and the customer), not everyone has the potential to become a great project leader. Therefore, we should provide general project management education to everyone, but only mentor those with a desire and the potential to become a great project leader.

This article covers why the authors feel many companies are in a position of having individuals who are just managing projects—rather than true project leaders. In addition, it identifies some of the requisite character traits and skill sets that a successful project leader should possess, and how an organization can best utilize its resources to ensure that the right type of individuals are leading projects.

The Corporate Need—A "Warm Body" Concept

More and more, the successful business is the one that can quickly and effectively react to a rapidly changing marketplace. It must be able to respond to its competitor's challenges in the market. This means it must be able to change rapidly, and to manage that change in such a manner that there are no downstream reverberations, thereby quelling the effectiveness of the change.

These changes are effected by means of projects—the business endeavor having a specific start and end date, producing a specific set of deliverables (changes), and consuming a predetermined number of corporate resources.

> Project management continues to become more challenging and we think this trend will continue. This means we have to pay special attention to the development of project managers who are capable of coping with jobs that range from small to megaprojects and with life spans of several months to ten years. At Fluor, a project manager must not only be able to manage the engineering, procurement and construction aspects of a project, he or she must also be able to manage aspects relating to finance, cost engineering, schedule, environmental considerations, regulatory agency requirements, inflation and cost escalations, labor problems, public and client relations, employee relations and changing laws. That's primarily on the domestic side. On international projects, the list of additional functions and considerations adds totally different complications (Fluor 1977).

It becomes obvious then that project management is as much an art as it is a science. The science aspects of project management include such areas as: planning, WBS techniques, creation of Gantt charts, setting and adhering to standards, creating CPM/precedence diagrams, performing variance analysis, doing earned value analysis—and the beat goes on. These are tools and techniques that can be learned, practiced, and honed. All that is required is the interest and ability to learn.

But project management as an art includes such diverse areas as: effective communications, trust, integrity, honesty, sociability, leadership, values, flexibility, decision-making, perspective, sound business judgment, and so on. How does one learn trust, honesty, or decision-making? True, there are thinking patterns and certain analysis techniques that can assist in some of these areas, but basically one has it or doesn't have it.

There are a number of techniques aimed at developing excellent project leaders (e. g., training, mentoring programs, experience, and more). Whatever set of techniques is selected for an organization's project management improvement program, there will be considerable expense involved in the process. It is therefore only prudent for that organization to take whatever steps are necessary to improve the success rate of the program. One such step is to *start with the right "raw product."* That is, to develop the right people. How have we gotten to the point where the question of selecting the right person even has to be considered?

Unfortunately, many companies have not evolved and developed their project management expertise along with the evolution of project management. Many of their competitors are in the modern project management era, whereas their own paradigm is one of earlier eras. They are playing catch up. They have more projects than managers. The most natural thing to do is to draft the person with a good reputation within the organization to lead the project. Generally this person is a good technician or a good administrative manager.

What's the next step? Orient, train, mentor, train, provide experience, train. In many cases, only with blind luck does an organization get a person having the right aptitudes into the project management development program.

It is apparent that there is a set of attributes or characteristics possessed by leaders—that is possessed by those that have the best chance of becoming excellent project leaders. Although understanding the concepts, tools, and techniques (the skills of project management) is important for everyone, not everyone has the potential to become a great project leader! Therefore, we should provide general project management education to everyone, but *only develop those with a desire and the potential of becoming a great project leader.*

A Better Solution—The "Right Body" Concept (Instilling Skills in the Right People)

In order to create a mutually successful corporate environment, it is important to create an environment for success by putting people into positions to succeed. Not everyone is destined to become a project leader, any more than everyone is destined to become the CEO. Projects are a team effort, and in any team initiative all team members serve valuable roles. There is a need for project leaders, project managers, technical leaders, project team members, and stakeholders. The corporation must acknowledge the value of all these roles and target professional development programs, training, and mentoring, as appropriate.

As we have defined before, there are distinct role differences between managing and leading. However, a leader must be able to do both, whereas a manager need only be proficient in management tactics. Given this logic, most often managers in the organization become the target pool for potential leaders. So, what does one look for in a potential project leader?

As noted earlier, we need to identify the character traits and the base set of skills that contribute to project leadership. We can then develop the skill sets to complement those traits in order to enhance success in project leadership. For example, a leader needs to:

- *Be adaptable and innovative.* This goes beyond the nature of man to be adaptable to his environment. In order to be successful, one has to be adaptable to change by embracing change and leading others through the transformation process. One can become an inspiration by the flexibility one portrays in finding creative solutions to a changing environment. To do otherwise is a disservice to the project team, left struggling with a new environment alone.
- *Have a facility for learning.* Everyone enjoys taking a class and learning something new. Not everyone embraces his new learning and applies it. One must be self-motivated and innovative in the way one changes her thinking by approaching the job from a new angle. Given that project management crosses all industries, one has to be able to absorb—in a short time frame—the nuances of each industry to which one is exposed and grasp the new technologies that one may encounter.
- *Be decisive and a problem solver.* This does not refer to rash decision-making, but rather once one has 40–70 percent of the information, one makes a decision and goes forward. A good project leader would also have a contingency plan and an ability to refocus the group, should that decision prove wrong. Being decisive means one is not afraid to make a wrong decision. If one doesn't make a decision, then life makes it, and control is lost. Being a problem solver means finding creative methods for discovering new solutions. Finding obstacles to be a challenge, instead of an overwhelming situation, is the sign of a good project leader.

However, character traits are not enough; they are merely the raw material from which a masterpiece can be derived. In addition to character traits, a base level of project management-related skills is required. For example, a good project leader should:

- *Be a good communicator.* We all propose to be great communicators. However, the art of being a great communicator includes the *ability to listen* to the ideas and concerns of others and to work toward win-win solutions. This is one of the core concepts of team building. A good communicator understands what is important to his project team, customer, and management. He learns how to speak their language, whether that is a detailed explanation or just the high-level facts. It is also important to determine the most effective means of communication (face to face, voice mail, email, written reports) and when these various means should be used.

- *Be an accomplished motivator.* Most people would like to see themselves as motivators; however, use of purse-string authority (authority to grant financial gains) is merely a carrot at the end of a stick and is not a long-lasting motivation technique. As a project leader, one must consider the needs and motivation factors of the team. In this, we mean a project leader must take a genuine interest in developing the skill sets of the project team, encourage team members to make mistakes and grow, and show overall support for team member decisions. Even if the decision is wrong, it can be reversed. However, berating an individual for having the courage to make a decision will ensure that the individual will be gunshy in the future, and fear is a terrible position from which to make a decision. A true project leader will encourage and not fear the team's development and skill-set growth.

- *Be multitasking with a broad knowledge base.* For many people it is difficult to successfully focus on more than one thing at a time. However, that is exactly the requirement for a project leader. The job description requires operating on different levels and having the foresight to know that once a task is completed, another is in the cue to start immediately, with no down time. The ability to organize one's time is a key attribute to multitasking. A true project leader is not only a good multitasker, but also prefers this mode of operating. With regard to a broad knowledge base, although one is not an accountant, a project leader needs a fundamental understanding of finances; although she may not be a systems engineer, the project leader needs a fundamental understanding of the functionality of the systems, terms, and concepts.

A technique that is most valuable in determining appropriately skilled resources is that of job expectations. These go beyond the general description of tasks (which should be considered an outline of general expectations, not a limitation of activities) to the results of the role. As we become increasingly global in our business endeavors and project orientation becomes the more common approach to work efforts, people and efforts are judged by the results. Just as we determine the acceptance criteria with a client for a project, we need to define the acceptance criteria for the individual by clearly communicating the results expected. In this way she understands the standards by which she is being measured and can take active steps toward becoming successful within her own eyes, as well as that of the corporation.

Bridging the Gap—Defining an Action Plan toward Effective Resource Utilization

Previously we have discussed the *problem* (the "warm body" concept) and the *goal* (instilling skills in the right person). How do we get from our current state to our desired state of enhanced productivity and results? We would submit the following as the project plan for this very important effort:

- *Assess the organization*. Measure the current state of project management maturity within the organization.
- *Select the leaders*. Measure the character traits and skills of those people interested in pursuing a project management career with the organization.
- *Specify the objectives*. Determine the specific objectives for project management improvements, both for the organization and for each person to be developed as a project leader.
- *Transition*. Document the change/transition plan to get from here to there and make the transition.

Assess the Organization

The goal here is to measure project management skills and practices of the organization against a "project management standard." This begs the question, "What standard?" PM Solutions has developed a project management maturity model, much like the Systems Engineering Institute's capability maturity model. The project management maturity model can assess an organization's project management skills and practices and plot them. This enables the organization to understand how it is functioning in several key areas, determine where it really should be, and devise a plan to get there.

Select the Leaders

We have laid a solid foundation for the fact that there is a set of characteristics and a base set of skills that is necessary in an individual if he is to become a *leader* and not merely a manager. Much as with an organization assessment, we have devised an appraisal vehicle that measures these characteristics and base skills at an individual level.

The organization needs to take a very difficult stand: not all the people having an interest in project management should be developed in that direction.

Rather, only those people having the characteristics and base skills should be trained/mentored.

This stand will be controversial and must be handled with much tact. It is akin to a best friend telling you that your lipstick is badly smeared on the left side. Your friend has earned the right and responsibility to share bad news as well as good news. In the same way, the organization has the right and responsibility to partner with an individual in assessing her skills and in creating a career progression plan. The organization must realize it is doing the individual a great service in being forthright about the likelihood of success in her career goals.

What does the organization achieve by taking this controversial approach? By doing an assessment for all those in the project management pool the organization understands which of these individuals *should* be in the pool. In addition, by administering such an instrument to others not yet in the pool, it may be possible to counsel them regarding the possibility of project management as a career direction. The organization will now be in a position to develop *leaders*.

Specify the Objectives

Having determined the organization's current project management state and targeting those individuals who have the potential for true project leadership, we must now define the future project management state for the organization and the future for the individual. Our assessment vehicles are specific and objective and provide for achieving higher levels of excellence. Objectives should be *S*mart, *M*easurable, *A*chievable, *R*ealistic, and *T*ime related (S.M.A.R.T.). An example might be a goal of having projects that meet the triple constraint parameters 90 percent of the time, or having 50 percent of the project managers/leaders within the organization Project Management Professional certified.

Transition

With the current and future state of the organization and individuals determined, we now need to manage this change and transition initiative in the same way we would manage a project, by putting together a project plan and managing to that plan. It is important to recognize that in any change and transition effort there will be resistance, which is a normal human response. Understanding why people are resisting change, creating measures for buy-in and commitment, and keeping the vision at the forefront are critical success factors. With regard to the buy-in factor, everyone wants to be on a winning team. Therefore, identifying quick hits by piloting new methods, approaches, or individuals is a good means of showing what the future state may resemble, thus minimizing resistance and concern. The project plan also serves as an excellent communication tool so that the project stakeholders understand what will occur, when it will occur, and what is expected of them throughout the process. The following section includes more rules for a successful transition (Schacht 1997).

Rules for Successful Project Management Transition of the Organization and People

Going from an organization with individuals who just manage projects to one of project leadership is a fundamental change and transition effort for organizations and individuals. As such, recognizing the success factors for organizational culture change is important to ensure long-term success. The more closely a structure is followed, the greater the chances for successful implementation.

- *Become a learning organization.* Embrace new ideas, new concepts, and new techniques, and make them available to everybody.
- *Establish clear communications processes and media.* Record and praise accomplishments and heroes who support and demonstrate the concepts required in the new culture.
- *Establish a flexible, central structure,* which provides a critical core for all implementation efforts.
- *Accept risk and proceed judiciously.* Strive to extend the culture throughout the organization, despite the inherent risk of change.
- *Know and publish boundaries for the culture.* Ensure a common understanding of what the culture is intended to be and what it isn't.
- *Evaluate and prove the economic value of the culture.*
- *Involve everyone.*

References

Moravec, Milan, and Richard Manley. 1995. Reinventing Leadership. *PM Network* (September): 15–18.

Fluor, J. Robert. 1977. Development of Project Managers. Keynote Address, Project Management Institute Ninth International Seminars & Symposium.

Schacht, Nicholas. 1997. Project Management Culture: An Anthropological Perspective. *PM Network* (September): 53–56.

Resource Managers: The Key to Your Success

Joan Knutson

PM Network 13 (March 1997)

The functional manager who owns the resources that you need assigned to your projects is known as the resource manager. These resource managers assure that the right people with the right talents are available and assigned to the right projects at the right time. Obviously, resource managers are very important in our world.

Yet, you say, you have no control over resource managers; that they often report to a different manager than you. True, but that does not lessen the reality of your dependence on them or absolve you from doing everything in your power to influence and support them in performing their resource management job to the best of their abilities.

However, the resource manager is often the forgotten cog in the project mechanism. When was the last time you made a special effort to have one-on-one meetings with your resource managers? When was the last time you brought all your resource managers together for a briefing especially designed for them, concerning the project? When was the last time you invited your resource managers to the training classes you offer your project team?

This article looks at the role of the resource manager in the project management discipline and the recommended partnership between the resource manager and the project manager.

The Basic Job of the Resource Manager

The resource manager's job is to see that his employees are successful and that his department meets its objective. In your organization, is it the functional department's objective to provide qualified resources to projects in a timely manner? If top management does not see this as one of the resource manager's major objectives, it will be difficult to elicit the resource manager's attention to the needs of your project. Let's assume that the resource managers have been asked by their management to support projects and project management to the best of their abilities.

Staffing, quality of work, meeting their internal organization's goals, and the growth and development of the resources are their key concerns.

Project Management-Related Functions

Resource managers perform three functions that are associated with project management. They produce long- and short-range staffing plans; hire, fire, and develop their staff; and perform in a matrix environment.

Producing Long- and Short-Range Staffing Plans

The resource manager must produce long- and short-term staffing plans that will assure that the right people with the right talents are available and are assigned to the right projects at the right time.

At the most strategic level, she staffs her department to accommodate project work and the functional area's operational work. The resource manager (hopefully, with input and direction from top management and the various project managers) determines the headcount required of her department for the period of time addressed in the budgetary process. During the functional budgeting process, the resource manager predicts how many people of what skill mix will be needed in order to accomplish the operational work of the department, as well as to accommodate the needs of the current and upcoming projects.

At the more tactical level, the resource manager, in conjunction with the project manager, assigns the right person with the right skill mix to the appropriate project. This requires that resource managers truly know the skills and personalities of their staff and understand the needs of the projects.

At the day-to-day operational working level, they prepare and track a schedule, manage the changes in their staffing plans, and move the players accordingly. During the project, as schedules slip, people become unavailable, and priorities change, those detailed staffing plans often become invalid. It is the job of the resource manager to respond intelligently to these changes and reschedule tasks and people accordingly.

Hiring, Firing, and Developing Staff

In conjunction with developing the staffing plan, the resource manager identifies the skills, knowledge, and competencies required to deliver the work "on the boards," match available skill sets, and perform a gap analysis. He needs to close the gaps by doing whatever it takes to get needed people on board:

hiring, negotiating transfers from other parts of the organization, isolating sub-contracted resources, and/or training current staff.

Once the anticipated work is broken down into specific assignments, resource managers groom, train, and "stretch" their staff. Forethought and preparation are needed to ensure that the staff members have time allocated in their schedules to participate in the professional development plan, which may include training, mentoring, or personal time to think and grow.

As the skill mix changes, certain resources may no longer be relevant to accomplish the anticipated operational and project workload. Hopefully, those resources have been "retrained" to possess needed new skills. If not, the resource manager has the unpleasant job of phasing them out of the organization.

Performing in a Matrix Environment

Resource managers tend to stay focused on their own empires. Why not? That is typically how they are reviewed. However, for resource managers to support the project management discipline, they need to be willing to function in a matrixed organization, be flexible to support other areas, and subvert their personal glories to contribute to the goal of the team.

The relationship between the resource manager and the project manager should be a partnership, with resource management the common ground. The goal of both is to provide resources properly, forecast resource needs, aid in the hiring process, and contribute to the performance appraisal process and growth and development of the staff.

The Project Manager's Role in This Relationship

If you are convinced that the functions described earlier, as performed by the resource manager, are crucial to your success, I suggest that there are two initiatives that you as a project manager need to take in order to ensure that the resource manager is capable of supporting you, your project, and project management. Those two initiatives are 1) provide training, and 2) provide position support tools.

Training

Provide a class for resource managers that addresses the resource management process and their role in the project management discipline. Position the course not only as a skills course to support the project effort within the organization, but also as a partnership course for project managers and resource managers. Focus on concepts, not methodology. Concentrate on the resource manager/project manager partnership, facilitating discussion between the two.

Topics to cover might include methods to create the staffing plan, types of reports to allow better communication, understanding roles and responsibilities, the link between strategic planning and tactical work, how to be flexible yet maintain control, just-in-time recruitment, and maintaining and growing the resources.

A training program designed uniquely for resource managers positions them to be active rather than passive players in the project arena.

Support Tools

More than a class is needed. To make the concept a reality, topics discussed in class must have support tools back on the job. Let's take one example. In order to perform intelligent staffing one must understand the concept of resource loading and leveling. Resource loading is the mathematical calculation of individual effort exerted on various tasks in a single time frame. After the resource has been "loaded" onto the schedule chart, some individuals may be overloaded, and the staffing plan must be "leveled." In other words, their schedules and perhaps other people's schedules must be changed to assure the availability of the right resources at the right times.

In the class, the resource managers learn about the concept of resource loading and leveling. They go back to their job better equipped to use the scheduling software on their computers. However, their scheduling software product does a nice job for one project at a time but doesn't have the power to deal with an enterprise-wide analysis. The resource managers have the desire and knowledge to intelligently manage the staffing schedules, but then they go back to the job and the necessary software support is not available. So they must try to do it by hand or with inadequate software, and they fail—or don't even attempt to rectify the situation. They feel even more frustrated because they now know how to fix the problem but can't, because they don't have the tools.

For those of you who want to focus some attention on the resource manager, what training do you offer and what tools do you provide? I suggest the following process.

1. Prepare an analysis of the resource manager's job in general.
2. Isolate those tasks that are specifically related to project management.
3. Determine how the resource manager would evaluate her success in these project management areas.
4. Question the resource manager's supervisor as to how the resource manager's success is evaluated, relative to project management.
5. Analyze the critical success factors that need to be in place in order for the resource manager to best support project management.
6. Work with the resource manager and his manager to implement a plan to provide those critical success factors.

If part of the plan is to change the resource manager's behaviors and enhance or expand her skill mix, create a list of the desired behaviors and skills and develop and/or provide appropriate training. If part of the plan is to provide tools, determine the tools that are necessary and make them available.

Resource managers are those people who provide you the resources needed to complete your projects. You owe them your attention.

Duties of the Effective Resource Manager

PM Network 21 (December 1999)

With the prominent role of project managers becoming increasingly popular, resource managers are becoming less sure of their role. Let's take a closer look.

The No. 1 reason why employees leave a company is that they don't feel appreciated. They don't feel like anyone is championing their cause or looking out for them.

Resource managers are the primary nurturers within an organization and company. They support their direct reports in helping them be successful in two key areas: meeting their project commitments and helping them to discover and achieve their potential in the organization and company. Let's look at a short list of the more significant duties of resource managers.

Hire and fire. Resource managers must invest the time to hire qualified people who can help the projects achieve their goals. Also important is the need to appropriately address poor performers.

Perform resource planning and allocation. Only resource managers can make job assignments. A project manager can, however, assign tasks and action items as they relate to a project member's assigned job. Resource managers must anticipate and plan for the future demands of their direct reports.

Define roles and responsibilities for direct reports. Resource managers ensure that their direct reports not only understand their jobs, but also understand how they will be measured against performing their jobs satisfactorily.

Support direct reports in meeting their commitments. Resource managers work with their direct reports to help them be successful. This includes reviewing their plans and routinely tracking their progress.

Are catalysts to resolve domain-related problems. Resource managers ensure that all problems within their domain are being addressed with the appropriate sense of urgency.

Evaluate performance of direct reports. Although verbal input from others can be solicited, resource managers are fully accountable for working closely with their direct reports to fairly evaluate their performance.

Compensate and award direct reports. Resource managers have the duty to appropriately compensate and award. Better to err on the side of too many and too large awards, than too few and too small.

Provide career counseling and development. Each human resource needs to be nurtured to reach his potential. Resource managers must be available and accessible to work with and help develop their direct reports, including areas of training and job opportunities.

Promote a productive work environment. Resource managers have the responsibility to ensure continual improvement in the productivity of direct reports, both on long-term projects and from project to project.

Serve as channels for company communications. Resource managers serve as conduits for the dissemination of company-related information to direct reports. The resource manager puts a *face* on the corporation with which the direct reports can communicate.

Execute company policies and practices. Resource managers are the *enforcement* arms for company polices and practices as they relate to the resource managers' domain of responsibility. This includes ensuring compliance with legal issues in areas such as products and services, workplace safety, and contractor relationships.

Secure future work opportunities. Resource managers strive to practice a full employment policy for direct reports whose performance is satisfactory. The best resource managers do not resort to downsizing as a standard or convenient method of managing the business. Instead, they accept responsibility for seeking and developing new business opportunities, while the direct reports focus on driving the day-to-day operations.

The resource manager has a nearly impossible job—with demands coming from every imaginable direction—yet a job that can have a profound impact on the organization's success.

Project Leadership and the Art of Managing Involvement

Michael K. Clark

Proceedings of the 30th Annual Project Management Institute
1999 Seminars & Symposium

Running an efficient organization requires that myriad tasks, projects, decisions, and plans be completed by teams or groups of employees. It requires the involvement of the right people at the right time to make certain that the components operate successfully. Above all, it requires the commitment of those involved. A well-orchestrated involvement of people leads to the high level of commitment required to move an organization toward common goals. Project management is about people and how they interact and plug into the organization's goals and objectives. Leadership is what breeds involvement, not project management software and endless Gantt charts. This article will review a research-based but practical way to improve project management leadership and effectiveness and better ensure the success of project implementation.

All of the intended value of a project is delivered during a project's implementation. The increase of project management software in recent years, however, has not significantly enhanced our ability to implement well. Our documented plans have improved, but it seems that the delivery of the benefits of those plans has not always improved. Current theories and improvements in strategic implementation and project management are distancing project managers from the messy business of leadership. It is my desire, through systematic and rational processes, to reengage project managers and their teams with a focus on what it takes to implement well—*leadership and project team involvement.*

Leadership development is undoubtedly the most crucial issue facing organizational- and management-development efforts over the next several years. More individuals than ever are being required to step into project management roles (often with little more than a few training classes and a crash course in

MS-Project). Organizations are operating lean, with more work being redefined into project-based work. This movement toward project-based work places a great price on project management talent and great pressures on project managers' abilities to lead. The organizations that can most quickly respond to the challenge of developing leadership within their project management ranks will be at a competitive advantage.

This article's primary objectives are to provide awareness of the alternative behaviors available to project managers, to foster effective leadership and involvement, and to provide the reader with immediate practical knowledge. It will also touch on the nature of decision-making, which is a primary component of effective involvement. I have seen entire organizations transformed once their approach to decision-making was rationalized and made visible. I am also hoping that you can begin to imagine how your organization can transform through the application of rational-thinking methods to business processes.

Implementation

It was Napoleon who quipped, "Plans are nothing, but *planning* is everything." There is a message there that has significant relevance to today's project managers. It is the *act* of planning, discussing, agreeing, and committing that forms the basis of effective project plans, not the document itself. Yet, so many of today's project managers are dazzled by the ability of software to beautify and present their plans in so many different ways that they lose sight of their primary responsibility: *to lead!* The focus of project management is seemingly in the wrong place. The focus is on tools and reports. The tools of project management, which are presented in great detail within *A Guide to the Project Management Body of Knowledge (PMBOK® Guide)*, are important, but they are not the primary determinant of success. It is the *act* of constructing those plans and how the project manager chooses to involve others in that planning that is the primary determinant of success.

The link between the activity of how the project is planned and the success of implementation is undeniable. Project managers who do not involve others in important decisions when plans are being established likely will not gain team commitment. This lack of commitment is what renders implementation unsuccessful. It is up to the project manager to ensure that the right people are involved at the right time to secure maximum commitment to the project plan. One of the most important characteristics of effective leadership, therefore, is the ability to balance the right level of involvement during the act of planning. And planning is nothing more than executing a series of decisions. Unfortunately, knowing when and whom to involve is not always obvious. Too much involvement in planning is also not good. Teamwork is not always appropriate. We were conditioned in the late 1980s and early 1990s to accept that teams were the answer to solving workplace difficulties. Before organizing your next planning team ask yourself, "What I am trying to accomplish here?" The project manager should make some decisions alone.

Now that we have established involvement during the act of planning as a determinant of effective implementation, let's step back and place implementation in the proper organizational context. The simple fact that involvement is important should be of no surprise to you. What may be of interest is the direct relationship between how involvement is managed during planning and the level of leadership effectiveness during project implementation. As was previously stated, implementation is what delivers a project's value. Senior management creates and establishes an organization's vision and strategy. Projects, through their planned structure and objectives, turn vision into action. The project resources are committed to consuming capital within the guidelines established by project managers and the team during the planning stage. Without commitment to the plan, organizational capital is misallocated and often wasted. The foundation of this process is the project manager, who guides, coaches, and manages the involvement of the team so that capital is most effectively utilized. Figure 1 summarizes the important structure of strategy, involvement, and implementation.

The glue that holds the most effective organizations together is the leadership ability of project managers who can best engage project resources within the critical structure outlined in Figure 1. The following section explains how to best execute the required mix of involvement to establish effective leadership.

Managing Involvement

What is common among the attributes of outstanding leaders? The identification of some common style among the diverse array of leaders in the world would be futile. Leaders employ different approaches, possess different strengths, and appeal to different groups. In fact, the worst place in which to look when seeking a successful approach to leadership is in the personality of a successful leader. This is especially relevant in organizations that are requiring more and more employees to take on project management roles. These organizations find themselves in the position of having to develop leaders from within their ranks.

Project Leadership Is about Behavior

There are three premises that organizations and project managers must address as they develop leadership both within their ranks and within themselves. The principals are as follows.

1. No one style of leadership is appropriate in every instance. Each project and management situation has variables that will determine the optimum behavior.

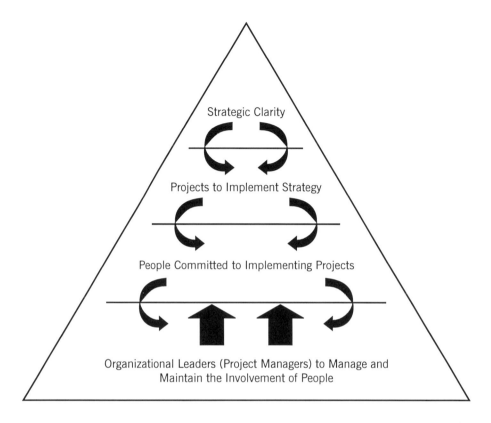

Figure 1. Strategy, Involvement, and Implementation Structure

2. Leaders are under tremendous time pressures and are constantly struggling with the choice between being time efficient in dealing with a particular situation or making a time investment that may help to develop the capabilities of others on the project team.

3. No leader can succeed by employing a style that demands talents they do not possess. Conversely, some project resources will not respond to certain leadership styles no matter how talented the project manager is at employing them.

Under these ever-present scenarios, how does a project manager increase her leadership effectiveness? Working with two noted experts in the area of participation, we have created an approach that has proven quite effective. Our research indicates that there is a defined range of five behaviors available to a project manager in any given situation. Misapplication of these behaviors is what often reduces the effectiveness of today's project manager. These approaches represent steps on a scale of participation—from no involvement from other project members to full participation.

A1. Resolve Alone

A leader behavior in which the project manager resolves a situation alone, without the participation of anyone else, or develops a recommendation without involving others. There is no opportunity for others to influence the resolution or recommendation. Example: The project manager privately draws up a work schedule and gives each project team member a copy. The "A" comes from autocratic; "1" is because this is the less participative of two autocratic behaviors.

A2. Ask Individuals

A leader behavior in which the project manager gets information from one or more other people, one at a time, before resolving a situation. The project manager need not inform the other(s) about the issue of concern. There is limited opportunity for others to influence the resolution or recommendation. Example: A project manager asks each team member individually about his current workload, and then draws up a work schedule. The project manager makes the final decision. "A" stands for autocratic; "2" because this is the more participative of two autocratic behaviors.

C1. Consult Individuals

A leader behavior in which the project manager discusses a situation with one or more other people individually, getting their ideas and suggestions before resolving the issue. There is some opportunity for others to influence the resolution or recommendation, although the project manager's decision need not necessarily reflect their input. Example: A project manager meets individually with team members to discuss how they think work should be scheduled, then draws up a work schedule. "C" represents consultative; "1" is because this is the less participative of two consultative behaviors.

C2. Consult Group

A leader behavior in which the project manager discusses a situation with other people in a group meeting, obtaining their ideas and suggestions prior to resolving the issue or developing a recommendation. There is significant opportunity for others to influence the resolution or recommendation. However, the project manager makes the final decision, which need not reflect others' input. Example: A project manager calls the team members together as a group to discuss how work should be scheduled, then draws up a work schedule after the meeting. "C" is for consultative; "2" because this is the more participative of the two consultative behaviors.

G2. Resolve as Group

A leader behavior in which the project manager discusses a situation with other team members as a group, and the group works together to develop a resolution or recommendation. The project manager may chair the meeting, establish boundaries for an acceptable outcome, and provide information and ideas. Each team member in the group can have significant impact on the resolution or recommendation. The project manager agrees to accept and implement any conclusion reached by the group. Example: A project manager meets with the team members as a group, and the group works together to develop a schedule during the meeting. "G" stands for group.

Take a Moment to Reflect

Our research indicates that leadership effectiveness is enhanced significantly when project managers apply the appropriate behavior at the appropriate time. Most project managers tend to stick with one or two styles based on their personal comfort and therefore miss opportunities to better guarantee implementation of their plans. A simple awareness of the leadership options available will have a significant impact on a project manager's effectiveness.

Along with the previous five leadership behaviors, there are also situation variables, which determine when a particular leadership behavior is appropriate. There are seven variables that can be grouped into two categories: quality and commitment. Quality factors affect the type of decision or solution required; commitment refers to the degree to which project team members will support the solution. The seven variables are:

Quality

1. Superior solution. Does it make a significant difference which course of action is adopted? Are all possible solutions able to resolve the issue equally well? For example, what color should the status report covers be? There probably is no one technically superior solution.

2. Adequacy of information. Does the project manager have enough information to find a superior solution or to make a quality decision alone? Information refers to all the data needed to analyze the situation.

3. Structure of the situation. Does the project manager know what information is missing and how to get it?

Commitment

4. Commitment. Is commitment by others critical to effective implementation of the solution? Does effective implementation require more than compliance? Conducting a research project requires judgment, independent action, and creativity. On the other hand, following specific guidelines or using a specified format may not require these elements. Sometimes commitment of others is not absolutely critical for an issue to be resolved. Filling out project time sheets is more of a compliance issue. Commitment should be distinguished from compliance, which is merely a willingness to follow set rules or procedures.

5. Commitment without participation. Will team members commit to a conclusion made by the project manager without their active participation? Is there a willingness to support a solution or decision and put in the extra effort to make it succeed without participating directly in determining that solution? Once you answer question #4, this helps to clarify whether team members will commit without direct involvement in the solution or decision. Project managers who have earned trust based on past actions may gain commitment without involving others. Sometimes people don't care which conclusion is implemented.

6. Goal agreement. Is there general agreement about project goals or task objectives between the team and the organization in this situation? Are the team's goals compatible with the interests of the organization? There are times when engineers want to design the heck out of things in order to create the end all, be all of solutions. However, time, cost, and commercial factors may not favor a highly designed solution. In this example, you may say there is lack of goal agreement.

7. Conflict about alternatives. Is there likely to be conflict about alternatives within the project team? There may be disagreement about which approach will provide a superior or acceptable solution. It may be in the project team members' best interests to come together as a group to discuss their differences of opinion.

The value of being familiar with these variables is that they can be combined to eliminate types of leadership behavior that could be damaging to the project team's success. The applicability of these variables will change from one situation to another. For example, if a project issue requires a single high-quality technical solution and the project manager does not posses complete information, then A1 behavior should be eliminated. Since it makes a difference which solution is chosen and the project manager has inadequate information, the project could be put at serious risk if the project manager chose to resolve the situation alone. If there is a single technically correct solution and goal agreement does not exist, then G2 behavior should be eliminated by the project manager as a leadership behavior option. Since it matters which course of action is taken and the project team members have different objectives from those of the organization, project success may again be placed at risk if the final decision is left to the group. Participation just for the sake of participation can be quite costly and can blunt the leadership effectiveness of the project manager.

By assessing variables within given project situations and evaluating the behaviors that make the most sense, project managers can significantly increase their abilities to implement projects well. Another worthwhile consideration for project managers in this context is the element of time efficiency versus the need to develop people. If tremendous time pressures exist, project managers would naturally favor those leadership behaviors toward the A1 end of the range. Autocratic decisions tend to be more time efficient. Each situation will likely result in a range of the five behaviors that can be selected. As long as the behavior is appropriate to the given situation, the time-strapped project manager would choose the appropriate behavior that is most time efficient.

Good leaders are also people who develop others. As we described previously, the development of outstanding future project managers is a critical issue for today's organizations. There will be instances when project managers have time to invest. Rather than choosing a more autocratic behavior, the project manager may give the team members an opportunity to decide or resolve the situation themselves or allow their measured input and recommendations. This helps the team members develop and exercise their own managerial and leadership skills. Once the project manager has determined the acceptable ranges of behavior in a given situation, she can then choose which is the best use of time: be efficient or develop individuals.

No one style or behavior will ever provide success in all situations. We all tend to default toward familiar behaviors when dealing with others. However, in critical project situations, choosing the wrong style adds significant risk to projects and can result in organizations failing to deliver against their strategic objectives. Leadership is dynamic and requires constant evaluation as project situations change. The stakes are high for organizations moving toward more project-based work. Every organization must have project managers that know the range of leadership behaviors that exist and can then effectively choose and move among those behaviors for the maximum benefit of the organization.

Kepner-Tregoe, Inc. obtained the rights to the research of Drs. Victor H. Vroom and Phillip W. Yetton and has applied the results of this research since the late 1970s in different organizational settings to further their initial findings. Decision trees used to guide managers through the process were also developed and copyrighted by Kepner-Tregoe, Inc.

How Can a Project Manager Be an Effective Negotiator?

Kent A. Dorr

Proceedings of the 30th Annual Project Management Institute
1998 Seminars & Symposium

Recent economic changes have made negotiating skills all the more important to the project manager. Bottom-line bids and proposals have driven contractors to be more aggressive in the increasingly competitive marketplace. Contractors are now challenging the client, citing scope changes, unforeseen conditions, schedule extensions, and any other reason to seek compensation—legitimate or not.

Any method of negotiation can be judged by three criteria: It should produce a wise agreement—if agreement is possible; it should be efficient; and it should improve, or at least not damage, the relationship between the parties. A wise agreement can be defined as one that meets the legitimate interests of each side to the extent possible, resolves conflicting interests fairly, is durable, and takes community interests into account (Fisher and Ury 1991).

Everyone negotiates something every day. It can be at work, at home, or at the store. Everyone wants to negotiate the issues and be involved with the decisions that affect them. People differ, and they use inherent negotiation skills to handle their differences. Unfortunately, most people lack effective negotiation skills, and their experiences often leave them alienated, dissatisfied, frustrated, or confused.

To be an effective and successful project manager, an individual needs to be a skilled negotiator. Whether it is negotiating with team members, resource support departments, or various contractors and clients, it is a large part of the job.

As a project manager, individuals must plan and prepare for controversy. Contracting by nature has complex requirements, various agendas, differing requirements, and unforeseeable developments. There are bound to be disagreements that are not easily resolved. Project managers tend to fall into entrenching themselves and not budging from their position. Contracting and claims are virtually synonymous. Project managers are often faced with the dual problem of running the project and trying to protect their company or clients from claims.

Negotiating contract disputes is one of the unpleasant tasks that face project managers. An effective negotiator needs to be knowledgeable and well prepared. A project manager needs to be realistic when preparing to negotiate any contract disputes. Claims cannot be won if the other person does not understand the claim or your position on the claim. If your point is not clear, concise, and effectively presented then both parties are faced with the difficult task of making decisions without a full understanding of the issue (Acuff 1998).

There is a systematic four-step approach that can be used to complement a project manager in negotiating disputes. This approach can assist a project manager in being prepared for negotiations and negotiating efficiently. This can result in a conclusion that is a win/win for both parties. The four tactics are:
1. Reducing the likelihood of contract disputes.
2. Recognizing potential disputes.
3. Preparing for negotiations.
4. Win/win settlements—closure.

How to Reduce the Likelihood of a Contract Dispute

A successful project starts during the planning phase of the project with knowing and understanding the scope of work to be accomplished. The statement of work for the project is to be written in sufficient detail so that the owner of the project is satisfied with the work performed by the contractor with little or no changes.

A document that can be used by a project manager is an Operations or Owner Requirements Document (ORD), which is a dynamic document and is to be used throughout a project's life cycle. The ORD is the foundation of the statement of work, which is the main contract document from which claims and disputes arise. Preparation starts at the beginning of the life cycle of a project, and continues through project closeout. Early planning and preparation of contract documents and keeping the documents accurate is the main ingredient in having a contract that can be successfully utilized. Then, if disputes arise, the disputes can be settled quickly and objectively. If your basic contract vehicle is weak, then the project manager is going to have a long, drawn-out project where scope creep and change orders are coming at the project manager constantly.

The success of a project and the reduction of the likelihood of contract dispute starts in the planning/conceptual stage of a project. Time and money are well spent during this stage to generate a concise ORD and then manage the project to the ORD. If the owner of the project continues to change the scope, then there are going to be costly delays to the project that will need to be negotiated and the contract amended to incorporate the changes.

Recognition of Potential Disputes

Anticipating disputes is not hard—it is almost impossible. There is no telling from where a dispute may arise and when it will appear.

Project managers have to look at the statement of work, contract documents, engineering specifications, and drawings with their bidding contractor hats on. With this approach, the project manager should then generate a pre-bid list of questions that he would ask at a pre-bid conference. This way the project manager can "head the dispute off at the pass" during the pre-bid phase.

It is beneficial to have a follow-up meeting, called an assumptions meeting, to provide to the bidders another chance to submit questions and state what assumptions are being made in preparing the estimates. Removing as many questions and unknowns as possible before the bids are submitted reduces the number of claims during the execution phase of the project.

The project manager can ask the project team to look at the bidding documents from a different view and ask the question, "If you were to bid this project, where would you see weak spots? Where are there holes or gray areas that a contractor could come at us with a claim?" What has been successful in the past is to perform peer review. The peer review should take a very aggressive look at the documents and challenge the project team to defend the bid package. The changes that will strengthen the project contract document for the project are then incorporated. In doing so, the project team is removing as many potential claims and disputes as possible. Ask for objective criticism from the peer review and remind the project team that it is not personal—it is good business sense.

The peer review is not limited to in-house resources, but can use exterior sources to provide feedback in support of generating a contract document that minimizes areas of potential dispute. It is possible to contract with another firm to review the package and provide comments on making the bid package better.

These reviews assist the project manager in recognizing areas of risk before a contract is awarded. After contract award, when the project is in the execution phase, the task of negotiating increases in difficulty. The project manager and the project team should have a feel for the project and how "things are going." It is hoped that they will be able to anticipate where difficulties will arise. Selection of the project team is an important factor in dealing with this aspect. As mentioned, experienced project personnel get a "feeling" for the project and can put into place changes to the scope of work that can either minimize or remove a potential dispute. Experienced members can bring lessons learned from past projects. Past errors will not be repeated in preparing the bidding documents.

The last area to cover in the recognition of potential disputes is risk management. Usually risk analysis is performed for the project during the planning or conceptual phase. The project team members should focus a majority of their time in managing the high-risk areas of the project, as this area is going to be the source of most claims and disputes. Managing the high-risk areas assists the project manager in the planning for the mitigation of disputes.

Preparing for the Negotiations

Each project manager prepares for negotiations in the way that she is are most comfortable; sometimes this is dependent on how much time she has in her schedule. The project manager should take the lead in the negotiating session, not the project engineer or the subcontract administrator.

Knowing and understanding the statement of work and other contract documents enhances the confidence level of the negotiator. Do your homework. Take your time to understand what angle the contractor's claim is taking. One way to prepare to negotiate is to break down the claim into separate line items to be negotiated. Then highlight in the contract documents where the areas are covered that support your position. Provide your disposition to the claim in a short, concise write up at the time of negotiation with your counterpart. The write up should cite specific sections, paragraphs, drawing numbers, and notes that disprove the claim.

This author does not agree with the commonly used tactics of only negotiating on your home turf or slightly outnumbering the other side. If the project manager is prepared and knows the project and contract documents, they should not care about where the negotiations take place, what time of day, or any other aspects. Allow the other side to make the plans. Simply state, "we should get together sooner than later," usually less than one week after the claim is submitted, and that "other issues are not important."

Having supporting documents at the ready is an immeasurable tool in assisting the project manager. Before the negotiating session the project manager should also have the project engineer review the dispute and provide a technical evaluation. It is also a good idea to have an independent cost estimate prepared. The project manager will use these documents for reference during the negotiation session.

Seek advice on the claim from a legal perspective. More times than not, this is covered by the subcontract administrator on the team. Citing actual past cases that are relative to the claim strengthens your position.

In preparing for the negotiation it is important to know your opponent. Try and determine what the main point is from his position and develop a contingency plan. The plan is to try and anticipate the main points that support his position and identify any weaknesses. Be prepared to make an opening statement where the project manager reviews the claim, the highlights of the claim, and then addresses his position, as the project manager understands it.

Before the negotiation session, the project manager needs to review the claim with the project team and decide who from the team will be participating. Assignments are then made as to what each member is going to be responsible for concerning the claim. The project manager then discusses how he expects each participant to conduct herself, what she should expect from herself, and the rules and guidelines are for the meeting.

The project manager should have an agenda ready to present at the meeting. The agenda sometimes becomes the first negotiated item of the session. Which side of the fence you represent usually dictates the agenda. The one with the money dictates.

The last thing, there should never be any contradiction between team members during the session. Input during a discussion is welcomed only when the comments strengthen and support your position (McCormack 1995).

The Win/Win Settlement

This is not a new term but a well-worn practice that this author strongly supports. The win/win settlement scenario is when the dispute is resolved to the satisfaction of both parties. Each side has neither won nor lost, but a fair and equitable settlement is reached.

In negotiations, the discussion is seen as a contest from which one side will emerge victorious and the other will be defeated (Jandt 1989). Each project manager negotiator should strive to help the other achieve a satisfactory agreement.

The project manager is responsible for keeping a professional, controlled attitude at all times during difficult negotiations. Staying focused on the agreed-to issues, being objective and fair, and not allowing oneself to be drawn into a "personalized dog fight" are the keys to having a successful session. Allow yourself to be flexible and open to new items introduced during the session.

At the start of the session, clearly state your perspective of the problem, then ask for the other side's view of the issue. Set some ground rules before items are discussed such as: no personal criticism, discuss one item to closure before addressing a new issue, stay professional, take a break of ten to fifteen minutes if tempers rise.

See if there are any questions from the opposing party, then ask your questions. Remove as many preconceived assumptions as possible, because this will alleviate mistakenly arguing over an issue.

When asking questions keep them open ended. Then probe with follow-up questions. Stay with the questions until you learn everything you need to know. Do not lose sight that the purpose is to determine your counterpart's position. This helps you in finding the "least" amount of what is acceptable.

Remember that the issue is not what you think the other side would accept, but rather what you yourself would accept. What is fair and equitable? Your levels of tolerance exist wholly independently of your adversary's situation. Keep in mind that you should try and relate to what your counterparts' circumstances are.

Summary

Project managers that have not had formal training, experience, or use of an organized approach to negotiating disputes usually experience an unsuccessful negotiation session. Sometimes an experienced project manager is a very successful negotiator because of self-taught techniques and past practices that have developed into a strategy that works. Today project managers do not always have the luxury of learning through past negotiations, but suddenly find themselves involved in a major contract dispute that they are ill equipped to manage and negotiate. This results in a settlement that is not in the best interest of their clients.

Do not let yourself forget that negotiations are not a debate, a trial, or a contest. Stay focused and deal with the person across the table. Place yourself in the role of treating your opposite member as a fellow project manager with whom you are working, trying to agree on a joint opinion.

The relationship between the two sides becomes more important after the negotiation session has concluded. Each individual's satisfaction depends, to a degree, on making the other side sufficiently content with an agreement that they can live up to. As a negotiator, you will almost always want to look for solutions that will leave the other side satisfied as well (Fisher and Ury 1991).

The philosophy that a win/win scenario is a successful negotiation is not a unique one or a new idea. It is a matter of keeping a professional relationship with all parties for the term of the contract that eventually leads to a successful project completion. The author feels that by using the four techniques presented in this article, a project manager can negotiate a fair and successful conclusion to contract disputes.

References

Acuff, Frank L. 1998. *How to Negotiate Anything with Anyone, Anywhere.* New York American Management Association.

Fisher, Roger, and William Ury. 1991. *From Getting To Yes: Negotiating Agreement Without Giving In.* New York: Haughton, Mifflin Company.

Jandt, Fred E. 1989. *Win-Win Negotiating, Turning Conflict into Agreement.* New York: John Wiley & Sons, Inc.

McCormack, Mark H. 1995. *Negotiating Beverly Hills.* Century Limited.

Negotiating the Right Decision

Andrc Long

PM Network 39 (December 1997)

As high-level decision-makers, project managers don't usually see themselves as negotiators. That's usually contract management's job. Yet, in fact, successful project managers are artful negotiators. They use dissent to search for alternatives and bargain among groups and individuals with diverse, and sometimes conflicting, interests to achieve consensus and commitment. For them, negotiation is not a process of giving in or compromising in order to secure an agreement but a method of obtaining resolution of a complete problem or project.

Individuals and groups bargain with project managers all the time. The Integrated Product Development Team (IPDT) is, in its very essence, participative management. The collective decision-making and shared responsibilities of an IPDT in many ways limit the project manager's authority by what the IPDT and other subordinates are willing to accept. In making the tradeoffs and reaching the right decisions, a typical project manager spends more time negotiating in his daily work than contract managers ever do. One could argue that successful project managers spend so much time harmonizing or reconciling needs that they have to be naturally gifted with an intuitive understanding of people and persuasion.

Clash and Conflict

Management theorist Peter Drucker said, "The right decision grows out of the clash and conflict of divergent opinions and out of the serious consideration of competing alternatives." Unlike attitudes, opinions are only a temporary way of perceiving something and should be susceptible to change by convincing arguments. Drucker believed that most people approached a problem with preconceived opinions before searching for the facts. He felt that this is normal since people experienced in an area should be expected to have an opinion. Yet if you ask them to search for facts first, they will often look for the facts that fit the conclusion they have already made.

As individuals concerned with the "big picture," project managers must think through and challenge opinions. Limited resources, diverse personalities, complicated issues, and other variables can make reaching the right decision a difficult challenge. When department heads beg for their engineering design and make promises of a financial or delivery nature based upon assumptions, project managers must test these needs and assumptions against reality. This process of examining, studying, and testing is in actuality a complex negotiation where the players argue, document, and consider alternatives. In project management there are always competing interests and stakeholders. For example, in the construction of a building, one functional area of an IPDT may want a more novel elevation design while another in a conflicting functional area, such as financial management, may feel it is not worth the extra time and cost involved in improving the foundation to accommodate the design. The two engage in a bargaining process eventually including the project manager.

To negotiate successfully, project managers must understand the bargaining process and how it is used by individuals and groups to get what they want. Motivation plays a large part in this since it is driven by personal needs. These needs can be ranked from highest to lowest priority starting with physiological, safety, social, and self-esteem needs and ending with self-actualization, which concerns the need for personal success. As these various hierarchical needs are satisfied, their power to motivate is diminished.

For example, let's consider socialization needs. Most managers are concerned with how they are perceived by their superiors. If taken to the extreme, this kind of manager will always agree with proposals that are perceived as having the backing of her superiors. Her socialization needs will prevent the manager from considering other alternatives that may be unpopular or controversial with the boss or peers. However, effective project managers must be able to counter this by testing opinions against facts and encouraging debate based upon merit.

This requires project managers who do not have a need to be liked by everyone, but who also are not loners. They must be team players that are not afraid of exercising independence from the group or individual department heads in order to meet team objectives.

In persuading others and reaching the "right decision," effective project managers must understand why there is disagreement and what the other party's argument is really about. Maybe the other party sees a different reality or is concerned with a different problem. Unfortunately, we cannot understand issues until we have first heard them stated. There is much truth to the adage that "we hear only half of what is said to us, understand only half of that, believe only half of that, and remember only half of that." Good listening skills cannot be overemphasized, especially in the field of project management where problems can be extremely complex. However, once they are mastered, good listening can also become contagious since people tend to listen better when they feel they are understood. It is natural to feel that a person who understands you is intelligent, sympathetic, and may himself have opinions worth listening to. A genuine understanding of another's perspectives, feelings, opinions, and attitudes helps release the productive potential inherent in people.

In Search of Something Better

The reason for negotiating is to get something better than we would have been able to get if we did not negotiate. While some project managers have complete responsibility with no direct authority, most have some authority to impose their decisions on various engineering/design activities. However, project managers negotiate with their subordinates and other functional groups to obtain worthwhile solutions and secure their participation in executing whatever was agreed.

Those with higher aspirations in life often end up with better results, and it is the same in negotiations. Our personal level of aspiration is a yardstick by which we measure ourselves. The more successful we are, the more we aspire. In negotiations, high demands and hard-fought concessions can lower the other side's aspiration level and also give a project manager or team more room to negotiate. However, being unreasonable, unrealistic, and unconvincing is also a formula for losing your credibility and influence. While it is common practice to give concessions on minor issues or in areas that are not important to you, demands and concessions are most effective when they are less predictable. Avoid tit-for-tat concessions. This does not mean that one should be arbitrary; cooperation, not arbitrary behavior, will lead to better project decisions.

When bargaining, it is common for parties to argue for positions, use tactics to seek a competitive advantage, and make concessions to reach a compromise. Tactics are nothing more than procedures, some ethical and some not, which assist a negotiator in gaining an advantage. This type of negotiation is often referred to as "positional," but is also known as "competitive" negotiation. It is often characterized by parties attempting to maximize their own gain, sometimes at the expense of others. The initial position for each party is usually to get everything and give up nothing. During the negotiation, information that does not promote a side's position is usually not disclosed. An arsenal of tactics are used to get large concessions while conceding as little as possible. This methodology has been successfully applied for thousands of years and is almost human nature to many people and cultures.

However, positional bargaining can severely impede IPDTs because the focus is on positions—such as, "I want a higher-grade steel"—and not on meeting the underlying concerns—such as, "Why do you think you need a higher-grade steel?" Project managers are supposed to be searching for optimal solutions, but positional bargaining often results in a minimally acceptable compromise or mechanical splitting of the difference rather than a win/win solution.

"Interest-based" negotiations involve separating the underlying needs of the parties from their positions. By knowing each other's interests, the negotiating parties can develop creative solutions that meet their legitimate needs. Instead of being a contest of wills and power, the process becomes a problem-solving endeavor where the give and take is based on merit. The results are outcomes produced efficiently and amicably. The method involves four essential points: separate the people from the problem, focus on interests and not positions, invent options for mutual gain, and use objective criteria or a fair standard to determine the outcome.

However, not all people communicate in such an open fashion. This is especially true of professional negotiators, who by their very natures are competitive people. For example, contract negotiators are usually selected for competitiveness and drive to win. Sharing their personal or corporate interests would be tantamount to suicide when dealing with another competitive negotiator.

Interest-based advocates argue that unless interests are discovered, the parties are only dividing up the pie instead of enlarging the pie before it's cut. Most experienced negotiators believe that the less they talk the better off they are. Since negotiations usually consist of a mix of common and conflicting interests, a competitive negotiator will look behind positions for the information and interests that are driving the positions being taken. This enables the negotiator to better meet his needs and also harmonize or reconcile the needs of the other party, when necessary or appropriate.

While some negotiations, such as the purchase and sale of a home, involve a short-term relationship with unrelated interests, IPDTs present a different situation. A large turnkey construction project may span many years and require cooperative problem solving at all levels within the organization and with the client. Project managers and IPDTs cannot afford to become polarized. They must build trust and gain commitment from each other through their mutual dependence. They must demonstrate high integrity and dependability and expect the same from others. The more confidence you place in others, the more they will justify your faith. Without trust and a good working relationship, it is unrealistic to expect participants to lay all their cards on the table.

When project managers and IPDT members do not have trust and confidence in one another, they are more prone to use tactics that finesse or manipulate the situation to their advantage. Take the use of time constraints as an example. The amount of time available to each party is one of the most significant factors affecting a negotiation. Time tactics can provide an enormous amount of leverage, even when the time limitations are not real. However, if an IPDT does not have enough time to plan, prepare, and negotiate, the negative effects can be absolutely disastrous. For example, project managers have been known to use artificial deadlines, such as funding and fiscal-year pressure, to push IPDTs into yielding favorable decisions.

It is not unusual during any bargaining to have items that are valuable to one side while unimportant to the other. For example, a mechanical engineer may intentionally include inflated hours to install the ventilation system when the real intention is to require a more rigorous design specification. The engineer may argue at length to support the need for the additional hours only to later concede the issue in exchange for the improved design specification. These are called straw issues and must be distinguished from the genuine needs of the party.

Another tactic is the use of threats. All threats are bluffs unless the negotiator issuing the threat is prepared to carry it out. It makes no sense to threaten unless you are reasonably sure that the other party believes you will follow through. By its very nature, negotiation involves various degrees of threats. The simple possibility of a project manager imposing her decision on the team constitutes a type of threat. Beware, however, that direct threats can inflame a problem and invite retaliation.

In general, any tactic employed must be used carefully and judiciously. If poorly conceived or executed, it can be counterproductive and damaging. The best approach relies not on slick maneuvers but instead on collaborative problem solving, where parties share their needs and work together in good faith.

The negotiation method detailed here is derived in part from the "principled negotiation" model developed by the Harvard Negotiation Project and detailed in the best-selling book, *Getting to Yes: Negotiating Agreement Without Giving In*, by Roger Fisher and William Ury (Penguin 1991).

Handling Unpleasant Project Tasks

Gregory D. Githens, PMP

PM Network 28 (December 1997)

Why consider unpleasant tasks? Project managers must frequently ask others to work in physically dangerous conditions, work overtime or with people they dislike, or change product designs. Effective project managers master the twin challenges of accomplishing the work while preserving (even enhancing) personal relationships. Handling unpleasant tasks is a supreme test of leadership ability.

I believe that our changed organizational environment means that people will increasingly need to perform unpleasant work. Why? Because modern organizations are shifting toward less specialization and more sharing of work. The new horizontal organization cannot tolerate the refrain, "That's not my job," and individuals must leave their comfort zones to grow in the organization.

Here are some strategies and guidelines to help project managers improve their approaches to communicating unpleasant project tasks. Applying these ideas will help people handle unpleasant tasks in a way that preserves dignity.

Influencing in All Directions

Influencing is a style of communicating and motivating others to accept and perform unpleasant tasks. It works in all directions: with superiors, subordinates, and peers.

In your role of project manager, you may request a senior person or a peer to perform an unpleasant project task. They might be the only one available, hold the needed technical expertise, or have the organizational position to make a commitment. For some executives, making a basic decision is unpleasant; it forces them into a commitment for which they might be held accountable!

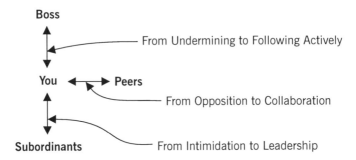

Figure 1. Influencing Behaviors Can Vary from Controlling to Empowering

Effective influencers provide information that is relevant to the needs of the senior person or a peer. Consider the manager of a product development process unable to get senior executives to commit support to an ISO-documented development process. For the manager the task of approaching senior executives was daunting, because he feared rejection and appearing incompetent. He zeroed in on the executives' needs to add value to the organization and avoid repeating project disasters. Next, he related the proposed change as a solution to the executives' needs.

By "following actively" and specifically connecting the objectives of the development process with executives' objectives for the organization's performance, he was able to secure their support and sponsorship for an organizational change program.

Influencing is a core project management skill, particularly important when one doesn't have a formal position of authority. Figure 1 provides a model for evaluating and identifying behaviors that promote or retard influence. The responses to an unpleasant task will vary whether you are in an ineffective, stressful, "trapped" condition or in a fully involved, organizationally effective "energized" state.

Trapped. When we are "trapped," we worry only about ourselves. We undermine the success of our bosses and oppose the efforts of our peers. We intimidate and micromanage our subordinates. We try to avoid unpleasant tasks. The role of the bearer of bad news only increases the isolation. Trapped managers regard unpleasant tasks as nuisances or threats and respond with defensiveness, avoidance, or minimal effort.

Static. A manager in a static situation is cautious and mechanical. "Let it happen" is a frequent strategy. We passively follow our leaders, protect our turf when dealing with peers, and direct our subordinates according to rigid rules and processes.

Energized. An empowered project manager has the authority, resources, information, and accountability to accomplish results, and does so in a way that maintains a big-picture, long-term perspective. Collaboration is the desired process. Build *and* exercise influence by actively leading—that is, helping the boss, peers, and subordinates to achieve their objectives.

Ten Guidelines for Improving Influence on Unpleasant Tasks

The following ten guidelines are for increasing effectiveness in communicating about an unpleasant task. These are real-world guidelines based on observing and coaching dozens of experienced project managers.

1. *Do your homework, particularly if the unpleasant task involves dates or cost.* Probably the worst unpleasant task (or at least the most frequent) is when a project manager confronts an executive or customer with the data that a project due date is late or unachievable. When you use good project scheduling practices and adjust estimates for quantitative and scheduled risk, you can build a sound, irrefutable case for establishing a realistic completion date. Many executives or customers would rather get the bad news than be surprised later.

2. *Getting their attention is a prerequisite.* A student of Samurai warriorship asked his Zen master the secret to learning the craft. "Attention!" commanded the master. Confused, the student repeated his question. "Attention! Attention!" replied the master again.

Getting your audience to tune in to your presence and message is a prerequisite to discussing an unpleasant task. If people know that bad news is on the way, they will avoid a meeting. Be dogged in getting the right people included, and (at least temporarily) remove distractions.

3. *Prepare for objections.* Objections have great value. They are signals that attention and comprehension are under way. Plan for and welcome objections, which can include questions such as the following: Is there really a problem? Is it important? To whom? Are the skills available? Why do you think we are competent to handle the task? Is there a simpler solution? What's in it for me? What are the inherent threats and punishments? What are the real requirements? Ideal outcomes? Minimum conditions? Will people "shoot the messenger"?

4. *Talk to people in person.* The medium of communication is as important as the message. An impersonal note or message suggests that the sender does not care enough to become involved and desires emotional distance. An informal memo, newsletter, or email is an ineffective and possibly counterproductive way to announce a change or to motivate and direct people to accomplish an unpleasant task.

Technology is making the process much more difficult because, although communications are rapid, they are impersonal. In today's project environment, we are increasingly seeing signs of the "virtual electronic sweatshop." An email message shouts, "Submit this immediately!" At worst, recipients feel, "I'm just an instrument of someone else's work."

Unpleasant projects are often threatening. They cause anger and resentment for individuals involved in the project. As uncomfortable as it might be for you, you need to speak to people personally. One of the most useful strategies I can offer is to plan for a period of venting anger and frustration, even if the group is directing it at you. Let people get mad and sound off. It's therapeutic!

There is an important role for formal, written communications in implementing unpleasant project tasks. Formal memos and other forms of formal documentation are often a good follow up, because people are "in denial" and have a hard time *hearing* information that disturbs their security. The written form provides formality, reinforcing the need to regard the work seriously.

5. *Ask for what you want.* Asking for what we want is common sense, but it's underused as a communication strategy. You want something. They want something. Negotiating is one approach to a workable solution. Remember this nugget of wisdom from Gerald Weinberg: "To want is natural, to get is negotiable."

Separate constraints from preferences when formulating requirements. Some things are "must haves" and others are "nice to haves." If you don't know whether a requirement is a constraint or preference, admit it and allow others to use that information in their design of the solution. A good project communicator structures the conversation to help the receiver make a choice. The sidebar, Structuring the Choice: Adoption and Attitude, provides key criteria for adopting an idea.

6. *Authenticity is the basis for trust.* Authenticity is knowing yourself and accepting your strengths and weaknesses. When we are authentic, we tell the truth about ourselves to others. We expose our vulnerabilities. The wizard in *The Wizard of Oz* is a perfect example of the fakery of an inauthentic person who has true power when he becomes an honest and caring person, rather than a manipulator.

People around you quickly perceive authenticity and are more open to trust. Trust is the glue of the relationship, and it comes from trustworthy people who have earned your trust.

To be trustworthy, you need to make a commitment to the truth. If you are hiding something, it will probably show (some people have an uncanny knack for seeing through you). Ignoring a question usually reinforces people's fears. A believable leader does not know everything. Don't be afraid to say, "I don't know."

While this guideline may be too "warm and fuzzy" for many, I encourage you to observe others who are authentic. You will discover that they are self-confident, nonneurotic, and effective. People are much more willing to place their trust in authentic people.

7. *Avoid bribes and sugarcoating.* Search out the underlying audience needs. Many managers mistakenly try to bribe (with money, recognition, and so on) to get others to adopt the desired decision.

"Sugarcoating" is trying to smooth-talk people by telling them that an unpleasant task will really be fun. Sugarcoating is dishonest and inauthentic. While this may have worked for Tom Sawyer, it is seldom effective in the workplace, where workers have learned to be cynical about the intentions of others.

8. *Recognize and address threats to security and well-being.* Many, many tasks are hazardous. The hazards might involve threats to personal safety, security, or ego. Threats to safety and well-being can command *all* of our attention. First, address the factors that would lead to dissatisfaction. Search for solutions that provide protection from these threats. Psychologist Frederick Herzberg called these dissatisfiers "hygiene factors," and teaches us that we must remove these dissatisfiers before we can apply positive incentives.

Often, there is no way you can offer a motivator for performing an unpleasant task. The best you can do is help make the task short, clean, and nonrecurring. First, identify what the audience wants to avoid, and preserve and focus efforts on minimizing the threat. After you have removed the threat, your audience may perceive a recognition program or a bonus as a positive reward and thus a motivator.

9. *Take the first step to lead the way.* When starting work on an unpleasant task, one of the best lessons is for the leader to participate in the solution. Specifically, be the first to step forward and deal with the problem. Followers look at actions more than words.

Telling and selling has limited impact. Remember Robert F. Mager's observation: "Exhortation is used more and accomplishes less than almost any behavior-changing tool known to man."

10. *Develop (and share) empathy.* Empathy is the ability or capacity to participate in another's feelings or ideas. It is a mutual understanding derived from shared experiences. Empathy underlies trust. People who have mutual empathy are more likely to accomplish the needed work and preserve good interpersonal relationships. Vulnerability and authenticity keep people participating in the communication process. Don't withhold information about your feelings. People want to know your reactions.

With the unique nature of the project setting, empathy is crucial. Since tasks are unique and temporary, you only get one opportunity to build the necessary empathy. You probably won't achieve a deep level of trust with strangers, but it is possible to cooperate and avoid manipulation. Stephen Covey's principle, "Seek first to understand and then to be understood," is valuable advice when communicating about an unpleasant task.

Implementation: Consensus Is Particularly Important

Why do we spend endless hours discussing problems and finding solutions only to discover that individuals have not taken action? One answer is that we are more skilled in analysis than synthesis (implementation). Consensus-building is a robust technique for assuring implementation.

Consensus is one of the most misunderstood terms used in today's organizations. It does *not mean* that everyone agrees on a decision, it means that *people agree to support the decision, even though they do not agree with the decision.* Every member of the group must visibly signal his agreement to support the implementation. This definition has a key corollary: The group defines its membership so that each member of the group knows *who is in* and *who is out* of the implementation group. The worst result of no consensus is muddling, nonparticipation, and inertia. The best result of no consensus is the accomplishment of the work via luck. It's incredible how much people rely on luck!

For consensus to work in a project environment, there needs to be a way to recognize the 100 percent agreement of project participants. The signs can range from verbal statements to physical signals.

Be forewarned that consensus-building is time consuming and sometimes painful, because it forces members of the group to expose and examine their assumptions, biases, and fears. It is effective because it assures that people will align their actions with their decisions. It is a basic discipline that surfaces and removes obstacles to full implementation.

Get their attention, *shape* their attitude, and *secure* their commitment. Common-sense principles? Maybe. But why do a surprising number of experienced, highly placed managers use very amateur strategies for communicating about unpleasant work? Often their egos and insecurities get in the way of basic civility. Choice and attitude underlie effectiveness. Attitude can change an unpleasant task to a learning opportunity. If we approach communications with a philosophy of civility and authenticity, we can get difficult, unpleasant work done without being manipulative.

Structuring the Choice:
Adoption and Attitude

"Push back" is a popular phrase that means "don't passively follow orders when they don't make sense." While some individuals deeply believe that they are compelled to follow orders, most are just over-worked or lazy thinkers. Effective modern project managers obtain project charters and make decisions within the charter's boundaries.

Many people perceive or assume that a threat to employment security is present. Thus, they become passive about accepting assignments, rationalizing that "they have accepted the lesser of two evils." Often their level of commitment is, at best, grudging compliance.

The truth is that we all have choices, and there is almost nothing that one person or group can compel another to do. The most important choice we make is our attitude. Each project participant can make the choice regarding her attitude in accepting and performing an unpleasant task. She can choose to perform an unpleasant task, retain dignity, and even grow along the way.

You can facilitate the choice process. Innovation scholar Everett Rogers identified five basic criteria involved in choice, which you can use as a framework for commitment.

1. *Simplicity*. The condition of simplicity exists when followers can see the issue as a straightforward, uncomplicated choice between two alternatives. Often we provide too much information. Eventually the "shades of gray" will emerge from the "black and white." Every good salesperson knows when it's time to quit selling and be quiet.
2. *Relative Advantage*. The choice is perceived as better than the alternatives.
3. *Observability*. Benefits can be observed, and observed quickly. Often benefits are too long term and abstract.
4. *Compatibility*. The decision is compatible with existing values.
5. *Trialability*. Followers can make a small commitment before making a major commitment.

Section 2

Organizational Planning: Identifying Roles, Responsibilities, and Relationships

The Fourth Constraint: Relationships

Russ Volckmann; Joan Knutson, Contributing Editor

PM Network 15 (May 1997)

Schedule, budget, and quality: these are the critical variables in project management, often referred to as the triple constraints. The core task in project management is to manage each of them, as well as the implications of the effect each will have on the others. If you decrease budget, there will be an impact on the schedule and/or on the quality of the product. When the budget is decreased or the schedule is tightened, some functionality will probably have to be sacrificed.

In the same way, effective relationships are critical to the success of our projects. The quality of relationships within a project and between a project organization and its external stakeholders will be manifested in the overall performance of the project.

What constitutes an effective relationship? That's a bit harder to define. We know that in managing conflicts, resolution is not always the best goal. Some conflicts are better avoided so that work can continue or that individuals can continue to work together on a bounded task. So it is with relationships. Relationships are dynamic and unpredictable. As a consequence, we must focus on how we sustain workable relationships over time, not on living up to some predetermined model of what constitutes a "good" or "bad" relationship.

Each project exists in a different cultural context, with a different set of core values, norms, and expectations. The qualities of relationships important to those cultures and for that particular project will vary. In one project, sharing information widely within the project may be important, but sharing information with the customer may be avoided. In another project, sharing information with the customer may be critical, since his input to changing conditions may be critical for the success of the project. Within the same project, the need for sharing may vary across phases.

A Cautionary Tale

A few years ago I consulted on the startup phase of a software development project. We assisted the project executives and project managers in gaining some agreement on their approach to the project. They chose a strong team strategy, which included collocation of technical and user staff, joint sponsorship from the user and technical branches of the organization, and joint project management (a user and technical project manager). Not long after our work was completed things began to deteriorate. This project that started with such high hopes ended up costing the parent company several millions of dollars, with no useful product. The leaders of that project are no longer with the company. The project was killed, and a new approach to meeting the organization's needs was undertaken under new leadership.

Luckily, there are lessons to be learned from failure. Here are some insights that this project provided into the importance of relationships in project management.

The executive responsible for the project established a very strong relationship with the project managers. Among them, however, they colluded to present senior executives with a "no problems" status of the project on an ongoing basis. Executive management was fooled into believing that the project was progressing very well. When the truth came out, the project managers and responsible executive left the company, and the embarrassed senior executives were left to search for a way out of their dilemma.

The project managers initially advocated a strong team approach to this project. As the project proceeded, however, the user and technical staff became upset about how the project was being managed and had growing concerns about the technical direction of the project. Their attempts to raise these issues were rebuffed. The project managers even proclaimed that the technical and user staffs were no longer to directly speak to each other, but they must communicate through the project managers. Within a year many of the technical and user staff members left the project and, in some cases, the company.

In both cases individuals were acting on sets of beliefs, values, and assumptions about relationships. The project managers believed and valued their exercise of control over relationships and the flow of information. The staff believed that it was important to share information and ideas across functional boundaries.

A Web of Relationships

It is critical to be clear about the quality of relationships that contribute to project success. This can be done by identifying who the players are and what their roles will be, by articulating the critical qualities of these relationships, and by designing support systems for these qualities.

To begin this process, you must examine the two "umbrella" groups within a project: the project team and project management.

The project team is composed of three groups. The first is the core team, composed of members who will take a continuing active role through much of the life of the project. In a space systems project this includes leaders in computer hardware, software, and materials and members of the project office. In-and-outers are those who make a contribution, leave, and return. This can happen several times over the life of a project. In a software development project, database leadership and technical staff may be in this position. Customers are often in-and-outers, as are quality inspectors. One aspect of relationships with in-and-outers is how information will be shared so that they can get up to speed. Another may be how these individuals are integrated with core team members with whom they must work closely. One-timers are those who come into a project, complete a task, and leave, never to be seen again on that project. In a construction project, a subcontractor for site preparation may be a one-timer.

The more complex the project, the more complex is the web of relationships. A major challenge for project management is to weave this set of relationships into a fabric that supports project success. The requirements for doing that will vary.

Project management consists of not only the project manager, but functional or resource managers and executives as well. Each has a role to play; each makes a contribution to the project. Yet project management really constitutes the web of relationships among these roles. What these roles are and what contribution will be required for project success will vary by project and context. By articulating these relationships, their shared purposes, and supporting requirements, we lay a foundation for project success.

Project charters were developed to assist in this task. My experience suggests that many executives and project managers develop charters as a bureaucratic task, without sufficient consideration to the web of relationships among those represented in this part of the model. The task is not so much to develop a complex document that spells out details about relationships and roles; rather it is the conversations that people have about the kinds of relationships that will help the project to be successful. The principles generated by these conversations may be included in the project charter.

When we recognize that project management is an activity that emerges from a web of relationships, this challenges our "hero" model of the project manager. Heroic acts are events in the life of a project: coming up with an effective solution to a problem; devising a way of effectively managing a risk; producing a creative design; or leading the team to meet a challenge. Heroic acts occur at all levels of a project organization, but the life of projects is more than a series of these events. Over the long haul relationships between project managers, resource managers, and executives provide for successful project management. That's why the quality of relationships within a project deserves to be elevated to the status of "the fourth constraint."

Actions We Can Take to Attend to Relationships on Projects

- Articulate roles. Are they project management roles or project team roles? Clarify how these roles relate to each other.
- Be clear about shared purposes and goals. They constitute the foundation for relationships that work.
- Converse with executives and resource managers to determine the roles they will be performing in project management and how they relate to other roles.
- Capture critical elements of these roles in the project charter.
- As the project unfolds or as new phases are entered, reexamine relationships by identifying what is working, what you have each learned so far, and how roles and relationships may be adjusted for the next phase of the project.
- Take the time during project startup to define the relationships within the core team that will contribute to success. Develop systems to support the quality of relationships you wish to support.
- Reward and recognize those who develop effective relationships. Build into rewards and recognition systems support for the development of valued relationship qualities. Reward and recognize all of those who contribute to making relationships work to support project success.
- Publicize ways that effective relationships have contributed to project successes. Talk about this in team meetings.

Relationship Building: A Key Technical Skill

Ron Rader and Cliff Vaughan

PM Network 47 (June 1999)

Are you a project manager who has risen through the technical ranks? If so, you're probably discovering that you have to develop and hone a whole new set of project management skills that weren't required just a few years ago.

Communications, networking, customer satisfaction, enlightened staff management, staff motivation, and managing a project for profit are vital skills in today's marketplace. In the past, about the only issues you heard of from your firm, your client, and your engineering university concerned technical skills and knowledge. The message was clear: The highest level of technical expertise always wins the project. While client surveys still rank a service provider's technical expertise as high in importance, the present-day client wants more. It's not enough to own and implement modern computer software to manage and track scope, schedule, and budget. The technical side must be coupled with people skills, especially if your project leadership could impact the future of the organization. And it will.

The project management challenge is now more global, more complex, and more customer driven than at any time in the past. Whoever best meets and exceeds the customer's expectations earns the best chance to win and keep the business. Technical skills to manage the project are not enough; most everyone in the business can make that claim. Your mastery and effective use of interpersonal skills can differentiate you from your competition.

An effective project manager must be able to organize a team effort, inspire each team member to perform at his highest level, recognize and manage the effects that personalities and styles have on group dynamics, and still meet the demands of scope, schedule, and budget.

In addition, a project manager must be sensitive to and help manage the client representative's requirements to report to higher management, orchestrate the internal selling of the project, and demonstrate control of the client company's resources in a prudent fashion. In short, the personal interaction that the project manager has with the client representative and with the project team can be a major factor in the ultimate success or failure of the project.

These expectations have swiftly engulfed organizations worldwide. Global competition, an insatiable demand for quality, and world-class customer service have merged to create a totally new paradigm for everyone responsible for ensuring that customers get what they pay for and are satisfied with what they receive. The new paradigm has brought a whole new list of requirements to the world of project management and to those of us who earn our living in that marketplace.

The client's often unspoken expectations sound like this: As your client, I place high value on the degree of concern that you demonstrate for my organization's success, as well as my personal success. Achieving success in this arena can be summarized in two words: *relationship building*. Customers want and expect the project manager to be interested in the goals of the client organization. They expect the project manager to understand their business and to actively help them meet their company's objectives. You must build personal and professional trust based on performance and personal interaction if you are to succeed.

There is a human side in all of us that asks, "What's in it for me?" The project manager should look continually for opportunities to help the client representative become a superstar in her organization. Never embarrass the client representative or place her in an awkward position. Such actions cast an unprofessional shadow on your ability to provide customer service and technical expertise.

Unfortunately, there are many organizations where the various elements of a healthy, dynamic customer relationship continue to be undervalued, overlooked, and, even more often, ignored by project managers who continue to rely on technical skills alone. The people skills required to develop client satisfaction are swept aside with negative terms such as touchy-feely, charm school, unimportant, waste of time, schmoozing, and a litany of others. "That's not a technical requirement" and "What's that got to do with my project?" are remarks often heard.

The truth is that it has *everything* to do with the project. In fact, the key to continuing success with most clients rests on relationship building. The successful relationship is built on mutual respect, confidence, and trust between the parties. The client representative must have complete confidence that the project manager will get the job done on schedule and within budget. The client representative must also believe that the project manager will make a personal commitment to success, will keep the client representative informed of project status, and will spring no surprises that will create awkward moments in front of client company management.

It's not the number of advanced technical degrees or past project experience of the staff that retains the client through multiple projects. Ask any experienced sales manager in a technical service organization and he will likely tell you that personalized service leads to continuing sole-source work. Technical expertise and relationship building must be balanced and operate in tandem to achieve long-term success. It is the project manager's responsibility to ensure the needed level of expertise is delivered to the project in tandem with the proper interest and respect for the client organization's internal requirements.

What are the skills that separate the best project managers from the average ones?

Negotiating

Successful project managers negotiate from a position of strength built through supplying accurate information. Successful project managers are always truthful, professional, and courteous. The client is often seeking information in order to explain the basis of a high cost to management. The project manager must be able to support the approach, as well as the estimated costs for a project, if the client representative is to become an ally and partner. An open and honest discussion of how a cost estimate was created and a willingness to explore alternatives can result in mutual respect and understanding of how the project will be accomplished. All too often, we see projects lost during negotiations by a project manager with a condescending "I am the expert, and you should do what I tell you" approach.

Listening

Project managers must be good listeners. They must be able to communicate with the client and with the project team. The project manager is responsible for the overall execution of the project. She must implement through the efforts of other team members. Project managers are expected to demonstrate high performance standards and understand the mission. That mission is communicated to the project manager by the client, and then to the project team by the project manager. The project manager must listen actively to the client and use follow-up questions to ensure understanding.

Often the complete requirements of the project cannot be transmitted adequately through a written scope document. Most certainly, the personal importance of the project to the client representative, along with other nuances, cannot be transmitted in a scope document.

Understanding Behavior Styles

Project managers must have a clear understanding of the client and project team's different personal styles. That knowledge provides valuable insight into how to communicate effectively and negotiate with specific individuals. Behavior styles, management styles, and individual types are real and can be managed for magnificent project success; or they can be mismanaged and ignored for a dismal procession of project failures.

Before any project team undertakes a major group endeavor, especially if it shares no history as a team, the members of the group should participate in a one- or two-day program aimed at understanding and appreciating individual differences, styles, and strengths. The costs of getting to know the other team members as people with names and faces will be recovered many times over as the project progresses. The results of group/team cohesiveness can often prove priceless in terms of project success.

In many projects, we execute seemingly endless documentation, make the required telephone calls, and send people who have never worked together as a team to a site and expect instant and magical success between the team and the client representative. There is little logic, rationale, or hope in this picture. It is a blueprint for failure. The manager of a major project who seeks the highest performance and continuing success will budget time for team training focused on styles, strengths, and personality types when the project involves multiple people from different locations and technical backgrounds.

Knowledge of styles can help you determine how to meet individual personal preferences for communication techniques. We have observed a number of instances when the project manager used knowledge of the client's personal style and correctly changed the approach. The change enabled the manager to quietly collect long, outstanding accounts receivable and obtain project change orders that were previously denied.

Personality clashes can creep into projects and lead to a competitive, divisive environment between the client's representative and the service provider's team. This creates almost certain failure for the project and the project manager. Learn to manage individual styles and you'll orchestrate harmony on project teams.

Understanding the Client's Organization

To be successful, you must understand the client's organization—its requirements, expectations, business style, culture, competition, profitability pressures, and other related characteristics. Learn the project's priority in the client's organization. To whom does the client contact report? Do you know the level of exposure for the client's project team, for your project team? How well is the need for information from these teams being managed?

Knowing to whom in the client's organization the project reports are made can also give you insight into funding priorities and the level of difficulty you can expect when seeking project decisions.

Understanding the Client's Internal Politics and Pressures

Understanding the internal politics of the client's organization and helping the client representative with those pressures will let you quickly build a relationship of mutual respect with your client.

However, becoming involved in or choosing sides in an internal political struggle within the client's organization can be devastating to your organization and to professional relationships between the organizations. Respect can be lost quickly, and future opportunities can go up in smoke.

Experienced project managers will be aware of and understand the internal politics of the client's organization while remaining apart from the struggle. The goal is to be seen as one who is a respected, reliable, professional, non-threatening, third-party ally when dealing with the client's organization.

Seeing Opportunities

Project managers not only have a responsibility to their own organizations to execute the project as contracted, but also a responsibility to create and acquire future project work. Every organization that provides any type of service has a need for new work to replace work that is being completed. Project managers have the best opportunity to be aware of and win future projects. We have personally observed instances where project managers ignored and showed no interest in a new project when it would have involved others or would have increased their workload. To ignore new opportunities with a current client demonstrates a lack of support for others in the project manager's organization. More importantly, this attitude could signal the client that this firm has no interest in a continually expanding working relationship. Professionalism creates a mutual respect and confidence that reassures the client firm that the project manager can produce desired results in the future.

Understanding the Client's Strengths, Weaknesses, and Expectations

Project managers must understand the client's strengths, weaknesses, and expectations in order to deliver the desired results. Project managers must be prepared to shore-up any weaknesses, make use of strengths, and otherwise ensure that client expectations are met. As the project progresses, open communication, education, knowledge, personal relationships, and the unfolding results of the project can all be used to meet client expectations that sometimes evolve with the project.

Communicating Continuously to Keep the Client Informed

Most service providers and their project managers are not in the same core business as the client organization. Therefore, if the client doesn't give the project the attention necessary to fully understand the deliverables that will be produced, there may be unpleasant surprises for both parties. All too often, and usually too late, the client discovers that the delivered services may not meet the need.

The experienced project manager will remain in constant communication with the client to ensure that there is a complete understanding of work in progress, work accomplished, and work that is planned for the near future. During project reviews, we have heard the manager of a project valued at over $5 million say that he had not talked to the client's representative in more than a month, since the representative knows how to contact him if she has questions.

A continuing status-report process (both written and informal via regular telephone conversations) enables timely, lower-cost modifications to be made and creates a happier, long-term partnership with the client. Communication is a major key to achieving client satisfaction and must be planned along with other project activities and monitored to achieve the desired results.

We have witnessed multiple disputes between clients and project management organizations that were centered on technical scope, change orders, and cost, when, in fact, the real issue was lack of communication early in the project.

Seeking Client Feedback

The successful project manager continually communicates with the client to ensure that needs and expectations are being met. The purpose is to solicit feedback on status and required changes and to help mold client expectations. Early feedback can enable modifications that will have little impact on schedule and budget. Failure to communicate and ask for feedback is too often at the root of project failure.

Helping the Client Achieve Superstar Status in His Company

The effective project manager must be willing to help meet the client representative's internal organization needs. A project manager must recognize her role as one of assisting the client representative to get the job done. The project manager's success becomes the client representative's success. A client organization's internal rewards (i.e., raises, promotions, commendations) may very well be linked to performance of the project manager's organization. Recognition of excellent performance can manifest itself in the form of repeat work, if the work is done well and a professional relationship is built through mutual respect.

The project manager is often a temporary player in the life of the client representative, and he must be willing to allow the client representative to share in the success of the project for the long-term benefit to his own organization.

Serving as the Orchestra Leader

Communication with the project team by the project manager is vital. In order to become a team, its members must be informed. They must be able to respond to scope changes, cope with schedule acceleration, and meet other internal needs. Without effective communication, the project team cannot hope to achieve a project's objectives. The project manager must also recognize and reward team members who help achieve the project objectives.

Following Up with Team Members

The project manager assigns tasks to team members to enable completion of the entire project. The wise project manager will not wait until each task is due for completion to request it. The project manager must communicate with team members on an individual basis to ensure that the task is understood, the schedule is clear, and there is no interference that could affect completion of the task.

The traits that enable project managers to win clients, keep clients, and develop additional business opportunities are very basic human traits. Often they are the same traits that drive our decisions in our everyday lives.

The technical skills and services of the individuals with whom you deal are generally equal. Gasoline prices are competitive, and all banks offer about the same rates. So why do you choose one over the other? In most cases, you select the person or organization that demonstrates a strong, friendly, caring, distinctive commitment to you and your concerns. Usually you choose the people who best personalize the service they provide you.

As project managers, our clients continually judge us and then select us from that perspective, once they believe we have the technical capabilities they need. Our abilities and opportunities to please the client have far fewer limitations when our work is grounded in strong interpersonal relationships with our clients. The key that will most often enable you to exceed customer expectations will be found in the interpersonal aspects of your relationships with clients, and will almost always lead to additional and continuing work from the same customer.

Anticipating Team Roles and Interactions When Planning a Software Development Project

Jeffrey H. Schweriner

Proceedings of the 30th Annual Project Management Institute
1999 Seminars & Symposium

Most projects, no matter what the industry, require a team. Every team member has specified tasks designed to carry out the development and implementation of the project. But for *successful* projects, every team member not only performs his specified tasks, but plays a specific role as well. By definition, a role is defined as a part or character to be played by an actor (Random House 1979). Indeed, project roles are defined not by what a person does, but rather by what *part* he plays.

Project roles become extremely important in highly technical projects such as software development. In software development the nature of the work becomes more complex and time constraints are frequently imposed. Although powerful programming languages and advanced engineering concepts are the available tools for producing good software, multiple developers are required to produce sophisticated software systems. How the human resources are organized and managed becomes critical in the success or failure of a software development project. This article identifies a model by which a manager can anticipate and build a software development team, and describes how the roles and interactions of chosen team members can contribute to the success, or failure, of a software project.

Building the Software Development Team

Complex software development projects require critical decision-making in the upstream portion of the development process, particularly during the specification and design phases. One of the most important upstream decisions is building the development team. From a managerial perspective, many factors must be considered when building the team. For more complex projects, knowledge from multiple technical and functional domains is a necessity (Walz, Elam, and Curtis 1993). Walz, Elam, and Curtis claim that in an ideal situation a software design team is staffed so that both the levels and distribution of knowledge within the team match those required for the successful completion of the project. Unfortunately, only under ideal circumstances can this be applied. In the real world, a manager is often faced with the technical and knowledge shortfalls of team members. In most situations, individual team members must acquire additional information before accomplishing their set tasks. To bridge the knowledge gap, formal training sessions, group meetings, and discussions frequently may be required. The most productive activities of the team come from the integration of knowledge.

During the knowledge-integration process, the manager is faced with handling multiple, concurrent, and often conflicting goals. The manager needs to be able to leverage the specific strengths of individual people while still maintaining the uniformity and stability of the pending project.

It appears that although technical expertise and knowledge of participants are necessary for a successful software project, the actual role a team member plays becomes a critical factor in the interaction of team members and how successful the team is in reaching project goals. In the team-building process, the manager is then faced with two very important questions: how do the group members interact to acquire, share, and integrate project relevant knowledge, and how do participation styles differ among team members?

Group Interaction Model

Several models have been published to aid managers in understanding how group members interact to achieve project goals. Constantine has devised a paradigmatic framework describing various types of groups (1993). According to Constantine, this framework provides a model for the organization and management of collective human activities. In other words, this model provides a general framework that can be applied toward building a software development team within the dynamics of the project and within the corporate structure. Constantine sets the stage by observing that everyday life affords us countless examples of groups of people carrying out joint activities or tasks in a coordinated manner. To emphasize this point, he compares a family dinner to a software project. He points out that the common thread between the family dinner and the software project is that there are always recognizably consistent patterns of interaction. From his observations, Constantine aims to establish a conceptual framework for understanding how a group of people jointly involved in a common activity or

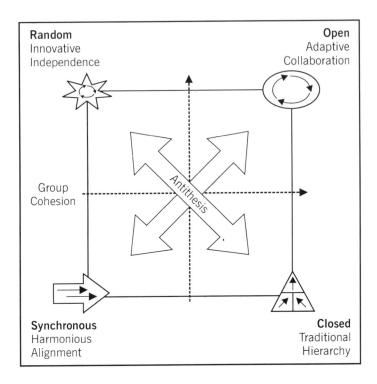

Figure 1. Constantine's Model

goal carry it to completion. Figure 1 is the paradigm that Constantine uses to describe how group members organize and coordinate daily activities.

The lower right corner of Figure 1 represents the traditional hierarchy or closed paradigm. Within this paradigm, continuity of a project is maintained through established standards and rules of operation. Stability is maintained by controlling for deviations from established norms and patterns. The purest example of a closed paradigm, cited by Constantine, is the military service; however, this type of paradigm also may be applied to groups in a large corporate structure that repeatedly produce the same type of product.

The random paradigm, which is the antithesis of the closed paradigm, is found on the complete opposite side (upper left) of the model shown in Figure 1. This paradigm heavily emphasizes innovation through creative autonomy of team members. By giving each team member the freedom to create and act independently, a manager can create a breakthrough project team, which may lead to developing a new technology. Hyman has successfully applied this paradigm (1993).

The open paradigm (upper right corner) in Figure 1 is a synthesis of the closed and random paradigms. The open-paradigm team is based on adaptive collaboration and the integrating of innovation while maintaining stability. Individuals with collective ideas and interests work together through negotiation and discussion. This type of team situation works best with small software development teams. Rettig and Simons have published an excellent example of an open-structured team (1993).

The final paradigm in the model in Figure 1, opposite to the open paradigm, is the synchronous or harmonious model. This model is based on harmonious and effortless coordination through the alignment of members with a common vision that reflects the collective vision. A synchronous or harmonious team is useful in simple projects, where each team member can program an independent piece of software, and the collective software completes the whole project.

From the various paradigms described in Constantine's model, a manager can begin to explore how effective project teams are established and how team roles fit within the organization of the project.

In a 1989 study, Larson and LaFasto interviewed team members to learn how the people who performed best within different kinds of teams were described. Constantine has reviewed Larson and LaFasto's conclusions, and has refined their results by incorporating his model coupled with his observations on programming teams:

> People who do best in closed paradigm (tactical) teams have been described as loyal, committed, and action-oriented. They seem to have a strong sense of urgency and respond well to leadership. People who work best within the creative environment of a random (or breakthrough) team are independent thinkers, often artistic or intellectual. They are persevering self-starters who do not need orders to get going or close supervision to keep going. People who thrive in the collaborative consensus-building or open (problem-solving) teams are practical minded but sensitive to people issues. They have integrity and are seen as trustworthy by peers, exhibiting intelligence coupled with good interpersonal skills. It appears that those who fit well in strongly synchronous teams are intuitive, somewhat introverted, yet people sensitive. They are good at linking the larger picture to specific action and work with quiet efficiency (Constantine 1993).

Constantine's model provides a manager with a more rational approach to building a team. Each paradigm reinforces and is reinforced by the behavior of individual team members.

Margerison and McCann define several team roles in *Team Management: Practical New Approaches* (1990). They developed a basic integrated-team model and identified nine key team roles, as shown in Figure 2.

Eight sections of the team management wheel shown in Figure 2 correspond to eight different roles or work preferences, which are grouped into four areas. The ninth role is a *linker,* which is most often associated with a project manager. Note

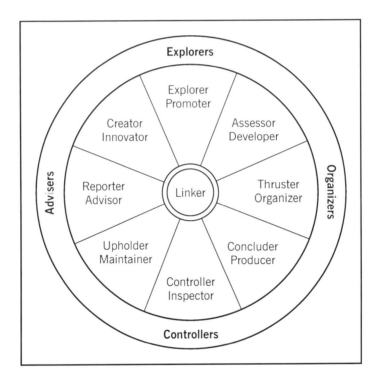

Figure 2. Team Management Wheel

that each role has a two-word description. The first word is used to describe a behavior description, and the second word is used to describe the work function. Each role is worth further discussion.

- Producer—Provides direction and follow through. Enjoys working to set procedures.
- Creator—Initiates creative ideas. Provides innovation and often needs to be managed in such a way that she is not constrained by the corporate structure.
- Controller—Examines details and enforces rules. Enjoys doing detailed work and checking facts and figures.
- Organizer—Provides structure. This person may be the project manager, the one to set procedures and systems. An organizer will set the process to ensure that deadlines are met.
- Adviser—Encourages the search for more information. This may not necessarily be an immediate team member, but rather an experienced old-timer who can advise the team on the correct way to move forward.
- Assessor—Offers insightful analysis of options. In software, an assessor may also be called an information architect, a designer who applies practical application to the ideas of the initial creative team.

- Maintainer—Fights external battles. An account executive for a software team often plays the role of a maintainer, someone who will defend the team against outside criticism and conflict.
- Promoter—Champions ideas after they're initiated. Plays a key role, exploring new ways of doing things outside the organization. In software development, this person might investigate new development tools.
- Linker—Coordinates and integrates. This role best describes the project manager in software development. Margerison and McCann (1990) describe eleven key linking skills: 1) active listening, 2) communication, 3) problem solving and counseling, 4) team development, 5) work allocation, 6) team relationships, 7) delegation, 8) quality standards, 9) objectives setting, 10) interface management, and 11) participative decision-making.

Conclusion

A project manager has several models from which to choose when organizing a software development team during the upstream portion of a project. Additionally, it is clear that successful software teams are more than just the sum of their team members performing their assigned duties; team members also play important roles that allow the team to function as a dynamic unit. In addition, team members (in small teams) will gravitate toward the roles that best fit their personalities.

Several guidebooks and publications can aid managers in forming a strong software development team. Margerison and McCann recommend a questionnaire for determining who on a team is best suited for a particular role (1990). Their Team Management Index poses a series of questions (based on the principles of the Myers-Briggs personality test) designed to gather information on the personal strengths and weaknesses of each prospective team member. In addition, *A Guide to the Project Management Body of Knowledge (PMBOK® Guide)* discusses organizational planning, in which team roles play a part. A project manager should consider what roles will be required and what roles will be dominant during the different phases of the project. Depending on how responsibility oriented the roles on a project are, the manager may decide not to document the role assignments. For example, a manager may decide to recruit a certain individual in the organization to play the role of adviser. This decision may be more appropriate for one's own personal journal than for a project plan. While it may take considerable effort to plan for project team roles, it can make the difference between a mediocre and high-performance software development team.

References

Constantine, Larry L. 1993. Work Organization: Paradigms for Project Management and Organization. *Communications of the ACM* 36: 35–43.

Hyman, Risa B. 1993. Creative Chaos in High Performance Teams: An Experience Report. *Communications of the ACM* 36: 57–60.

Larson, C. E., and F. M. J. LaFasto. 1989. *Teamwork: What Must Go Right/What Can Go Wrong.* Newbury Park, CA: Sage.

Margerison, C., and D. McCann. 1990. *Team Management: Practical New Approaches.* London: Mercury Books.

Project Management Institute. 2000. *A Guide to the Project Management Body of Knowledge (PMBOK® Guide)* – 2000 Edition. Newtown Square, PA: Project Management Institute.

Random House, Inc. 1979. *The Random House College Dictionary.*

Rettig, Marc, and Gary Simons. 1993. A Project Planning and Development Process for Small Teams. *Communications of the ACM* 36: 45–55.

Walz, D. B., J. J. Elam, and B. Curtis. 1993. Inside a Software Design Team: Knowledge Acquisition, Sharing, and Integration. *Communications of the ACM* 36.

The Project Manager/ Functional Manager Partnership

George Pitagorsky, PMP

Project Management Journal 7 (December 1998)

The collaborative relationship between functional managers and project managers is critical to effective project performance and to the well-being of any organization. This article defines project manager and functional manager roles, discusses issues regarding project manager/functional manager relations, and offers recommendations that promote collaborative relationships aimed at furthering the organization's success. There is no cookbook approach—project managers, functional managers, and their management must creatively adapt project management ideas and practices to their situations.

The Challenge

Project management and management by projects have emerged as major trends in the ongoing search to improve performance in organizations. Some organizations have a long history of project-centered activity while others are new to it. My findings, based on anecdotal information from hundreds of functional and project managers attending project management seminars across the country, is that conflict between project managers and functional managers is common.

The organization's challenge is to find a structure that suits its needs. Structure, the foundation for behavior, includes role and responsibility definitions, organizational boundaries, relationships, policies, procedures, and an effective reward system. In the context of project management, the roles of and relationships between functional and project managers are among the most critical aspects of the structure. These roles vary across the spectrum of industries and individual organizations performing projects.

Radical versus Incremental Change

Radical structural change may be necessary. Often, though, the structure is sound, and the attitudes and beliefs of the people in the organization are the root of the problem. What is needed is a renewal of the understanding of the organization's goals and how already-defined structures can help to meet them. Renewed understanding leads to more conscious relationships; more conscious relationships lead to better performance. The challenge is to engineer the organization's structure to fit its needs. Organizational structure is a means to an end; it should not be cast in concrete. It is a factor that contributes to the organization's ability to perform projects successfully. Underlying the structure is the common intention of all participants—to achieve the organization's objectives. Although, based on anecdotal evidence, it is clear that with this common intention most organizational obstacles can be overcome. In other words, people who want to cut through the politics and interpersonal conflicts that get in the way of effective performance can do so.

Project Success

The degree to which an organization's structure is working is measured by the degree to which projects are successfully performed. A successful project satisfies its clients and sponsors with an outcome that achieves objectives within time and cost constraints, produces a quality product, ends when appropriate (i.e., avoids wasting time and money), maintains and promotes harmonious relationships among project stakeholders (including project performers and management), and contributes lessons learned to the organization. Project success is measured in terms of:

- Project performance efficiency (e.g., meeting time and budget constraints, minimizing costs).
- Product quality and effectiveness (e.g., whether the project outcome actually helps to achieve the business objectives it was initiated to achieve, whether operational and maintenance costs are within reasonable expectations, and the degree to which quality specifications of the product have been met).
- The degree to which the project prepares the performing organization for the future (e.g., lessons learned) (Shenhar, Levy, and Dvir 1997).

Figure 1 shows the relationships among key success criteria.

Are projects consistently successful? If not, how does the organization's structure, particularly the relationships between project managers and functional managers, contribute to any shortcomings? What changes need to be made to improve performance?

Figure 1. Project Success Factors

Functional and Project Management Roles

There are three primary project-related management roles: program manager, project manager, and functional manager.

Program Manager

The program manager is responsible for the overall success of a program. A program is a set of projects and often ongoing operational activities (manufacturing, support, and so on) related by a common theme. The program manager generally has primary contact with the client and is responsible for the program planning (at the higher levels of the work breakdown structure), administration, and management. Product managers are program managers when the program is the development and life-cycle management of a product.

Project Manager

Project managers or project leaders are responsible for the planning and performance of individual projects. Project managers may:

- Administratively report to functional managers (possibly a manager of project managers) and to program managers with respect to their project(s).
- Report directly to functional managers who act as subcontractors to program managers.
- Report directly to program managers while managing resources from functional groups.
- Report directly to executive management.

Functional Manager

Regarding projects and programs, functional managers are responsible for ensuring that the resources in their areas are properly trained, evaluated, and motivated; that core processes within the function are effective; and that sufficient resources are available for program performance. In some organizations, functional managers are responsible for the performance of ongoing operations that are not related to projects. Sometimes functional managers are directly responsible for performance of project tasks, and sometimes they are responsible for providing resources to be directed by project managers.

There are two facets to the functional manager role: administration leadership, and technical/discipline leadership. Managers of non-operational functional groups that act as resource pools for projects are primarily administrators. Sometimes they are experts in a functional discipline who set functional standards and coach functional resources. In groups that perform project work as subcontractors, both the administrative and performance leadership roles must be performed. Often these two roles are best played by two different people.

Functional managers are custodians, not owners, of functional resources. They are responsible for ensuring that capable resources are available to fulfill project and operational needs. Functional managers are in a service role when it comes to providing resources or deliverables to project managers. As simple and obvious as this may seem it is often misunderstood or forgotten.

It is the responsibility of functional managers to assess operational and project requirements for resources over the next planning period (at least one year out), and to make sure that there are sufficient resources to fulfill them. To do so, functional managers need estimates from project managers, data on past experience, priority criteria from executives, an appropriate resource budget, and a source of resources.

Project Manager/Functional Manager Conflict

Project managers and functional managers are partners in the business of making projects succeed. As in all partnerships, there is an opportunity for conflict. Conflict can be healthy and useful if it is candidly addressed and leads to better decisions. Unnecessary conflict, which is often based on misunderstanding of roles, responsibilities, and mutual objectives, should be minimized if not eliminated. Conflict resolution requires both a forum at which to raise, define, and discuss issues and a commitment from senior management, functional managers, and project managers to actually resolve the issues.

The following sections discuss the principle conflicts between functional managers and project managers, as reported by several hundred attendees at project management seminars.

- Contention for resources.
- Functional manager involvement in project planning.
- Functional manager involvement in project performance.
- The tendency of functional managers and their staffs to take a narrow, discipline-centered view rather than a holistic view that places the discipline within the context of a multidiscipline project.

▪ The failure of project managers to take a holistic view that places the project in the context of a multi-project environment within an ongoing process.

Contention for Resources

Conflict over resources is based on the need by project managers to rely on the availability of project staff from functional areas. The availability of resources is a critical success factor in project performance. Functional organizations provide both human and other resources for project performance. Project managers plan, control, and coordinate project performance, based on commitments made by functional managers and external contractors, to provide people, products, or services within time, cost, and quality constraints.

If functional-manager commitments are not met, project commitments will not be met. If the project is important to the organization, the organization must hold functional managers accountable for fulfilling commitments. However, this accountability must be balanced with the authority and support needed by functional managers to deliver.

Functional managers schedule staff and other resources. Programs and projects compete for resources and services from functional groups. There is a need to shift resources as priorities and schedules change, causing delays in existing projects.

When faced with growing demand, functional managers may overcommit their resources. This tends to overwork people, resulting in degraded performance on projects, excessive costs, burnout, and turnover. Schedule slippage in one project often will result in delays in other, seemingly unrelated, projects as the transfer of resources is delayed. Pressure from upper management to meet tight or irrational deadlines leads to additional over commitment.

Project slippage is inevitable and when promised resources or subproject deliverables are delayed, their slippage intensifies conflict between project managers and functional managers. Project managers blame functional managers for the slippage; functional managers blame project managers for being insensitive to the big-picture needs for resources across and between multiple projects and internal or operational activities. Often, functional managers and project managers will augment their staffs with consulting services and/or overtime, increasing costs beyond originally budgeted levels.

To manage the contention for resources and services, functional managers must maintain master schedules. These master schedules allow each functional manager to see where and when resources are committed. Negotiation between functional managers and project managers regarding the staffing and scheduling of new or changing projects can then be based on objective criteria rather than on politics, pleading, haggling, and arm-twisting. A higher-level master schedule, consolidating functional group schedules and cutting across all programs and functional groups, may be useful in organizations where the staff and number of programs make it feasible.

The master schedule is a schedule that includes all of the work assignments (current and planned) for a group. The assignments will generally cut across projects and should address any nonproject activities that are performed by or use resources. The master schedule shows the degree to which resources (human and other) are allocated and their availability for further assignments.

In addition, the master schedule shows the relationships between projects based on resource dependencies—projects that are related to one another because they use common resources. When there is no master schedule, resource dependencies are often overlooked by project planners and functional managers. This, in turn, leads to impossible commitments.

It is the functional manager's responsibility to make sure that resource commitments are feasible and that they are either fulfilled or that project managers are made aware, as early as possible, when they will not be kept and why. Functional managers may facilitate negotiations among project managers vying for resources. Functional managers must be consulted before their resources are committed to project schedules.

Executive management is responsible for ensuring that the desire for "lean and mean" organizations doesn't lead to an irrational relationship between project objectives, resource availability, and operational requirements. Unrealistic demands from executive management are among the most damaging factors in organizational performance.

Functional Manager Involvement in Project Planning

Authority is a factor in any organization. Many project managers believe that the more authority a project manager has over project resources, and the more dedicated those resources are to the project, the more likely is project success. In complex projects, however, it is rare to find project managers with authority over all resources. In fact, it may be more effective to have functional managers responsible for their resources' performance, freeing project managers to manage the big picture and client relations. Project managers without direct authority over project resources can manage through accountability.

Project and program managers must have the minimal authority to get formal commitments from functional managers for resources or, when functional groups are responsible for performing work on the project, for deliverables. Commitments for deliverables must be accompanied by plans that show enough detail to give the project manager the ability to monitor progress. To monitor progress, project managers must have the authority to require functional managers or functional resources to report progress against their plans.

With this authority and an efficient reporting system that delivers candid reports to senior management, program management, and functional management at various levels, accountability will motivate functional management and resources to make reasonable commitments and to keep them. When it is not possible to keep previously made commitments, the reason must be stated candidly as part of the reporting system. Functional managers, project managers, and management share the responsibility for adjusting schedules and/or resources as necessary.

To balance this project manager authority, functional managers must be *asked* to commit to schedules and budgets. Program or project managers who make commitments for project deadlines before consulting functional managers cannot expect to pressure functional managers into compliance. The attempt to do so puts a wedge between project managers and functional managers, creating an adversarial relationship. Furthermore, it leads to a continuous juggling act by functional managers as they borrow resources from one project to try to make the deadline on another. Ultimately, the system breaks down, and projects run late or, worse, the product is released before it is ready—quality is subordinated to schedule, and everyone loses.

For projects in which most or all of the work is performed by functional groups, functional managers and/or project managers who report to them should do most of the planning. The program manager coordinates the intergroup planning process. The project manager makes sure that functional groups collaboratively perform dependency analysis, all of the work needed to fulfill project objectives has been identified and is covered by a responsible group, and the project's time and cost constraints are being considered by the functional groups as they formulate their plans and then work the project.

Project planning involves negotiation between functional managers, project managers, clients, and project sponsors. Each party to the negotiation process must have the ability to candidly present arguments for why project activities can or can't be done within desired constraints. If any one party has too much power, it is likely that the planning process will be dysfunctional. Dysfunctional planning leads to dysfunctional performance and unnecessary interpersonal conflict.

Functional Manager Involvement in Project Performance

In my seminars, the most frequently reported performance-related conflicts revolve around the definition of requirements and the acceptance of results.

Sometimes feedback of requirements to clients and/or project managers is bypassed—"We know what you want. We're in a hurry." Some functional groups object to having others scrutinize their work, making project quality control a political issue. "We've tested our piece, and it works. If there is something wrong, it must be a hardware, software, or interface problem. Get someone else to fix it."

In order to accurately estimate and avoid unnecessary rework, it is necessary for all parties in a project to have a mutual understanding of what needs to be done and what an acceptable outcome will look like. This means that both deliverables and the approach that will be taken to achieve them must be defined and verified in a dialogue among the client, sponsor, program manager, functional manager(s) and/or their staff, and other stakeholders. The level of detail of this dialogue depends on the type of work being done and the nature of the relationships.

Generally the program manager is the facilitator of the dialogue. The client is responsible for articulating the project objectives and product definition. Performers are responsible for documenting these requirements in a way that makes it possible for the client to verify that the performers have an accurate and complete understanding.

Depending on the functional groups' roles, they may be directly involved with the client or given their requirements by the project manager. In any case, it is critical that functional groups document their requirements and feed them back to the project manager and/or the client so that the possibility of producing erroneous results is minimized.

Acceptance criteria should be documented and agreed upon before work is started. Rework and much of the conflict between functional performance groups and project managers can be avoided if acceptance criteria, quality control methods, and responsibilities are clearly defined and communicated early in the project's life. Performers should be reminded that errors found by quality control people from outside their discipline were put there by the performers. Quality control people should be reminded that they don't make up acceptance criteria on the fly.

Project managers are responsible for the project's overall outcome. Functional managers are accountable for the outcome of the work performed under their responsibility. Quality control may be performed by the project manager or by an independent quality control function.

Tendency to Take a Narrow, Discipline-Centered View

In many organizations, functional managers and staff are specialists in a particular discipline or operational area. They may view project work only in terms of their specific efforts rather than as part of a larger effort. As a result they may object to or ignore project manager efforts to take part in quality control and assurance activities and monitor project progress.

Continuous reminders regarding the overall goal of the organization, as obvious as they may seem, are necessary to avoid the tendency toward taking a narrow, discipline-centered view.

Failure to Take a Holistic View

Just as functional managers and staff must take a project-centered view, the project manager must remember that functional managers serve multiple projects and may be responsible for operational activities. Project managers have the responsibility to negotiate with functional managers for resources or deliverables, not to demand or create unrealistic pressures. When project schedule goals conflict with the ability of functional groups to comply, higher-level priorities are used to settle the conflict.

Creating a Collaborative Relationship

There is no formulaic approach, no magic wand that will resolve all problems. Each organization is unique and needs its own specific solutions based on sound project management principles. The organization's goal should be to promote and support collaborative relationships.

Furthermore, a holistic program is needed to improve project performance. No one aspect of the organization and its performance can be addressed in isolation. Individual projects are performed as if they are autonomous rather than parts of higher-level programs. While this may be more efficient from the point of view of the individual project manager, it is detrimental to the program as a whole.

Project leaders and their functional managers have a great deal of autonomy and often view the program manager as an administrator rather than a true manager of the program and its component projects. Project leaders work with staff members who also report to functional managers. While most of the project staff is dedicated to specific projects, there are also performers who simultaneously work on multiple projects. Some functional resources work on internal projects, mostly focused on process improvement and research and development.

Functional managers want to limit the role of program managers and retain control of project performance. To make matters more complex, they have a history of dealing directly with customers in a way that sometimes contradicts the aims of program managers. Program managers want more direct control over project leaders, more influence in performance, and to reduce and closely coordinate direct contact between functional managers and clients. The functional managers, who are senior scientists in management and administrative roles, often value their scientific discipline expertise over their administrative management expertise.

The organization needs to become more program centered because programs are its source of income, and the organization is facing significant competition for the first time in its history. At the same time, the performance of its knowledge workers (the realm of the functional groups) has been the substance that allowed the organization to succeed. The organization needs to retain its competencies and make the most efficient use of these specialized, scarce, and expensive resources. Functional managers must give over to program management some or all of their autonomy, control, and authority as their group's efforts are seen as integral parts of interdisciplinary programs.

A change initiative is necessary to create lasting improvement. The initiative is a complex program that may be as complex as a business-process reengineering project. The changes required, the degree of resistance to change in the organization, and the degree to which senior management, functional managers, and project managers are committed to change are all factors that determine the level of complexity, difficulty, and risk for the initiative.

Change Initiative Objectives

To directly address project-manager/functional-manager relationship issues:

1. Appropriately balance authority between functional managers and project or program managers.

   1.1. Avoid—particularly in large cross-functional projects—having a project manager report directly to a functional manager that is providing resources or services to the project manager's project.

   1.2. Ensure that there is a clear escalation path and criteria for when to escalate issues between project managers and functional managers. Generally, this means identifying a steering group or a higher-level executive with the authority to break ties and adjust priorities.

   1.3. Clearly define project manager authority in a project charter.

   1.4. By requiring functional manager involvement and approval of project plans, ensure that functional managers have the authority to "push back" when they are forced to comply with schedules and budgets that conflict with their resource availability and preexisting commitments.

2. Clarify and regularly review roles and responsibilities, particularly with regard to functional management involvement in project initiation, planning, requirements definition, customer contact, and the direction of functional resource performance.

   2.1. Perform post-project performance reviews in which the effectiveness of role and responsibility assignments is one of the items addressed.

   2.2. Perform cross-project performance reviews that assess the organization's track record and correlate roles and responsibilities and organization structure with project success and the occurrence of problems.

3. Ensure that everyone is accountable for achieving their commitments via a project reporting system that requires functional managers and their resources to regularly report progress against relatively detailed plans to project managers, who candidly report results to interested stakeholders.

   3.1. Implement a tool-based reporting procedure that gives the project manager the ability to incorporate their group's work plans into the overall project plan and that enables a relatively seamless reporting of progress against these plans.

   3.2. Eliminate, if it exists, the attitude that the project manager is breaking some code of silence when he holds functional groups accountable for slippage.

   3.3. Make the identification of the cause(s) of slippage a normal part of all progress reporting.

4. Ensure that project managers have a formal and candid input to the performance evaluation of individual functional resources and of functional groups.

    4.1. Institute a regular procedure by which project managers give formal (written) performance evaluations for functional resources reporting directly to them and for functional groups performing tasks on their projects.

    4.2. Institute a procedure to give functional managers the ability to give candid feedback on project manager performance.

5. Change incentive systems to motivate functional resources' project performance.

    5.1. Require that evaluations of functional staff and functional group performance by project managers be used in performance and salary reviews.

    5.2. Continuously reinforce the need for collaborative efforts in cross-functional projects by highlighting the criticality of these efforts to the organization's bottom line.

    5.3. Include project performance and support in the mission statements of functional groups.

    5.4. Include functional groups and resources in project bonus plans.

6. Buffer projects from unnecessary contention for resources between project work and operational work.

    6.1. Assess staffing levels to ensure that functional groups have sufficient resources to satisfy ongoing operational requirements (including proposal and estimating support) and project requirements.

    6.2. To the extent possible, structure the organization so that operational and project work are performed by separate people.

    6.3. When allocating resources to projects, account for operational work. Don't assume full-time availability unless there is a realistic probability that the resources are fully dedicated.

7. Maintain master schedules for functional groups to enable accurate estimating of resource availability.

    7.1. Require that each functional group keep an up-to-date master schedule that accounts for all project and nonproject effort and shows how resources are allocated over time.

    7.2. Ensure that when responding to project manager requests for commitments that functional managers use their master schedules to justify the response.

    7.3. Provide adequate administrative support to functional managers (perhaps via a project office) to enable them to manage their resources more effectively without having to sacrifice technical leadership and human resource management effectiveness.

8. Clearly prioritize projects to de-politicize the assignment of resources among competing projects.
   8.1. Establish appropriate steering groups or project executives to prioritize projects and make other decisions to avoid or break deadlocks between functional managers and project managers.
   8.2. Require senior management and internal clients to document the priorities of the projects they initiate.
   8.3. Require that the impact of changes in priorities be reported across all effected projects.
9. Clearly define requirements and acceptance criteria for projects and tasks within projects and validate that they are mutually understood and accepted.
   9.1. Establish standards and procedures to clearly identify who is responsible for documenting requirements for task performance, including processes for clarifying and verifying requirements.
   9.2. Require that acceptance criteria for deliverables from and to functional groups be formally defined.

Roles and Responsibilities

The work to create a collaborative relationship requires commitment and effort from the following principle participants.

Senior management must fully understand the issues and support the plans to improve relationships through organizational change. The nature of the changes is such that without senior management involvement, the changes would not be possible. A member of senior management should act as the sponsor of the change initiative. Senior managers should be involved in the development of procedures for project prioritization.

Functional managers and project managers must take an active role in the development of role and responsibility definitions and procedures. Without their direct involvement and commitment to change, any improvement program will be marginally successful, at best.

The human resource function must participate to develop or revise and implement procedures for performance review, incentive systems, and any other aspects of the program that impact human resource-related issues. Further, the human resource person may be a good facilitator for the change initiative.

A project office function, if one exists, should be involved in the initiative to ensure coordination and to negotiate its role and responsibilities under the new system. If there is no project office, consider the development of one to provide minimal administrative support and coaching and possibly to be the "home" of the project managers.

A program manager for the initiative should be appointed to direct and drive the initiative through the change process. Depending on the size of the organization, and the degree to which the functional managers and project managers can be relied upon to take proactive roles, dedicated resources reporting to the program manager should be provided.

Ongoing Dialogue and Continuous Improvement

Healthy relationships require an ongoing dialogue among functional managers, project managers, and program managers and their management and clients. This dialogue is part of a formal quality-assurance process that, among other things, evaluates the organization's performance and identifies desirable changes to the organization's structure, based on what is best for the organization as a whole.

Holding onto old structures for the sake of tradition, or to perpetuate "silos," is impractical and counterproductive. There is a need to take a fresh view that permits the organization to regularly redefine itself so as to minimize politics and the inefficiencies that go along with political infighting between people who should be acting as partners, not competitors.

Adaptive structures evolve as the organization matures and as the staff changes. Performance analysis and dialogue among managers and executives will lead to the most effective organization structure, given the work to be done, the nature of the resources available, and the need for clear accountability for planning and performance.

References

Project Management Institute. 2000. *A Guide to the Project Management Body of Knowledge (PMBOK® Guide)* – 2000 Edition. Newtown Sq., PA: Project Management Institute.

Shenhar, Aaron J., Ofer Levy, and Dov Dvir. 1997. Mapping the Dimensions of Project Success. *Project Management Journal* 28, 2: 5–13.

Setting Expectations: Initiating the Project Manager/Client Relationship

David E. VanEpps, PMP

PM Network 101 (September 2000)

I used to believe that project management was about plans, schedules, budgets, contracts, and the like. Freshly equipped with project management training and a working knowledge of *A Guide to the Project Management Body of Knowledge (PMBOK® Guide)*, I was ready to tackle the world. Over my next several years of managing numerous software projects, I learned about the other side of project management.

True project management comes from the heart. It is a passion to do the right things and to do things right. It's a deep-seated inspiration to lead teams to deliver superior products while exceeding customer expectations. Don't get me wrong; the technical skills of project management are essential. Your clients deserve a project manager who has mastered both the technical skills and soft skills of project management, much like you deserve a physician who not only is passionate about medicine, but also did pretty well in medical school.

Proper expectation setting involves establishing a relationship with the client, creating a project culture with the stakeholders, and maintaining open communication channels. It helps to establish and maintain a positive relationship, improves team morale, and prevents countless hours of rework. It is often the difference between a highly successful project and one laden with misunderstandings, misinterpretations, and destructive communication.

The Problem

Although project managers are often exceptional when it comes to executing the technical skills of requirements management, schedule planning, and tracking, we often fall short when it comes to setting proper expectations. By changing a few simple behaviors, we can greatly improve the odds of completing projects successfully.

One survey found that 10 percent of all projects are canceled because of unrealistic expectations (The Standish Group 1994). Clients will mold their own perceptions or misconceptions prior to the kickoff meeting. These can originate from a lack of software development knowledge, past experience with other similar projects, pre-established deadlines, and pre-established budgets set by senior management.

Pre-Kickoff

Prior to a project kickoff meeting, the project manager should make a point to have a separate, pre-kickoff meeting with the client to mutually establish expectations. While the project kickoff meeting typically includes sharing information about the project with the entire team, the pre-kickoff meeting has a different focus.

The pre-kickoff meeting must be well thought, well planned, and well executed. The goal is to establish a solid relationship between the project manager and client. The intention of the meeting is not to solidify specific project deliverables (e.g., don't gather requirements or estimate schedules), but to establish the human relations aspect of the project. This is the place to state how you want to work with the client. Make it a statement of intent and spirit (Block 1981).

To accomplish this objective, the project manager and client must establish their roles and responsibilities for the project, and share past experiences and lessons learned. It is an opportunity for the project manager to stress the importance of the client's roles. Too often the client assumes that his role ends once the project manager enters the picture. The client must realize that his input into the requirements analysis, estimating, and planning stages of the project is fundamental to the success of the project. During the pre-kickoff meeting, the project manager and client must also discuss any risks and assumptions that are critical to the project, and determine how these factors will be managed throughout the project.

Communications

A key ingredient to expectation setting is properly preparing for and planning communication. Most project managers spend approximately 90 percent of their working hours engaged in some form of communication: conferences, meetings, writing memos, reading reports, and talking with team members, top management, customers, clients, subcontractors, suppliers, and so on (Stuckenbruck and Marshall 1997). Given this premise, shouldn't communication be planned as thoroughly as a budget or schedule?

In the pre-kickoff meeting, set the stage for how communication will be planned. Open your door to bad news from the client and encourage the client to openly communicate without fear of reprisal. In turn, assure your client that you can and will communicate openly, even when the news is bad.

Channels for open and honest communication should be primed early across the entire project team and stakeholders. Much of this is cultural, which is why the project manager and client must lay the foundation prior to the kickoff meeting. Establishing a culture of openness and honesty takes time and leadership. It takes a true leader who is empathetic to her team and passionate about her projects.

Risk Management

I challenge you to find a successful, large project that doesn't practice open and honest risk management. Risk identification is one of the most challenging tasks on any project and essential when setting project expectations. It also requires a cultural and behavioral change from the team members. The project manager must prime the client before the kickoff meeting as to the risk-management approach.

Like communication, this is another culture change that requires inspired leadership. During the pre-kickoff meeting, the project manager and client should plan a strategy by which they reward and praise those who are honest about identifying risks. The project manager and client should also agree not to "shoot the messenger" when these risks are openly presented.

Perceptions and Assumptions

With every project come some preconceived perceptions and corresponding assumptions. In fact, these perceptions often speak louder than facts. Perceptions are often very different from reality, usually due to diverse expectations, false assumptions, and ineffective communications.

Perceptions are established by the expectations that begin as soon as the project is conceptualized. The key is to understand the various perceptions and communicate through them. Prior to the kickoff meeting, the project manager and client should spend some time talking about any known perceptions within either the client's team or the project team.

Assumptions are what often make or break the project. The project manager and client should have a clear plan by which they collectively identify and document assumptions from the pre-kickoff meeting throughout the life cycle. Since assumptions deal with the very heart of our thought processes, this is critical to establishing and maintaining realistic expectations. Assumptions help the client to understand how and why delivery schedules and budgetary estimates were derived, which is often a source of conflict. Sharing assumptions helps minimize the perception of unfairly padding schedule or cost estimates.

As a side effect of a well-executed pre-kickoff meeting, the client will likely walk away with a positive impression of the project manager.

Expectation setting is more than project planning and tracking. It is more than scoping and communication. Successful project management requires a passion for excellence. It requires a burning desire to exceed all expectations. This type of passion demonstrates your commitment to your client and helps instill a sense of confidence that you are an advocate for the client's best interest.

References

Block, Peter. 1981. *Flawless Consulting.* Pfeifer & Company.

The Standish Group. 1994. *Charting the Seas of Information Technology.*

Stuckenbruck, Linn C., and David Marshall. 1997. *Team Building for Project Managers: Principles of Project Management.* Newtown Square, PA: Project Management Institute.

Engage! Involve the Customer to Manage Scope

Dean Leffingwell

PM Network 27 (August 1997)

In the requirements college program that I teach, I always ask participants—experienced analysts, project managers, product managers, applications developers, testers, and quality-assurance personnel—some key questions about the most significant ongoing challenges they face. Without fail, they report that managing project scope is among their most challenging issues.

The Problem of Project Scope

Fortunately, a number of useful techniques for managing scope exist. In particular, engaging customers in scope management can be one of the most effective techniques for solving this pervasive software-development problem. Given the definition of project scope in Figure 1, the question I ask is: "At the start of application development, what amount of scope are you given by your management, customers, or stakeholders?"

In response, only one requirements-college attendee has ever answered "under 100 percent." The others have responded with numbers that vary from 125 to 500 percent. The median and the average for each session is the same: approximately 200 percent. This data correlates remarkably well with the 1994 Chaos Report by the Standish Group, which discusses why projects fail. This study found that "53 percent of the projects will cost 189 percent of estimates."

What happens when a project proceeds with a 200 percent initial scope? Two major outcomes are possible. Only half of the committed work may be accomplished, with the consequence that customers are dissatisfied, marketing and product launch promises are missed, manuals and promotional materials are inaccurate and must be reworked, and the entire team is frustrated and demotivated. Or, at

Figure 1. Balancing Functionality with Available Resources

deadline time, only 50 percent of each feature works. The consequences are that nothing useful works at the time the deadline passes. The deadline is missed badly. In the worst case, the entire team is fired (after working 50 percent overtime) and the non-participants get their ill-deserved promotions.

The Toughest Question

Clearly, scope must be managed before and during the application development effort. However, given the facts above, the task is daunting. For the average project to have any hope of success it will be necessary to reduce its scope by a factor of two.

This leads to perhaps the toughest question faced by application developers: "How does one manage to reduce scope and keep the customer happy?"

Engaging Customers to Manage *Their* Project Scope

Reducing project scope to at least within shouting distance of available resources and time has the potential to create an adversarial relationship between the application development community and our customers, whose needs we must meet. But it doesn't have to be that way. We can actively engage our customers in managing *their* requirements, and *their* project scope, to assure quality and timeliness of software outcomes.

This conclusion is based on two critical in sights: 1) It is in our customer's best financial interest to meet her external commitments to her marketplace. Therefore, delivering a high-quality—and if necessary, a scope-reduced application— on time and on budget is the highest overall benefit that we developers can provide; and, 2) the application, its key features, and the business needs that it fulfills all belong to *the customer*, rather than the application development team.

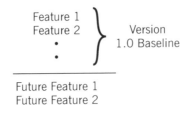

Figure 2. Requirements Baseline

Developing the Baseline

The first step in scope management is to create a requirements baseline. A requirements baseline is simply an itemized set of requirements or features that is intended to be delivered in a specific version of the application, as shown in Figure 2.

Establishing the baseline for the project is a requirements elicitation effort. We must understand the features and specifications that are necessary for the application to meet our customer's needs. Techniques for requirements elicitation can include interviews, questionnaires, requirements workshops, storyboards, role-playing, use cases, quality function deployment, and prototyping.

The choice of technique will vary, based on the nature of the application, the skill and sophistication of the development team, and the customer. The result is the set of items that must be delivered to satisfy the customer. An additional benefit of the process is that we show customers that it is important to us to understand their needs, that we are deeply committed to the application, and that we manage the development process in a professional manner.

An effective elicitation process will determine not only what the application must do, but will also establish relative priorities of the features. Techniques for "triaging" the feature set include cumulative voting, wherein the stakeholders are allotted a certain number of virtual dollars, with which they can "buy" those features that are most crucial to success, or ranking priorities in categories such as critical, relevant, important, or useful (see Table 1). In the latter case, the process must permit only an equal number of votes of each priority type, or the result will quickly tend toward everything being critical. An example of a triaged feature set is shown in Table 1.

Reducing Scope

The next step is the trickiest. If, as we expect, the features add up to 200 percent scope, then we must chop the baseline in half or more. Communicating this to customers requires both negotiation skills and a total commitment to the schedule.

Feature	Benefit	Risk	Effort
Feature 1-The New Configuration	Critical	Med	High
Feature 2-A New Capability	Critical	Med	Med
Feature 3-The Operator	Important	Low	Med
Feature 4-Windows 95 Compatible	Important	High	High
Feature 5-Project Structure	Relevant	Low	Low

Table 1. A Triaged Feature Set

The guiding principle in these negotiations should be "underpromise and overdeliver." With scope negotiated to an achievable level, and with the customer's "must haves," the team will establish credibility by meeting schedules with quality, and occasionally with utility, that could not be committed to before.

Manageable Threats

Failure to provide sufficient margin for error, feature creep, and extreme work cultures, in which even attempting to negotiate scope is considered career limiting, is difficult, but these are manageable threats to project success. Successful development managers create margin for error in estimating effort and allow time to incorporate legitimate change during the development cycle. Effective managers also resist feature creep, which Gerald Weinburg notes can increase scope by as much as 50 percent after the start of a project (1995). Even hostile political environments can be mitigated by focusing the development effort on the customer's critical priorities. At deadline time, at least the most important features will be working reliably.

Change Happens

Even in the best of scope management processes, change is inevitable. The reasons for change may be because we failed to ask the right people the right questions at the right time; the problem being solved or our understanding of the problem being solved changed; the users or customers changed their minds or their perceptions; the external environment changed; or we failed to create a process to help manage change.

While the potential for change in even a well-managed process can be discouraging, the point is to simply "get over it" and move on with a process for managing change. This process engages the customer in helping control change or supporting the necessary change with an increased budget or an officially changed project timeline.

One mechanism for controlling change may be as simple as a Change Control Board (CCB). A CCB is a committee of team members responsible for analyzing and approving appropriate change before it is incorporated into the project baseline. Alternately, the baseline is owned by a project champion who will defend the application, and its associated schedule and budget, against unnecessary change. Either technique creates what Weinburg calls an "official channel" through which all change is funneled to assure project success (1995). The response of the project team to a request for change is a professional "can-do attitude," followed by a similarly professional request for funding, schedule extension, or elimination of some element of the project baseline that is of less importance than the new item.

Of course, your customer should chair the CCB or help the project champion evaluate change proposals. After all, it's his feature, his budget, and his schedule. Our job is to help the project champion make the tradeoffs inherent in all projects. By doing so, we move the problem of managing scope to his doorstep rather than our own.

We cannot expect that this process will make the scope challenge go away any more than any other single process will solve the world. However, the steps outlined can be expected to have a material effect on the scope of the problem, allowing application developers to focus on critical subsets and incrementally deliver high-quality systems that meet or exceed the expectations of the user. Further, engaging the customer in helping to solve the scope management problem increases commitment on the part of both parties, and fosters improved communication and trust between the customer and application development teams. The result will be higher-quality applications, on time and on budget.

References

Weinburg, Gerald. 1995. Just Say No! Improving the Requirements Process. *American Programmer.*

Enhancing Supplier Relationships

Todd K. Walles, PMP

PM Network 60 (October 1998)

The days of being everything to each customer are fading. Companies cannot afford to maintain noncore services that drive up overhead costs. The shift to removing noncore services is noteworthy, because companies are relying more on external suppliers. To outsource, partner, and team have become fashionable trends. This means that suppliers are now strategic resources, not merely providers of products or services. Companies often solicit participation from suppliers during the business-development phase in order to properly plan and implement projects. As one project is successfully completed, many companies and their suppliers begin collaborating on the next opportunity.

Project managers are responsible for assembling winning teams and defining the required resources. As a company's backlog increases, the availability of key staff and resources diminishes. This trend leads project managers to search for help. The creation of long-lasting relationships with suppliers is a solution that requires effective communication and the sharing of information. For the purposes of this article, let's define *suppliers* as all consultants, subcontractors, vendors, and specialty trades that are retained from outside firms.

The days of accepting low-bid offerings are quickly vanishing. Sure, it remains essential to retain suppliers that offer fair and reasonable pricing; however, the selection criteria also include performance metrics. Compliance with the specifications and having the lowest price may not be enough to add value to a project. Project managers want responsive suppliers that will collaborate and share creative solutions. This requires commitment, partnering, and effective communication.

Project managers routinely find themselves entangled with procurement agreements and contract modifications when working with suppliers. Nowadays, the type and complexity of the agreements may necessitate assistance from legal specialists, buyers, and contracting experts. Procurement may be the single most-demanding responsibility for project managers today.

The Networking Frenzy

A true measure of intelligence is not only what you retain, but also—perhaps more so—whether you know how to find solutions and implement them. Welcome to the networking frenzy, a fast and reliable way of retaining help. When internal resources are stretched near capacity, or a team is in jeopardy of not achieving expectations, look to outside suppliers for help.

Suppliers can be integrated with a project team in many ways. Project managers may retain suppliers to address resource imbalances, to obtain products or services that are not available from their company, or to enroll technical expertise. In order to make sound decisions when outsourcing work, project managers should be familiar with the capabilities of many companies in relevant work areas and disciplines. These external contacts should be employed, as necessary, to supplement any project team.

Knowing where to obtain assistance and how to approach suppliers is a challenge to all project managers. The response to this challenge may vary from one organization to another. To establish or expand a network of suppliers, it is important to retain vendor information, contacts, and references. If a procurement solicitation or supplier list is unfamiliar, consider reviewing the scope or capabilities with colleagues. The combined knowledge and experiences of others will generally facilitate retaining the best supplier. Additional information can be obtained by accessing supplier databases, contacting trade or industry associations, and reviewing business journals, directories, or buying guides. Many companies maintain databases to tabulate supplier information and performance measurements; most include specialty data pertaining to small, disadvantaged, or female-owned businesses. Be cautious, however, as the accuracy of the databases can be flawed if the feedback and input are not provided in regular, timely intervals. Use all of these techniques to expand your network of contacts so that assistance is only a phone call (or an email) away.

The most effective technique for assessing suppliers is through previous work experience. Word-of-mouth and referrals are still reliable tools to evaluate performance. Knowing the capabilities and limitations of suppliers will pay handsome dividends during implementation. However, even the best suppliers can become overcommitted, and project managers must be able to recognize this occurrence and take necessary actions.

Several factors can influence potential suppliers, such as company name recognition, visibility of a project in the marketplace, and the attractiveness of the work (to be contracted). At times, companies can leverage multiple opportunities to encourage participation or interest. By proactively seeking relevant information from suppliers and then soliciting their participation to bid, most suppliers will be responsive to the next request.

New Trends in Procurement

There are numerous types of agreements, alliances, or partnerships for retaining external suppliers. The specifics of these agreements are beyond the focus for this article and therefore not discussed here. The quest for most project managers involves integrating the suppliers with in-house resources while maintaining the delivery, quality, and costs expected by the customer.

In the past, low-priced offerings were accepted. Today the objective of low cost remains, but the method for arriving at competitive costs has changed. Companies are working together to define scope, schedule, and performance measurements. Perhaps most noteworthy, suppliers are participating in preplanning activities with companies to develop creative solutions. This type of involvement fosters mutual gain and long-term business relations.

The management of supplier relationships can dictate the success of a project. Project managers should demonstrate the importance of effective communication and leadership. The project teams should promote synergy and share relevant information with suppliers, as required, to achieve customer goals.

Consider these objectives when establishing a supplier relationship:

- Carefully define the statement of work. It is essential in order to meet the expectations of the customer and to avoid claims or disputes.
- Balance the amount of work with the capabilities of the supplier. Too large or small an assignment may lead to performance problems.
- Provide adequate time for the supplier to respond to the solicitation. Rushing the supplier's response will undoubtedly result in less competitive costs or overlooked items.
- Establish reasonable terms. Take into consideration the scope, the amount of risk, and the project's technical requirements. Also, clearly define pricing and risk-sharing parameters such as bonding, insurance, and payment terms.
- Solidify delivery. Insist on responsiveness, open communication, and collaboration and resolve issues in a timely manner.
- Communicate the business strategy, project objectives, and milestones. Let the suppliers participate and make a difference.
- Manage the relationship. Share information, build credibility, and keep an eye toward the next opportunity.

Creating and maintaining effective supplier relationships is another example of how today's project managers must own their projects, and thereby reduce the downside exposure caused by changing project environments.

Relationship Building

Often, companies will examine their best clients and strategize about ways to improve performance and secure new business. Many solicit feedback or appraisals pertaining to past performance or customer satisfaction, and then strive to redefine and improve the relationship. Similar evaluation techniques can prove valuable toward improving external supplier relationships. Many project managers face the pressure of completing one assignment and swiftly moving on to another, and, as a result, the post-performance appraisal is forgotten. Even when the appraisal is prepared, the feedback isn't always shared with the supplier to benefit the relationship in the future.

Consider the development of a supplier relationship in terms of succession planning. Instead of grooming the next leader to assume your position, train and develop the supplier to deliver continuity and enhance the next business opportunity. To retain new clients, most companies strive to intimately know their customer's business, along with how they buy and what makes them successful. The same philosophy holds true for managing supplier relationships. The company and the supplier should strive to be advocates for each other and align the relationship toward common goals.

Companies need to regularly identify and assess the capabilities of suppliers. It is essential to expand the network and provide opportunities to new firms, meanwhile challenging the suppliers that regularly exceed expectations. Procurement should be more than a project start-up activity. Here are a few suggestions to improve a supplier network:

- Sponsor a breakfast meeting for suppliers, and provide information on contracting, technologies, or similar topics of interest.
- Support small business fairs, and encourage participation from your company to identify and learn more about new businesses, including small and/or disadvantaged firms.
- Promote the distribution of supplier information between staff located at different geographical offices. Hold technology-transfer sessions at lunch or other common meetings.
- Try to meet periodically with suppliers and discuss ongoing work as well as upcoming business opportunities.

Partnering for performance is not just an overused phrase. Partnering can be casual, informal business relations. The climate is ripe for companies to establish reliable working relationships with suppliers that complement your own. By developing long-lasting supplier relationships, companies will be better prepared to assemble winning teams and thereby minimize the impacts caused by changing project environments.

Section 3

Human Resource Theory and Charts

Post-Planning Review Prevents Poor Project Performance

David Antonioni

PM Network 43 (October 1997)

Project managers are usually encouraged to conduct evaluations of their project management processes at the closeout of projects. Although end-of-project evaluations are valuable, there is another approach that may contribute more to project success and at the same time improve the organization's overall project management practices. Post-planning project management reviews can be more effective at achieving both short- and long-term company goals.

Project Management Evaluations

Project management evaluations are usually conducted by project managers and their project team members at the end of the implementation phase or at the close of a project. An evaluation differs from a project status report because it addresses the entire project life cycle: conception, planning, implementation, and closeout. Objectives are evaluated; budget comparisons are made; documentation is examined; and outstanding issues are identified, discussed, and possibly resolved. An evaluation usually recognizes factors that contributed to the success or failure of the project. Some project managers also evaluate and complete performance appraisals for each team member based on the accountabilities established at the beginning of the project.

Project evaluations tend to be just what the name says—evaluations—with an emphasis on feed*back*. Project evaluations may occur too late to do much good. Post-planning project reviews are recommended because they serve as feed*forward* information that can prevent problems during the project's implementation.

Post-Planning Project Management Reviews

A post-planning project review is conducted at the end of the planning phase by reviewers who are experienced professional project managers. Planning, as specified in this article, includes defining the problem to be solved, developing objectives, creating strategies for achieving objectives, and constructing detailed work plans to attain objectives. Unlike a status report, a post-planning project review is conducted by someone from outside the project, not from within the project team. Project managers receive direct, customized feedback and support from highly qualified reviewers. The reviews are intended to help project managers and team members improve their project management skills through on-the-job feedback and coaching. The reviews can also provide senior management with information about organizational systems issues that may affect project management throughout the company.

Post-planning project reviews may also help reduce big-impact scope changes by ensuring that the planning process is done correctly. A project plan review is a proactive problem-prevention approach, while a project evaluation is a problem-detection approach. Therefore, post-planning project reviews should minimize the possibility that project scope changes might occur during the implementation phase by making sure that the project was well conceived and planned. This should significantly increase the likelihood that projects are on time, within budget, and meet or exceed customers' expectations.

A Survey Assessing Project Management Evaluations and Post-Planning Reviews

Approximately 200 project managers attending seminars sponsored by the University of Wisconsin-Madison responded to a brief survey assessing the extent to which they conducted project management evaluations and when they conducted the evaluations. The majority of these project managers worked on product development, engineering, or information technology projects.

The results of the survey indicate that only about half of the respondents conducted project management evaluations and that the majority of these evaluations were conducted after projects had been completed. Post-planning project management reviews are rare. However, respondents to the survey indicated that post-planning reviews were more powerful in contributing to project success (on time, within budget) than evaluations conducted at the end of the project.

The most common format used by the respondents for conducting project management evaluations involved project team discussion facilitated by project leaders. One-on-one interviews, focus groups, and questionnaires were less likely to be used. The evaluation data was primarily collected from team members and project managers, although in some cases customers, clients, or end users were included in the feedback processes.

Based on the results, it appears worthwhile to invest resources when conducting post-planning project reviews.

Establishing a Post-Planning Project Process

An organization needs to first develop a methodology or standard operating procedures for project management. The methodology provides a frame of reference for project managers and establishes guidelines to follow when reviews are conducted. Lessons learned from reviews can then be used to update project management methodology.

The organization should then form a project management review board consisting of the project management director, an experienced project sponsor, an experienced project manager, and a project team member. Ideally, a past customer of the organization's project results would also be on the board. If the organization does not have the resources to form such a board, then the project management director and two experienced project managers should serve as the review team. If the organization does not have a project management director, the review board could include experienced project managers. Some of the organizations in the study reported hiring a project management consultant to be a member of the review board.

Next, a project management review team should be named. This team consists of at least two experienced project managers who have good interpersonal skills as well as technical project management skills. As reviewers, the managers need to be skilled at interviewing and listening, and must be prepared to teach and coach others. Some organizations contract with a qualified consultant to conduct and teach staff members how to do the reviews.

Ideally, organizations should evaluate every project. However, because of limited resources, only select projects may be reviewed. Some of the criteria used for selecting the projects include risk, financial impact (profitability), complexity of technology, and client sensitivity. In some cases, a project manager's experience may determine the need for a review. A review team can help a project manager develop knowledge and skills at the same time that it increases the likelihood of project success.

What Occurs during Post-Planning Project Reviews

During the project review all project management documents are examined: the description of the project mission, client expectations, project scope, risk analysis, work breakdown structure, master schedule, budget development and tracking, contracting strategy, procurement process, monitoring and control procedures, meeting schedules, skill assessment, team formation, information distribution, and project implementation plans. In structured interviews, reviewers ask the project manager and the project team specific questions to assess the work completed in the conception and planning phases of the project. Reviewers should prepare a list of standard questions, such as those listed in the sidebar. In addition, reviewers can also ask questions based on information they receive during the interviews.

The review data is summarized to point out strengths and areas for improvements. Reviewers can then make recommendations to help project managers adjust their procedures. A copy of the evaluation results is then sent to the project management review team or to the person in charge of the organization's project management process, so that lessons learned can be disseminated to other project management teams. The organization should update its project management methodology based on information from the project reviews. The organization's culture may affect reactions to the idea of sharing the lessons learned. In some situations project teams may find it difficult to share information about their mistakes with other teams because of distrust about how the information will be used.

Employee Responses

Organizations most likely will experience some initial resistance to conducting post-planning reviews until benefits are experienced. Experienced project managers generally work the best as reviewers. However, these individuals may complain about the amount of time needed to conduct the reviews. Therefore, it is essential that the organizations commit staff and time to conduct the reviews. As mentioned earlier, some organizations hire a qualified consultant to conduct the reviews. As a guideline, it takes approximately two days to conduct a thorough review; therefore, the project managers involved must have time allocated to the review process. The organization should make sure that project managers are recognized and rewarded for their work as project reviewers.

Organizations should begin to experience benefits from the reviews after the first year. Project success rates should increase, and project managers and team members should experience skill development. Reviewers, too, should experience personal development from coaching others. As one reviewer said, "I've learned from teaching. I have a better overall understanding of the project management process because I'm conducting these reviews."

It makes good sense to conduct a review at the end of the planning phase in order to prevent potential problems in the implementation phase. However, conducting project-planning reviews requires management to modify its mindset. It is a radical change for reviews to be conducted by experienced project managers from outside the project team. It is also a change to conduct this type of review before the end of the project. Management needs to pay heed to the axiom that proper planning prevents poor project performance. One of the benefits of

---

Questions to Ask During Project Plan Reviews

- Is there a formal problem statement written for the project?
- Was the problem statement shared with the customer?
- What process was used to make sure that there was a clear understanding of the customer's requirements?
- What steps were taken to make sure that the project team understood the problem statement?
- What is the specific mission of the project?
- Who are the stakeholders of the project?
- What are the criteria for success of the project for different stakeholders?
- What discrepancies of expectations exist?
- How have the discrepancies been resolved?
- What are the objectives of the project?
- What are the specific deliverables of the project?
- How are the end results of the project going to be used by the customer?
- What is the scope of the project?
- What are the risks of the project?
- What is the contingency plan to address the risks?
- Who has signed off on the project plan?
- What are the reporting timelines?
- What knowledge, skills, and abilities do you need from project team members?
- Have team members' roles been defined?
- What is the communication plan to ensure sustaining sponsorship?

---

reviews stems from a feed*forward* approach—the information can be used immediately on current projects.

For best results, both project reviews and evaluations should be done. Both provide opportunities to gather information useful for improving the organization's project management process, thus increasing the probability of project success and giving the organization a competitive advantage.

PM Stands for
People Motivator

Carol L. Grimes

*Proceedings of the 27th Annual Project Management Institute
1996 Seminars & Symposium*

Project managers face hard tasks every day. Most can be dealt with by using the skills that the project manager has learned (scope, budget, WBS, Gantt charts). When dealing with a team, however, a project manager does not have a chart or other simple solution for managing the people themselves. The project manager *must* manage the people who are on the project team, and usually does not have any true power to hire and fire in a matrix management environment. Thus, the project manager must learn how to effectively motivate people to perform to the project solution. Have you ever had people like this on your project teams?

This is the fourth project to which Tom Techie has been assigned in the last month. Mary Mom cannot work past 5 P.M. because she has to pick her children up at daycare. Gary Gladhand says he is thrilled to be on the project, can volunteer most of his time, but his reputation is that he never follows through or meets a deadline. Nancy Negative has worked with you in the past, and you know her to be a disruptive influence, always a "nay sayer," but a hard worker. And Patty Perfect is...! No one knows all that she knows, nor is she ever wrong—or so she says. Do you recognize any of these people? How about Manny Moaner, who constantly tells anyone nearby how much "real" work he has to do and cannot make meetings, or Harry History, who can always say how it was tried in the past and failed. This guy always gets on my teams.

If you have the ability to grant financial benefits to each of the participants on your project team, you probably think that that is all you need to use. A study by Kenneth Kovoch presents the surprising results in Table 1 (1992).

The project manager must learn what people really want and need in order to be an effective people motivator. Let's talk about two motivation theories.

What Managers Think Employees Want		What Employees Really Want
1	Good Pay	5
2	Job Security	4
3	Promotion and Growth	6
4	Good Working Conditions	7
5	Interesting Work	1
6	Tactful Discipline	10
7	Loyalty to Employees	8
8	Full Appreciation of Work Done	2
9	Help with Personal Problems	9
10	Feeling of Being in on Things	3

Table 1. What Employees Want

The first theory to consider is Maslow's Hierarchy of Needs, shown in Figure 1 (1954). This begins with the *physiological* needs—hunger, thirst, sleep, and relaxation. Only when the lowest, most basic needs are met can the person move up the hierarchy.

The need for *safety* is the next level that humans must address. This involves not just physical safety, but also the predictability and orderliness of the world.

The next step up is that of *love and belonging*. Does this mean that the project manager has to love everyone? Absolutely not. It means that the project manager must develop an effective working relationship with each team member. Understanding group dynamics also contributes to the effectiveness of the project manager in meeting this need.

The stages of group dynamics are basically the same regardless of the reason for the formation of the group, as shown in Figure 2. Stage 1 is forming—testing, dependence, and orientation. Stage 2 is storming—this is where conflict begins among the team members. Stage 3 is norming—characterized by the development of team cohesion, team identity, trust, and risk taking. Stage 4 is performing—the team members have a sense of task and of their roles within the team; they produce solutions. Finally, Stage 5 is adjourning—the task is concluded, and the team disengages.

Now that you know how teams form, let's go back to the Hierarchy of Needs. The fourth level up is that of the need for *esteem*. This is the desire for achievement and competence.

The highest level of need in Maslow's theory is that of *self-actualization*. This is where the project manager really begins to see the true creativity and ability of the team members. This is the performing stage of group formation.

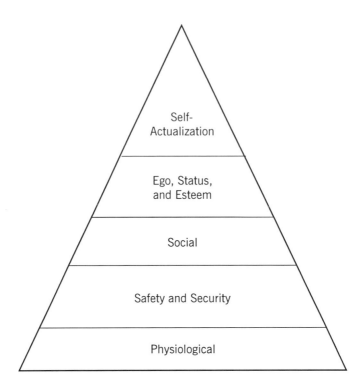

Figure 1. Maslow's Hierarchy of Needs

Another theorist, Herzberg, looks at motivation a bit differently (1959). His two-factor theory addresses the workplace specifically. This theory states that there are two different kinds of factors that must be considered in dealing with workers: motivation and maintenance.

Motivation factors will *satisfy and motivate* employees. These include achievement, recognition, the work itself, responsibility, and opportunity for growth. Motivation factors are the ones that *move the employee to improved performance.*

The other factors are those of hygiene or maintenance. Maintenance factors are job security; salary; working conditions; status; company policies; quality of technical supervision; quality of interpersonal relationships among peers, supervisors, and subordinates; and fringe benefits. These factors can create dissatisfaction with the job and must be met in order to keep the worker on the job.

Those are the theories. Next are some practical suggestions on how to put the theoretical information to work.

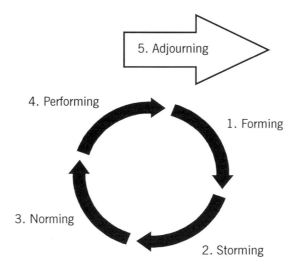

Figure 2. Group Dynamics

Criticism

Criticize the process, not the person. Try to sandwich a negative comment between two positive ones. Focus on what went well in the project. "Catch" a person doing something right. Remember, even the worst person may have a good writing style; focus on the positives.

Money

Bucks are not good motivators; better ones can be found by talking to the person. As shown in Table 1, people want to have interesting work and to be recognized for doing a good job. "My work would be better if I thought anyone ever looked at it."

You Reap What You Reward

Doctors get paid for having sick people. What would happen if they only got paid when you were well? In China, where this is the case, the doctors are experts in preventive medicine; here they are experts in surgery. What if lawyers were paid by the case, at a flat rate? Do you think trials would last for months? What if teachers were paid for the scores their students receive on their SATs?

Clear Directions

Directions should be clear, concise, and understandable. It is hard to hit a moving target.

Fear

Fear is a powerful motivator. Some things that people fear are that they won't be trusted or respected, they will lose their jobs, they will fail, or their boss will find someone better. Some ways people use fear are by refusing to give praise, making excessive demands, flying off the handle, and embarrassing someone. Fear should never be used as a motivator; *care rather than scare*.

Time Management

Some people are motivated to do what they are supposed to do but don't manage their time wisely. Steven Covey, in *First Things First*, says to make a to-do list every day (1994). Put an A beside the highest priorities, a B beside the next most-important items, and a C beside all of the others. Spend your time doing the A items until they are done, then work on the Bs. The Cs go in a drawer and are reviewed at the end of the day. Any Cs that have not moved to A go back in the drawer.

Concentrate on one thing at a time, relax, and give yourself some time to revitalize. Delegate, or ask for help. Remember that 80 percent of your time will be spent on 20 percent of the work.

Communicate

Develop a communication plan at the beginning of your project, and stick to it.
1. Define your audience.
2. Define the key thought or message.
3. Give that message three times and in three ways.
4. Don't forget to save a copy (either electronically or on paper, not both) for records management.
5. Select the right time and place. Never have anything due on Friday afternoon. You won't look at it until Monday morning anyway, and having it due Monday morning will give the person two more days to work on it if needed.
6. Use bullets and graphics.
7. Try to use one screen to get your information communicated if using electronic media.
8. Preplan your voice-mail messages. No one likes to listen to rambling.

Ego/Self-Actualization

Listen to what people tell you. Show appreciation. If you must turn down an idea, do it gently and explain why. Whenever possible, ask for input from your team on how to handle specific problems.

Get Unstuck

Sometimes people just get stuck. Have the team help them through this by having brainstorming sessions. Bring in a consultant or an expert. Have the person write down all of the issues and possible solutions, then all of the pro-and-con points. You may need to give that task to someone else, but be sure to have a new task for the "stuckee."

Make It Fun

People will be more likely to do a good job when they enjoy what they are doing. Laugh at yourself, and add humor to as many situations as possible. Add a line to your status reports, using silly sayings like: "Be nice to your kids; they are the ones who will choose your nursing home."

Rewards

Finally, the project budget should always include dollars for rewards, but this need not be a $1 million per day bonus. That is what the state of California paid over the contract estimate during each day of improvement for completion of the interstates after the last earthquake.

Here are some suggestions for other reward ideas:

- Certificates of recognition that can be printed on a laser printer.
- A pizza party, or any lunch, catered to the job site. (No alcohol; it could set a bad precedent.)
- Tee shirts, hats, pens, key chains, coffee mugs, or mouse pads that are printed with something related to the project. This also supports the need for belonging.
- Gift certificates to sporting-goods stores, restaurants, or shopping centers.
- Turkeys, hams, or special types of candy (such as Godiva chocolates).
- A thank-you card, signed by all of the project stakeholders.
- The person's name and a brief description of the activity or accomplishment being recognized included in the project status report.

In conclusion, it is hoped that with increasing awareness of the factors that motivate people to be their best, your project solutions will also be the best.

References

Covey, Steven. 1994. *First Things First.* New York, NY: Simon & Schuster.

Herzberg, F., B. Mausner, and B. Snyderman. 1959. *The Motivation to Work,* 2d ed. New York, NY: Wiley.

Kovoch, Kenneth. 1992. Motivation in the Real World. *Advanced Management Journal.* In: Gellerman, Saul W., New York, NY: Dutton.

Maslow, Abraham H. 1954. *Motivation and Personality.* New York, NY: Harper & Row.

Using the Learning Curve to Design Effective Training

Fred Borgianini, PMP

PM Network 50 (July 1998)

Training is a major activity in many types of projects, especially those that develop and deploy new business processes, computer systems, or software applications. For example, implementing a new order-entry system can change the process of accessing customers' information, entering orders, and tracking product sales. Employees performing the ordering process must learn new methods and procedures, new user interfaces, and new ways to access information. Training activities should include hands-on exercises that will allow employees to productively use the new system.

But how many exercises are required? How much training time is needed? And how productive will the employee be at the completion of training? You can use the learning curve concept to answer these questions and help design an effective training course.

The basis for the learning curve concept is "practice makes perfect." The more you repeat a process, the more efficient you become, and the less time it takes to perform. Businesses use learning curves to forecast costs, price, or work hours relative to the number of units produced (output) over time. In Measuring Learning Costs, Ken M. Boze wrote, "The 80 percent learning curve is standard for many activities and can serve as an average for forecasting learning costs" (1994). The same applies to forecasting learning time. When applying the learning curve concept to training design, you can estimate the number of training exercises needed to gain a desired productivity improvement level and the total time required to complete the exercises. Let's look at how the learning curve works.

Figure 1 is an example of an 80 percent learning curve. The horizontal axis shows the cumulative number of completed exercises (output), and the vertical axis shows the expected time to complete each exercise. In this example, it takes

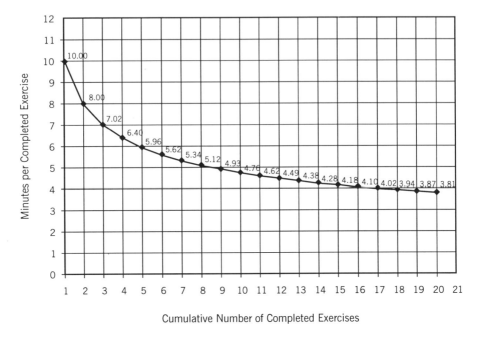

Figure 1. The 80 Percent Learning Curve

ten minutes for a person to successfully complete the first exercise. When the output doubles to two completed exercises, the expected time falls from ten minutes to eight minutes, 80 percent of the first exercise (or a 20 percent decrease in time). When the output doubles again, to four completed exercises, the expected time falls to 6.4 minutes, 80 percent of the second exercise. Each time the number of completed exercises doubles, there is a 20 percent decrease in time.

Notice that the slope of the learning curve is initially steep, then begins to flatten. This is because a person learns quickly at first, but with more and more practice becomes proficient at a task. Productivity—in this case the time it takes to successfully complete each training exercise—improves rapidly with the first few exercises, and then tapers off as the individual gains proficiency. Therefore, learning happens at a decreasing rate.

So how many exercises are required for an individual to become sufficiently productive? According to Boze, "The data tells us training programs should contain at least eight to ten exercises for each activity, which should move the individual well down the learning curve" (1994). You can see why by looking at Table 1. Column A shows the cumulative number of completed exercises. Column B shows the percentage of expected productivity increase from the previous exercise. Column C shows the cumulative percentage of expected productivity improvement from the first completed exercise. Note that percentages in Columns

A	B	C
Cumulative Number of Completed Exercises	Expected Productivity Increase from the Previous Exercise	Expected Cumulative Improvement from First Completed Exercise
2	20.00%	20.00%
3	12.20%	29.80%
4	8.80%	36.00%
5	6.90%	40.40%
6	5.70%	43.80%
7	4.80%	46.60%
8	4.20%	48.80%
9	3.70%	50.70%
10	3.30%	52.40%
11	3.00%	53.80%
12	2.80%	55.10%
13	2.50%	56.20%
14	2.40%	57.20%
15	2.20%	58.20%
16	2.10%	59.00%
17	1.90%	59.80%
18	1.80%	60.00%
19	1.70%	61.30%
20	1.60%	61.90%
21	1.60%	62.50%

Table 1. Expected Productivity Improvement

B and C apply to any 80 percent learning curve. Looking at Column B, notice how the rate of productivity improvement decreases with each completed exercise. The second exercise shows a 20 percent productivity increase from the first, but the twentieth completed exercise shows only a 1.6 percent productivity increase from the ninetieth. Column C shows the total effect on productivity. For example, it takes only ten completed exercises to gain a 52.4 percent total productivity increase, but it takes ten *more* exercises, for a total of twenty, to gain only an additional 9.5 percent increase to 61.9 percent. This means that the benefits gained from each additional exercise after ten may not be worth the additional time and cost to your project.

The complexity of the activity may determine whether you include more than ten or less than eight exercises. For example, from a data-entry perspective, creating an initial order for a new customer is usually more complex than canceling an existing order. Use Table 1 as a guide for choosing a desired productivity-improvement level for each activity. For establishing a new order, you may want to include twelve data-entry exercises to achieve a 55.1 percent total productivity improvement from the first exercise. For canceling an order, six exercises for a 43.8 percent total productivity improvement may suffice. This gives you the flexibility to vary the number of exercises to achieve a target productivity-improvement level for each activity.

How much training time is required? You can estimate the total time to complete each person's training by adding together the expected minutes to complete the total number of exercises for each training activity. Table 2 shows the 80 percent learning curve as it applies to three training activities for our new order-entry system: establishing a new order, changing an order, and canceling an order. Column A shows the cumulative number of completed exercises. Column B shows the learning-curve factor for each exercise. Note that the learning-curve factors shown are the same for any 80 percent learning curve.

Before you apply the learning-curve factors you will need to estimate the expected time to complete the first exercise. You can do this by using parametric (historical and statistical) methods or other available estimating tools. Once you've determined the expected time to complete the first exercise, multiply it by the learning-curve factor for each subsequent exercise to get the expected number of minutes. For example, Column C shows an estimated time of fifteen minutes to complete the first "new order" exercise. The second exercise is expected to take twelve minutes, .8 x 15. Exercise three is expected to take 10.53 minutes, .702 x 15, and so on. The same logic applies to Columns D and E, changing orders and canceling orders, respectively. The totals at the bottom of each column reflect twelve exercises for entering new orders, nine exercises for changing orders, and six exercises for canceling orders. Column F shows the total time it takes to complete all twenty-seven exercises, 192.57 minutes (or three hours, thirteen minutes). With start-up activities and breaks, you can plan on a four-hour training class.

At this point you've estimated the number of exercises and the time required for individuals to achieve a certain productivity-improvement level at the end of their training. How do you give your students the best chance at continuing to improve in practice? Timing! According to Boze, "Added time between training and practical application shifts the learning curve up, as does time away from the job. Therefore, it is important that users apply what they learn quickly and get plenty of practice. Training should be timed with this in mind" (1994). Ensure that training sessions and deployment of the new system are closely linked in your project plan. To take full advantage of the learning curve, employees should move from the classroom to the workplace in the shortest time possible.

A	B	C	D	E	F
Cumulative Number of Completed Exercises	Learning-Curve Factor	Expected Minutes to Complete New-Order Exercises	Expected Minutes to Complete Change-Order Exercises	Expected Minutes to Complete Cancel-Order Exercises	Total Expected Minutes per Person
1	1.000	15.00	10.00	6.00	
2	0.800	12.00	8.00	4.80	
3	0.702	10.53	7.02	4.21	
4	0.640	9.60	6.40	3.84	
5	0.596	8.93	5.96	3.57	
6	0.562	8.42	5.62	3.37	
7	0.534	8.02	5.34		
8	0.512	7.68	5.12		
9	0.493	7.39	4.93		
10	0.476	7.15			
11	0.462	6.93			
12	0.449	6.74			
Totals	>>>>>>>	108.39	58.39	25.79	192.57 or 3 hrs, 13 mins

Table 2. Estimated Training Time

Remember the learning curve is primarily a useful estimating tool. While the concept provides a general model for the effect of practice on productivity, it does not account for variables such as employee motivation and resistance to change. Careful communications planning and management will help prepare employees for the rollout of a new system. The learning curve will help you design the training they need to use the system effectively.

References
Boze, Ken M. 1994. Measuring Learning Costs. *Management Accounting.*

QFD in Project Management— A Pragmatic Approach

R. J. Levene and K. R. H. Goffin

Proceedings of the 27th Annual Project Management Institute
1996 Seminars & Symposium

Intense competition and more-demanding customers are increasing the pressure on companies to bring innovative products to market faster. Consequently, many companies are looking for ways to accelerate new product development and at the same time ensure that the resulting products closely match customer requirements. Any techniques that can assist in faster, more effective product development have wide implications for industry.

A widely applied technique is Quality Function Deployment (QFD). It captures customer priorities—*the voice of the customer*—at an early stage in a project and uses them to drive all subsequent design decisions, especially those that involve tradeoffs between particular product features. QFD yields a detailed matrix that can be used as the basis for all project discussions and when used correctly, this articulates the link between customer requirements and the scope of the project. QFD can reduce rework and redesign; *getting it right the first time* was a key factor in the success of Japanese manufacturing in the '70s and '80s, and some of this success was attributed to the use of QFD (Hauser and Clausing 1988).

There is a wide body of literature documenting successful projects attributed to QFD. However, the link between QFD and project management techniques, in particular the need to integrate Work Breakdown Structures (WBSs), has been almost entirely ignored. Additionally, few papers have addressed the difficulties in implementing QFD because "[QFD] is not the panacea that some proponents would have managers believe" (Griffin 1992). Consequently the aims of this article are to:

- Propose how new product development could be changed by linking QFD and WBSs.
- Define a research agenda for further investigation of the importance of linking QFD and project management techniques.

The Essence of QFD

QFD is much more comprehensive than just taking account of customer requirements; its initial focus is aimed at the design stage of a project by correlating the customer needs with engineering design features. Excellent descriptions of the method exist in the literature (Hauser and Clausing 1988; Daetz 1990), so that only a brief description of the technique will be given here.

QFD involves identifying customer requirements ("WHATS"), grouping them into categories and entering these on the left of the QFD matrix (see Figure 1), with the priorities shown on the right. Design attributes ("HOWS") that can deliver the customer needs are mapped into the top of the matrix. The relationships between the customer and design requirements are then entered ("WHATS & HOWS"), as are correlations between the "HOWS." The resulting matrix summarizes all key project data, and further stages of QFD can improve design, process, and production planning.

The Value of QFD in the Development Cycle

The early beginnings of QFD, in the '70s, concentrated on correlating customer requirements with design attributes, it then developed rapidly in a variety of industries in Japan and was extended from design attributes through to parts, processes, and production. Most documented applications of the technique are in the area of product development (Kathawala and Motwani 1994), although applications in software development (Haag, Raja, and Schkade 1996), educational program design, and the service industry (Graessel and Zeidler 1993) have been published.

The technique is widely seen as the answer to the ills of product development. Quicker time to market and the right product are the ultimate goals of the competitive product developer, and theoretically QFD has all the components needed to achieve those goals. Those publications that claim success of the technique, in the main, are directed toward the product development area where the developer can get close to the real customer and when the product that is to be developed has no major technological challenges associated with it. However, this is not to say that its application is limited only to those types of projects.

In an analysis of the positive and negative aspects of using QFD, Griffin puts forward a series of factors that contribute to the success or failure of the technique (1992); some of these depend on project characteristics and some on the

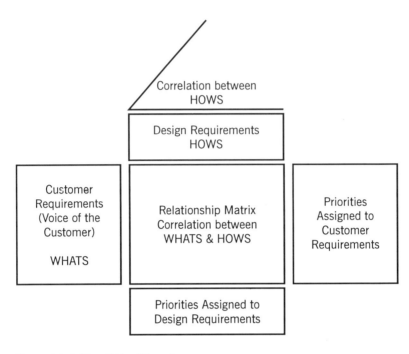

Source: Adapted from Zairi and Youssef

Figure 1. The House of Quality

way in which organizations implement QFD. She also suggests that there are important intangible benefits that arise from QFD, such as reduced cross-functional barriers, and these are also echoed in the process of building a WBS.

QFD and Project Management

Project Definition

Although research has identified a number of factors that influence the success of projects, it is not surprising to find that project definition is one of the major factors that contributes to project success (Morris and Hough 1987). It is not only definition but also definition in association with *client* consultation that is important (Pinto and Slevin 1988), and so it would seem sensible for project managers to use appropriate tools to aid the conceptualization and definition of projects. This principle is applicable to every class of project, not just those aimed at developing products. WBSs have been used extensively in the definition of *what* needs to be done in the project. Although their original purpose was to break the project into more manageable chunks of work, an important side benefit of WBSs is an exposure of any weaknesses in the project scope. The formulation of the WBS can be viewed as the pivotal stage of any project, linking the goals and objectives of the project to the subsequently more detailed planning stages typified by schedules and budgets.

Project success is often viewed simplistically as the adherence to schedule and budget, but without adequate project definition the agreed schedule and budget set at the start of the project have little chance of being met. Therefore, correct understanding of the goals and objectives of the project and a well-formulated WBS should not only lead to success but should also minimize potential changes to the project.

Weaknesses in Project Formulation

If the goals and objectives of a project are poorly formulated, then subsequent customer satisfaction with the results of the project (i.e., the product) is likely to be low; therefore it is essential that customer needs are properly incorporated into the project objectives and fully accounted for in the planning process.

Project management is applicable to a wide range of industries and sectors, and in many the real end user is distant from the project management team. For example, the chain of connections could be: end user, department, owner, contractor, subcontractor, and project. The goals and objectives of the project may be formulated as comprehensively and verbosely as a project specification—often through a tender process. There is no guarantee that the real project requirements from the end-user viewpoint have been successfully translated into the specification. The WBS frequently reflects this, but its formulation is not a rigorous process and is often carried out too late in the project and in formal contractual situations, even frequently after the contract award. Blending the QFD and WBS processes could bring significant advantages to many projects by focusing the formulation of the WBS with end-user needs in mind and by carrying it out earlier in the conceptual phase of the project. The resultant WBS would be more structured and produce a formulation of work packages that are easier and have more appropriate work-package boundaries.

Work Breakdown Structures—Enhanced with QFD

The benefits of QFD have been extolled by many authors; most identify that the emphasis on cross-functional teamwork is not just an added benefit, but also an essential part in the implementation of the technique. Daetz summarizes this well: "QFD specifies the use of cross-functional teams so that a more complete and balanced view of customer/user needs, the competitive environment, and possible company responses is developed and used in the product definition, design, and production processes" (1990). Product definition by consensus is imbued in the philosophy of QFD and is reflected in its deliverables (tables and matrices). Consensus is also an essential part of any project planning process.

Daetz also identifies some benefits associated with the output from QFD that correlate well with the benefits of a WBS (1990):

- Identifying areas where the team needs to acquire better information.
- Storing the results of decisions that the team makes.
- Using the QFD matrices to communicate the product plan.

By comparison, some of the benefits of constructing a WBS include (Levene 1996):

- Exposing any weaknesses in the project scope.
- Visually communicating the "what" of the project.
- Providing a basis for measuring future change.

The philosophy of a WBS is one of manageability and control. The resultant work packages are formulated so that they can be assigned to a person in the organization who takes responsibility for full delivery of that work package. Implicit in this formulation is that they are put together so that they are a good fit for the organization. Techniques to aid such a formulation are sparse; such a formulation is done either in isolation by the project manager or (better) by the project team, with much discussion and brainstorming. Globerson describes the WBS as the taxonomy of the project and emphasizes the effect that the WBS-building process has on the success of the project (1994). Although he identifies guidelines for its construction, his overall conclusion is that the WBS has to be the result of discussion between the (cross-functional) members of the project team.

Formulating the WBS

Constructing the WBS can be approached in a number of ways (Levene 1996; Globerson 1994); the most common are project life cycle, functional use, component or product, and geographical area. Frequently there is a mixture of these approaches with, for example, a functional or system breakdown at level 2 of the structure and component at the next level down. The work packages must be unique and clearly distinguishable from each other. In breaking the project into its component parts or products, any associated management services should be included to encompass all the project costs. The work packages can be defined so that they have their own set of goals and objectives and other associated information; a typical work-package description can contain any of the following information.

Work Package Content
Design Philosophy and Assumptions
Brief Description of Work and Context

Cost Estimate
Work Hours and Materials
Subcontracts

Time
Overall Span

Resources
People/Key Personnel
Equipment

Deliverables
Key Documents
Specifications
Reports

Quality Assurance Criteria
Procedures
Client Involvement

Criteria for Success
Guarantees
Performance Specification

Some of this information falls naturally from the project specification, but in practice many project teams would find it hard to provide the detail. However, implicit in the QFD process is the closeness to the customer or end user, often in projects where the project team is distant from the customer. For example, in a construction project, the contractor responds to the client, who may be providing a facility to an unknown end user. In such cases the design formulation becomes the most important influence on the project time and cost. Yet many projects fail due to the lack of communication between client and contractor, with the subsequent lack of poor project definition. It is unlikely that a client would provide a WBS for the contractor, and in such an event, it is likely that it would not be appropriate for the contractor. However, a joint QFD session between client and contractor that identified not only product attributes but also project attributes distilled from the project specifications should go a long way toward providing not only design parameters for the project but also indicators that would help formulate an appropriate WBS.

View of the WBS/QFD World

With today's market pressures, achieving the product launch date (i.e., adhering to project schedule) is absolutely vital to product success. Since time is inviolate, then either cost and quality have to be compromised or the work scope reduced. Reducing the work scope implies fewer product features, and a well-formulated WBS can help considerably in such cases. Consider the work packages to be oriented around the features of the product—if a feature can be removed in order to reduce scope and maintain schedule, it can be thought of as a *pruning* exercise. (This is quite appropriate if the WBS is viewed as a tree structure.) In this way not only will schedule be achieved, but also the quality of the rest of the project—the other work packages—need not be threatened. This approach can be compared and contrasted to the actions of a poorly constructed project where scope reductions are carried out across the project, inevitably leading to quality problems or even rework.

The output from the QFD "house of quality" exercise would be invaluable in such cases, as the priority levels of features are part of its outputs. Thus, a link between QFD and project management techniques would not only influence the form of the WBS, but it also could help prioritize the sequence of work and, in a tight schedule situation, reduce the amount of wasted work.

Conclusions

The research described in this article is the first stage in an investigation into the need for linkages between project management and QFD. The objective is to enhance the benefit from QFD and maximize its value in project formulation. From the literature it can be seen that there has not been enough investigation in the past, so that a future research agenda is clear: there is a need for empirical study of the importance of integrating QFD with project management techniques in new product development. One thing is clear from the research: QFD is not a panacea, and companies need to be pragmatic about the advantages it can and cannot bring.

References

Daetz, D. 1990. Planning for Customer Satisfaction with Quality Function Deployment. *Proceedings*. Eighth International Conference of the ISQA (November).

Globerson, S. 1994. Impact of Various Work Breakdown Structures on Project Conceptualization. *International Journal of Project Management* 12, no. 3: 165–71.

Graessel, R., and P. Zeidler. 1993. Using Quality Function Deployment to Improve Customer Service. *Quality Progress* 26, no. 11: 59–63.

Griffin, A. 1992. Evaluating QFD's Use in US Firms as a Process for Developing Products. *J. Prod. Innov. Manag* 9: 171–187.

Haag, S., M. K. Raja, and L. L. Schkade. 1996. Quality Function Deployment Usage in Software Development. *Communications of the ACM* 39, no. 1: 41–49.

Hauser, J. R., and D. Clausing. 1988. The House of Quality. *Harvard Business Review.* (May–June): 63–73.

Kathawala, Y., and J. Motwani. 1994. Implementing Quality Function Deployment. *The TQM Magazine* 6, no. 6: 31–37.

Levene, R. J. 1996. *Project Management. The International Encyclopedia of Business and Management*. Routledge.

Morris, P. W. G., and G. H. Hough. 1987. *The Anatomy of Major Projects*. UK: John Wiley.

Pinto, J. K., and D. P. Slevin. 1988. Critical Success Factors Across the Project Life Cycle. *Project Management Journal* 19, no. 3: 67–75.

A Parallel WBS for International Projects

Cornelius Grove, Willa Hallowell, and Cynthia J. Smith

PM Network 37 (March 1999)

Team members arriving from abroad face many difficulties in acquiring housing; using metric specifications, which proves far more difficult than anticipated; dismissing an unproductive local worker and running seriously afoul of local law; government functionaries performing at a snail's pace unless "compensated"; the local joint-venture partner having a distressingly flexible view of the contract; local workers remaining unmotivated by pay-for-performance schemes; training events that worked well at home yielding poor results; and the key local manager being enraged, while the international project manager (IPM) can't figure why.

The first four items in this list are cross-border challenges: obstacles grounded in the logistical necessity of relocating employees and in unfamiliar governmental policies and regulations, legal structures, and business practices. They are easily recognizable because they have a certain "in-your-face" quality (including, in some cases, official sanctions for noncompliance).

The last four items are cross-cultural challenges: obstacles grounded in the differing assumptions, values, habits of thought, and patterns of behavior of the various national/ethnic groups cooperating on the project. These are *not* easily recognizable because they are outside of people's conscious awareness.

Comprehending and overcoming hurdles such as these is rarely mentioned in an IPM's job description. Yet, experienced IPMs will attest that the efficiency and effectiveness with which projects are completed is definitely affected by their success in handling cross-cultural and cross-border challenges.

Preparing for the Inevitable

The types of obstacles listed are inevitable in projects carried out across national and cultural boundaries. Significantly, most of these difficulties are predictable; business anthropologists and cross-cultural researchers have devised ways of reducing or even avoiding their negative effects. Now, at the turn of the millennium, IPMs have an unprecedented number of resources that can help them plan wisely for managing across mindsets.

To draw on these resources, an IPM and his direct reports must become educated about what is known from research and experience. However, learning to think about project management in a culturally sophisticated way cannot, by itself, reduce risks. The IPM and his firm must commit time, effort, and money. Culture *can* be managed, but not merely through educated thinking.

A Parallel WBS

We recommend a parallel work breakdown structure (WBS) for managing the international dimensions of a project. By *parallel* we suggest that every such project can benefit from *two* WBSs: an extensive one for the principal project, and a modest one for managing the project's international dimensions. Each has a budget, assigned personnel, and delivery dates. Completion of the parallel WBS ensures that the principal WBS is completed well, on time, and on budget. Think of it as low-cost insurance for risks that are certain to occur.

A budget for this parallel WBS should incorporate expense categories for which international projects customarily allocate funds: translators, language teachers, welcoming and milestone events, assistance for team members from abroad, and certain kinds of training. "Atypical expense categories" need to be added, as this need will become apparent. An adequate budget for managing these risks will be a tiny fraction of the budget for completing the principal project.

The Culture Risk Management Team

Our generic model calls for the direct involvement of project team members in managing the risks inherent in the project. The culture risk management (CRM) team is headed by a culture risk manager who should be a high-potential employee with aspirations to become an international project manager. Her CRM responsibilities should be on a part-time basis. CRM team members need to reflect the major ethnic and national groups working onsite. Team members can be rotated periodically, enabling more employees to learn firsthand the cultural realities of international project management.

The culture risk manager needs to be held accountable for reducing or avoiding cross-cultural and cross-border risks. She needs both human resources (team members, clerical help) and material resources to make good on that accountability: an office, a library, communication and travel capabilities, formal reporting requirements, and an adequate budget.

Information Management

As the principal project gets under way, the CRM team needs to gather reliable information about cross-cultural and cross-border challenges. This responsibility need not be theirs alone. Existing resources within the firm, such as the human resource, training and development, legal departments, and/or the firm's technical librarian, can assist. Cross-border information will be relatively easy to locate because much of it is legal and regulatory in nature. We anticipate perplexity about where to find information about cultural differences in assumptions, values, habits of thought, and patterns of behavior. Besides print and online sources, such information can be acquired from experienced people through interviewing. A cross-cultural consultant can assist by identifying pathways to information and knowing productive questions to ask informants.

Information undigested is as useless as information undiscovered. In order to skillfully perform their next critical function—risk assessment—CRM team members must dedicate time to understanding the information collected.

Risk Assessment and Strategy Planning

The objective of the CRM team is to predict potential risks then plan to reduce or avoid them. We're talking here about everything from the obvious (foreign exchange regulations), through the easily discoverable (whether local workers are accustomed to participatory or authoritative supervisory methods), to the subtle and obscure (whether the cultures represented onsite tend to value harmony or accuracy in communication, and how this may affect relationships).

Another category of risk to assess concerns the reaction of local nationals to the business practices and social values being imported into their environment. The authors recognize how typical it is for Americans to be guided by the unexamined assumption that their values and ways of life have universal applicability. However, this may not be the case, and since people in many cultures value harmonious relationships more than Americans do, the degree to which locals *actually give voice* to their concerns may not be a reliable gauge to how well they will cooperate in the long run. Two examples: Being from an individualistic, accomplishment-oriented culture, Americans use performance evaluations to reward employees, and they are accustomed to promoting young fast-trackers over older plodders. How does this play out in other cultures? And consider the cutting-edge technology that most projects introduce into their host communities: How might local people react to this?

A third category of risk assessment involves a direct examination of the formal project statement, objectives, work breakdown structure, and resource requirements to determine if any create, accentuate, or fail to account for risks associated with the project's international dimensions. Three examples: Is the time projected to complete certain phases unrealistic, given that local workers are far less driven by the clock than Americans? Has a step believed essential by local people—such as a *feng shui* evaluation of a building site—been omitted? Have face-to-face visits been planned with key players located offsite so that good personal relationships can lead to loyalty and trust?

Perceived risks need to be transformed into risk-reduction strategies and recommended to those in authority over the project's objectives, budget, and timelines. Regardless of whether the risk-reduction strategies are adopted, all perceived risks should be documented to better facilitate organizational learning.

International Project Personnel Support

The support of project team members arriving from abroad is a key function of the CRM team. The cultural coaching and relocation support of such people is a well-developed, well-documented blend of art and science that can easily be applied in the case of international project personnel. There are two significant questions. The first is whether any support will be provided for project personnel beyond the bare minimum that delivers them physically to the project site. If "yes," the second question is, "To what extent and at what level of quality will support be provided?"

No international assignee program is state of the art unless it delivers coordinated coaching and support in both host (project site) and sending countries. Note, however, that *any* level of support beyond the bare minimum is preferable to none at all, and that support delivered in the host country is more cost effective than support delivered before assignees leave home.

The CRM team's fundamental objective is to do whatever is necessary so that recently arrived assignees from abroad are not preoccupied with the details of settling into new living and working environments (cross-border issues) nor with the frustrations of rubbing elbows daily with people whose values and patterns of behavior are different (cross-cultural issues). An orientation handbook, face-to-face advice and assistance for team members from abroad, and procedures for handling routine and emergency situations are all helpful. To the extent that a CRM team can communicate or even coordinate these services with human resource departments in the sending countries, so much the better.

Integration of Project Personnel

Integration of project personnel should address not only those working onsite but also those at other locations worldwide who are contributing substantially to the project's eventual success. Onsite integration involves relatively simple, enjoyable events such as banquets or other social events (consistent with local practice) for welcoming newly arrived assignees, milestone events to celebrate successes, and holiday events drawing on the traditions of the various cultural groups onsite. Onsite integration also involves more substantial concerns such as investigating work-relationship and problem-solving patterns of the different cultures and developing hybrid "third ways" of getting things done.

Since 1990 researchers have been addressing the challenges faced by "global teams," people working together on one project from several distant sites. Such teams encounter major hurdles to communication and trust building. To the extent that a project has "virtual" participants, such issues are grist for the CRM team's mill.

It is unlikely that the work of any CRM team will totally eliminate every possible cross-border and, especially, cross-cultural risk. As its final responsibility, the team needs to give advance thought to the processes it can put in place to contain the damage from a major misunderstanding or conflict.

Toward Organizational Learning

A CRM team can be thought of as an expense—or as an investment. Any large firm completing one international project is almost certain to be planning or completing others as well. The information and expertise gained by a CRM team is transferable to other projects, but only if its work is evaluated, documented, reviewed by senior management, shared verbally and in print with other IPMs, and cataloged in the firm's archives.

To this end we recommend that 1) the CRM team's progress be formally assessed in quality assurance reviews, 2) team personnel be rotated, 3) the culture risk manager occasionally brief senior policymakers, 4) periodic CRM team reports be disseminated to project personnel, and 5) annual CRM team reports be disseminated to all the firm's employees and other stakeholders.

Applying the tools of project management to the human issues of cross-cultural work gives us a structured way to tackle a confusing issue. It's just one way in which project management will play an important role in our rapidly globalizing economy.

Section 4

Staff Acquisition and Kickoff

How Are You Handling the Resource Shortage?

Deborah Bigelow, PMP

PM Network 19 (January 2001)

As we begin the new year, we will undoubtedly face many new challenges within our organizations. One of the most significant challenges, and one that's gained increasing attention over the past few years, is that of attracting and retaining employees. The workforce simply is not growing as quickly as it has in the past. Compared to a 3.5 percent net increase in 1979, we will be experiencing a net decrease in employees by 2012. How will this affect your projects and your organization's success? And what can you do to proactively help your company meet this challenge?

First you need to understand our environment. The employee of the twenty-first century has certainly changed course from the employee of the mid-twentieth century. My dad worked for the same company for over thirty-five years. He never would have thought of changing jobs. He was just thankful that he had one; changing jobs would have been viewed as unstable. This is not true in today's world.

The human resource specialist of my company recently attended the Society for Human Resources 2000 Conference in Washington, DC. At this conference she heard a paper presentation titled Commitment in the Workplace—The 2000 Global Employee Relationship Report Benchmark, by Marc Drizin, vice president, Business Alliances Walker Information. According to the study, conducted by Wallker Information Global Network and the Hudson Institute, the average employee has twelve to fifteen jobs over the course of his career. The average employee stays in a job for 3.6 years. Employees in virtually all industries have shown a decrease in tenure over the last fifteen years, except government employees, who currently remain in their jobs for an average of 7.3 years.

The same study concluded that only one-third of all employees are truly loyal to their organizations, and only half of those loyal employees feel a strong personal attachment to their organizations. A disturbing underlying question here is: What is happening within our society when two-thirds of all employees feel no loyalty to those who employ them? Have we become so cold-hearted that employees are only important if they can positively affect the profit-and-loss statement? I do believe that businesses have to make business decisions, but have we swung the pendulum too far? Will it hurt businesses in the long run? Have we been too shortsighted?

Another conclusion of this study is that only half of all employees feel their organizations care about developing them for the long term. An underlying message here is that you have to train your people … or they will leave. I know my experience validates this. Potential employees are generally focused on what kind of commitment the organization is willing to provide in terms of professional development. Once they become employees, they will pursue what was promised, and organizations are obligated to honor their commitments or pay the consequences of a high turnover ratio.

Although organizations have no control over the number of resources that are available in society at large, they can be proactive in dealing with their resource issues by increasing the job-satisfaction levels of those employees already working for them. They need to be cognizant of *why* their employees stay and what drives them to leave. According to Drizin's study, five influences on employee loyalty are:

1. Fairness at work (including pay).
2. Care and concern for employees.
3. Satisfaction on a day-to-day basis.
4. Trust in employees.
5. Reputation of the organization.

So what does this mean to you? If you have any influence on recruiting or retaining employees or team members, it should mean a lot. Especially since Drizin reports that a Mercer study put the cost to replace a lost worker at over $30,000. It costs less to retain an employee than it does to replace one.

As a manager, you need to be aware and proactive in positively influencing your employees, especially in the five areas noted. Employers, as a whole, need to measure and manage what drives the loyalty of their employees. The expense of retaining workers should be viewed as an investment, not a cost. The labor pool is diminishing; be proactive in meeting this challenge!

Human Resources: How Are They Faring on Your Project?

Deborah Bigelow, PMP

PM Network 16 (January 1999)

In a lessons-learned meeting after the completion of a major software implementation project, I asked, "What was the major challenge on this project?" The response, without hesitation, was "human resources."

I should not have been surprised, but I was. With all the complexities of the project, this project manager still felt that management of human resources required much more energy and skill. The project manager emphasized that human resources were, by far, the most valuable resources.

I requested more explanation of how and why the human resource issues evolved so that I could more clearly understand and avoid this problem with future projects.

Challenges on the project included:

- Adequate staff not in place at the onset of the project.
- Current staff overloaded with daily work.
- Staff not perceiving the project as a priority.
- Temporary personnel added to support project but, when not utilized immediately, placed in other projects, and then it was almost impossible to get them back
- Lack of team-building skills.

Project managers tend to underestimate the resources required to complete a project. Oftentimes we do this out of fear that if the human resource need is too great the project will be not be approved. It is management's responsibility to ensure that the estimates provided are realistic and that any external help brought in to assist is quickly assigned and monitored.

A week after this conversation, I attended a Project Management Institute chapter meeting where the topic was Lessons Learned from Complex Projects. The overwhelming consensus of the eighty participants present was that team-building issues were by far the most pressing issues in most projects.

As a profession, we have tried to focus attention on team building to address the critical area of human issues. Teaching teamwork began almost forty years ago, with early efforts focusing on experiential learning. The idea was to force individuals to rely on other members of the team in a realistic situation, such as a "tug of war."

The next approach in teaching teamwork was in using experimental techniques targeted at building trust among team members. While effective for some, this approach was clearly not for everyone. Says Douglas Lowe, independent human resources consultant in Havertown, Pennsylvania, "I still run into people who roll their eyes back when you mention team building. They immediately think that they will have to hug someone or fall helplessly into someone's arms!"

Then came the cognitive approach—standing in front of a classroom and talking *at* people about why they change and why they don't. As you might surmise, this approach toward team building added little excitement or motivation to change.

In our current workplace, there are many methods of teaching teamwork: electronic mazes, role-playing, wall climbing, and Lego-building, to name just a few. What we're finding now is that it really doesn't matter what exercise you use, but rather how you debrief *after* the exercise to understand what you learned and then to *apply* what you learned back on the job. A project manager should build teamwork in a similar manner that a sports coach might: stress the plays (or process); then define the player's role and responsibility in the play (or project); then, like a coach, motivate team members to excel in the process.

The bottom line: In today's corporate environment, where resources are scarce, we must be proactive in avoiding human resource issues on projects. Management must take responsibility for providing realistic estimates of human resource needs, and then supplement regular staff with external resources to fill any gaps that might arise. Management must make an investment in team building, and the exercises learned in training environments must be applied and considered a critical success factor in good project management. The investment will certainly be worth it. And the success of your project may ultimately depend upon it.

Finding and Keeping the Best Employees

Edited by Joanita M. Nellenbach

PM Network 7 (June 1999)

Hiring used to be a fairly straightforward matter: You selected the people you wanted, put them to work, and waited for them to sink or swim. Like much of life, however, the hiring process has become increasingly complicated. In the strong economic climate in many regions, finding and keeping good employees is extremely difficult.

For growing companies, hiring just one unqualified employee can have a terribly negative effect on productivity, profitability, and morale. The time required to duplicate work and rebuild customer relationships because of employee incompetence is costly. In addition, losing good employees to competitors is expensive. With each departure, you forfeit whatever you invested in training and an amount of knowledge and information that even the experts haven't dared calculate. Furthermore, increasing governmental and legislative involvement in labor and employment issues means that business owners must be prepared to defend hiring and firing decisions in court.

Business owners can minimize their legal and financial risks by complying with federal and state regulations that govern employee-related policies and procedures. Although most large companies maintain a human resources department or in-house counsel to keep them up to speed on labor and employment issues, growing companies often don't have the time or resources to dedicate to creating or implementing structured human-resource guidelines.

By taking a few common-sense steps, however, any business can safeguard itself against making costly legal mistakes in hiring, managing, and firing employees. These steps provide a quick, efficient, and cost-effective system to establish a paper trail of written records that can be used to document employee-related issues if legal disputes should arise. Business owners should:

Demonstrate a businesslike approach from a prospective employee's first involvement with your company. This means providing an easy-to-understand employment application and explanation of your hiring timetable and a straightforward interview process. Offer a clear job description and avoid loaded terms that could suggest discrimination, such as salesman, Girl Friday, or young. In addition, you should state at every opportunity your company's intent to be lawful.

Make sure your job advertisements and application materials communicate clearly that your company is an equal-opportunity employer. Confine your questions to job-related matters: Will the candidate be comfortable doing lots of heavy lifting or data entry? Can she work late shifts or weekends?

Provide materials that explain all established company policies, from a list of paid holidays to attendance requirements. In some cases, the policies will cover areas required by government regulations. For example, a number of states now require that companies provide formal policies for identifying and reporting sexual harassment. Keep the policies in a notebook or manual. When you hire someone, be sure to have the right forms on hand for the new employee to fill out. These include I-9 and W-4 forms. The message is not only that you are organized, but also that you follow the law to the letter.

Maintain complete and up-to-date records on each employee. Keep job performance files that include written information on such matters as attendance, changes in duties or salary, and job performance. Save any written inquiries or statements from employees. Document any warnings you give an employee, even if the warnings are oral. Use and file written performance appraisals that reflect an honest assessment of an employee's job performance. Document all job-related accidents or illnesses. Write down exactly what happened, how the problem was treated, how the employee described the situation, and who else was present.

Keep your employees well informed. Make sure they know about changes in the law, especially those related to minimum wage, overtime reporting, and safety standards. Mount in prominent locations safety and health posters that advise employees on how to comply with state and federal safety, waste disposal, and other related regulations. This can help head off legal problems if an employee claims he wasn't informed about these matters.

Sharing information with employees sets the stage for encouraging more open lines of communication with them. Simply making employees feel that they can talk frankly about their problems or concerns can prevent many potential problems. Employees don't necessarily expect every problem to be solved; what's typically more important is that they feel you are listening to them.

Pump Up Your Project Scheduling

Marilee Camblin, PMP, and Thomas Schrimsher, PMP

PM Network 36 (January 1998)

Weak scheduling is a project management liability. Few project managers will deny that fact because more than a few have suffered the consequences of a flimsy scheduling system. Successful managers understand that a robust system holds significant project control potential beyond its fundamental applications of planning and performance measurement. Even when basic scheduling is relatively strong, a project's management can benefit from enhancements and efficiencies that maximize system capability and products.

When project control is the primary function of a scheduling system, credibility is its most important attribute. A certain fate awaits the project manager who must depend on less-than-solid information. A system that's not reliable or which is being manipulated may be worse for project management than no scheduling at all. Experienced managers know that the technical methods applied to produce the schedule network can directly influence the credibility of products from the network. Benchmark scheduling systems are sound in their application of detailed processes that ensure consistency and discipline, since these are what sustain network integrity and credibility to provide the basis for realistic, comprehensive project control.

But what of systems not up to benchmark standards? What approaches are suitable to improve an existing scheduling system that supports project management but is not altogether effective and efficient in doing so? Our recommendations address systems of this type, and they are readily adaptable for specific situations. Excluding a core set of six, these suggestions may be implemented separately. Scheduling pump-up can encompass as much or as little effort as the initiator decides. Certainly, it can be even more extensive than assimilation of all the tips presented here. The key is to preserve whatever gains are made and not let them shrivel away.

A Reality-Based Set of Best Practices

These recommendations evolved from a scheduling improvement initiative for the Department of Energy's Hanford Site, undertaken for the Tank Waste Remediation System Project. The government environment compelled certain requirements and processes for the subject program, and recommendations were developed under a process to "design" the system to achieve certain objectives, or outputs. Each prospective technique can be adopted or not, based on how well it serves to implement or enhance a scheduling function that supports discrete objectives for the system to be improved.

Here we present some of the recommendations that resulted from this government initiative. These suggestions generally assume a sizable program that schedules multiple projects of duration greater than one year, using computer software that calculates full-range cost/schedule data for performance measurement. The scheduling system is presumed to support summarization for a hierarchy of schedules; some prevailing budget cycle; baseline management—including change control; and some regular performance-measurement update cycle. Any assumption, and tips related to it, may be ignored if it does not apply for a particular system.

Pump Up Proposals

Recommendations can be adapted and combined in multiple ways to condition and beef up a scrawny scheduling program. However, just as the lightweight is cautioned to consult a doctor before undertaking serious physical exercise in an effort to muscle up, the manager wanting to implement these recommendations is cautioned to consider how well the prevailing project situation will accommodate the initiative and whether there is need to plan scope and estimate costs.

Implementation of proposed approaches will build effectiveness and efficiency to continually improve overall program capability. A core strategy, meant to ensure the essential prerequisite system, is the basis for all subsequent recommendations. Certain core techniques directly reinforce scheduling as a central function of project management. The impact of any recommendation on an existing program depends upon the degree to which the system already conforms to the suggested convention.

Core Strategy

The core strategy is fundamental to success in meeting the required outcomes for scheduling: real products, integration with cost and scope factors, and credibility. Especially for large projects, these six essential concepts must be in place to sustain credibility and provide an appropriate basis for project management.

- *Apply the critical path method for scheduling,* incorporating logic sufficient to integrate all schedule levels; constrain networks only as necessary to accommodate legitimate schedule drivers.
- *Develop hierarchical levels of schedules from top down* (preferably with the work breakdown structure [WBS] as the basis for vertical integration), and establish summary networks that allow electronic integration. Before proceeding with each lower level of development, validate the newest network against the upper-tier schedule from which it derived. After all levels are developed, report progress only on the lowest-level schedule and then electronically summarize progress for each higher level.
- *Load resources at the lowest schedule level available,* and provide for resource summarization. (Potential exception: level-of-effort resource loading may be designated for one specific network only when a hierarchy allows this limitation. See #4 in the following section.)
- *Develop standard code structures,* enforce their consistent application, and ensure that network dictionaries are fully developed. Practical discipline in this area is the basis for summarization on code. (For example, code by work breakdown structure, and summarize for each tier. See #1 in the following section.)
- *Apply configuration control* to establish baselined schedules as targets, limit access to baselines/targets, and enforce a schedule change-control process. Consider a routine process for independent backup—controlled by someone other than the project scheduler—of baseline schedules, on approval and after updates.
- *Proceduralize scheduling processes,* addressing even detailed mechanics/techniques that support critical path and credibility; document the procedures or desk instructions; and ensure compliance to them.

A manager is likely, at first glance, to believe that some or all of the core techniques are part of the project scheduling system. However, if the system has been identified as needing improvement, the first step is candid review of current methods to confirm that all core elements are being accomplished adequately to sustain the recommended intent for the system. Any elemental process not in place, or judged to fail intent, should be corrected in time to support subsequent implementation of any improvements related to it.

Scheduling Effectiveness

The dominant intent for this set of suggestions is scheduling effectiveness to serve project control. With the core strategy, execution will structure scheduling capability at the standard recognized for project management applications. For some projects, the first recommendation—install a product-oriented WBS—may be an "improvement" that is not a scheduling system prerogative. But overall project management should benefit if the WBS is product oriented, to facilitate control of work scope and, in turn, cost/schedule performance. Identification of schedule activity flows inherently if approved technical scope is broken down as work and its products, and, typically, a product-oriented WBS implies precursory integrating logic for precedence schedules.

1. *Product-oriented WBS.* Develop and define a product-oriented WBS that is comprehensive at every level for all technical scope. Establish WBS classifications according to endpoint product (not organization or function). Apply the WBS as the factor for integrating the schedule with cost and scope. Note that all work should be traceable through every level of the WBS and schedule. Example: Work described at the lowest WBS level as "pour concrete" can be followed through higher-level endpoints such as "build foundation," "erect hangar," and "construct airport."

2. *Schedule basis for performance measurement.* Eliminate opportunity for progress reporting based on actual costs, and otherwise strengthen project control by insisting that schedule networks be the primary source of performance data and calculations and the source of milestone status reporting. Establish electronic interface with the project's cost collection system so that actual costs can be incorporated into the network for calculation of integrated cost/schedule performance measurement, but ensure that schedule status is reported prior to the incorporation of actual costs. Provide electronic transfer of data to any other tracking systems that require status reporting.

3. *Centralized scheduling.* Centralize the scheduling organization for control and consistent development, especially for large or multiple projects. Generate and baseline separate schedules for each project (or a single project), based on groups, phases, or other logical division; merge these subordinate schedules into an integrated schedule network; and baseline the integrated schedule as the performance schedule subject to change control.

4. *Level-of-effort (LOE) criteria.* Establish specific criteria for incorporating LOE activities in schedule networks, and code LOE activities for selective exclusion from schedule graphics when omission is desirable for presentation purposes. When such limitation is appropriate, designate a single schedule network for LOE resource loading. For example, "operations" activity may impact a project generally, but not the schedule itself. Separation of operations tasks may be desirable to facilitate control of resources and costs at a level higher than for work segments needing to monitor schedule performance more closely.

5. *Prioritization.* Determine the appropriate bases for prioritization of scheduled work scope, and code schedule activities to indicate priority. This technique supports decisions based on "what if" scheduling scenarios where calculations move out some activities with flexible dates while maintaining early finishes for priority tasks with potential to impact the schedule end date.

6. *Analysis/trending.* Establish processes for regular analyses of critical path and cost/schedule performance, based on reports from networks at all schedule levels. Ask schedulers to describe the system's capability for products easily obtained or developed, and apply them as tools to accommodate management of the project. Provide for performance trending by maintaining readily available historical cost/schedule information, or as applicable, regularly export cost/schedule data to a non-network database.

Scheduling Efficiency

These recommendations further augment the core strategy and other suggestions given. They focus on process improvements expected to enhance overall capability and efficiency of the scheduling program.

1. *Quality assurance.* Establish processes and specify responsibilities within the scheduling organization; this is for quality assurance verifications such as peer review, review of nonconforming networks and products, and off-line checks of updates/changes/summarizations before their submittal to master networks. Consider assigning a "code cop" who maintains a routine to review network listings and reports for nonstandard codes, constraints, and so on.

2. *Scheduling technicians.* Use schedule technicians as the primary resource for data entry, especially if project schedulers are too often performing tasks not cost effective. Use of technicians frees schedulers to do other project control work, such as performance analysis, that better serves the project and the project manager.

3. *Activity identifiers.* Apply a standard scheme for unique schedule-activity identifiers (activity ID) that incorporates "intelligence" to readily indicate information about the scheduled activity, and ensure comprehensive development of the codes dictionary to support the activity ID scheme. For example, certain characters in the activity ID can show project, responsibility, or task number. (This suggestion expands upon the fourth core strategy to free up code fields previously used for information now embedded in more effective activity IDs.)

4. *Standard terms/symbols.* Establish standard terms and symbols, and develop a base set of reporting formats to be generated consistently for different management levels and multiple applications. Although reporting to individual standards and needs of various managers is sometimes necessary, potential for efficiency should be developed. Inconsistent application of graphics/reports and terms/symbols often confuses the comparison of performance data from period to period, or between projects.

5. *Dollars as a resource.* Indicate dollars as a resource in schedule networks by pricing out resources for activities, totaling the cost of all resources for each activity, loading that dollar figure as a separate resource in the activity, and summarizing the dollar resources for higher-level schedules. This technique is particularly useful when it is applied for review of high-level schedules that relate summary costs to summary activities.

This method provides a basis for budget-driven, what-if analysis that facilitates summary planning. When a project's duration extends over several years it may be advantageous to generate a spreadsheet database from the schedule network. Then dollar amounts are summarized for long-range planning and budgeting that is tied to the schedule and the resources it incorporates, which may be preferable to a budget-only spreadsheet basis for cost planning.

Just Do It!

Whew! Just reading about pumping up a scheduling program is hard work! How much tougher will the actual execution be? The best answer is to make pump-up exercises as tough as the scheduling program can stand without adversely impacting the project. If full implementation is not necessary, or not practical, the line-item presentation facilitates selection of a composite set of improvements.

Whatever combination of improvements best accommodates identified scheduling-system needs, initial planning for implementation can begin immediately after decisions regarding which, how, and when recommendations are executed. The manager who believes that proposed techniques are already part of the system should first determine whether incorporation is truly adequate to meet all suggested intents.

Recommendations presume two things: 1) project control is the primary function of the scheduling system, and 2) credibility is its most important attribute. In the government case, various managers interviewed with regard to their expectations for their scheduling systems confirmed these themes, and a survey indicated that benchmark systems were well grounded in their support for both contexts. Lack of commitment to the concept of schedule credibility as the basis for effective project control is likely to limit application of the high standards and best practices that characterize systems of merit.

Make a pump-up commitment. Implementation may well be a challenge that entails significant change, particularly for an established system, but these tips are worthwhile because of the overall project control benefits they hold. No pain, no gain! Just do it! Because project management *is* vulnerable to weak scheduling.

Kick Off the Smart Way

Paula K. Martin and Karen Tate, PMP

PM Network 25 (October 25)

You're about to hold a kick-off meeting. Will you do it the smart way or do you prefer the "kickoff for dummies" approach? It's not so much a matter of what you do at the kickoff that's important, but how you do it. Do you know how to build trust within the team? How to begin to create buy-in and commitment?

The kickoff is the first impression that the team has of the project and of you, the project leader. It sets the tone for the whole project. Therefore, it's important to do it right—the smart way.

First, we will examine the "dummy" or directive approach to leading a kick-off meeting. Let's eavesdrop on Dave as he conducts his meeting. See if you can identify Dave's mistakes.

"I think you all know me; my name is Dave. I'm the project leader on this project. Since we all know each other we can skip the introductions. I'm handing out the charter document that our sponsor provided. If you have any questions, just let me know. ...Clint, I don't think your concern about the customer requirements is valid. The customer has spelled out what she wants. Let's talk about how we can pull together and provide it to her."

Bonnie asks a question, and Dave replies, "That's not really relevant to the discussion at hand; I think we'd better move on."

Dave responds to Dwight's concerns about the deadlines by saying, "I understand your concerns, but there is nothing we can do about the deadline dates. I've outlined a schedule that I think will allow us to meet the deadlines. Look it over. I'm sure if we work hard, we can produce the deliverables on time."

Dave continues his directive approach, turning off one team member after another in the process.

Let's examine some of the things that Dave has done wrong:

- He has not included introductions or an icebreaker in the meeting.
- He cuts off any discussion of concerns or issues.

- He presents the charter as being cast in stone.
- He has created a schedule without team participation.
- He has not set up a "parking lot" to park ideas, issues, or concerns that are not relevant to the discussion at hand.

In order to get the results Dave needs for the project, he's going to have to make some changes to his approach. Maybe he can learn from Sam, a project leader who uses the smart approach.

Sam starts his kickoff meeting by saying, "Although we all know one another, let's spend a few minutes catching up on what each of us has been doing lately, and then I'd like to play a 'thinking styles' game. This will provide us a profile of our own and our team's thinking styles. I've set up a parking lot so that we won't lose any of the ideas, concerns, or issues that you have. We will address each one before the end of the meeting.

"I've worked with the sponsor on the charter, which I sent out to you ahead of time. I'd like to collect your comments, questions, concerns, and ideas about the charter. I'll record each one on a Post-it Note and place it on the banner paper I've tacked on the wall. Once we resolve any issues that we have with the charter, we'll begin creating the project plan together, as a team."

Sam acts as a facilitator rather than a director. He encourages team participation. He solicits issues and ideas. Sam treats each individual on the team with respect. He listens to their concerns and makes sure that each one gets addressed. In this way, he validates for each team member that his concerns are real and important. Sometimes this is all people are looking for. They want to be heard.

Facilitating is a different skill than directing. By paying attention to the team process, the smart project leader delivers better results than the directive project manager. The smart project leader pays attention to both the people and the tasks. In this way, she ensures that the project gets done on time and within budget. She also ensures that the people on the team feel a part of the project process.

So the next time you're preparing for a kick-off meeting, take a few minutes to think about what type of project team you want to foster. Then pick the approach that will get you to your goal.

Little Things Make the Biggest Difference

Catherine L. Tonne, PMP

PM Network 17 (April 1998)

Did you ever notice that it is always the proverbial "*straw* that breaks the camel's back"? Usually this occurs after a string of seemingly small and insignificant events. Chronic tardiness, not returning phone calls, missed commitments, unkept promises, and just general unreliability could individually be insignificant. However, over time, taken as a whole they can bring the walls of professional and personal credibility tumbling down. And once the fortress of credibility has fallen, it is a long and arduous task to build it up again—brick by brick by brick.

I am sure that all of you have your own pet peeves and hot buttons that promote shaky confidence or lost faith in either friends or coworkers. Even though I am pretty easygoing, I have mine, and they flow pretty seamlessly between my personal and professional life. I find it easier to keep a consistent set of personal performance standards and expectations of others (and myself) whether on a project, at work, or at home. It makes life less stressful and more consistent, as I do not have to remember to switch back and forth between the two. And we all know we could do with less stress these days!

It is usually the small things that chip away at one's credibility. And if you think about it, this makes sense. I once heard a speaker say, "It is the mosquitoes in life that get us—not the elephants." I would apply this to specifically mean the little things we *do* on a day-to-day basis are more important than what we *say*. People's true colors and capabilities are evident by their actions and not their words, even though they are spoken with the best intentions. This becomes critically important on projects.

Project managers must be very perceptive in reading and interpreting people's actions and evaluating how they line up with verbal inputs. We are bombarded with a flood of information and words, but the real data comes from what we see people do. This is some of what I call "soft data" versus "hard data"—what is written or quantified. We need to collect and use both in managing projects and making critical decisions. If what we see is consistent with people's words, then we begin to trust them and their abilities to follow through to completion. Credibility is built (or lost) by how people perform over time—one day, one encounter, and one project at a time.

We must also be mindful of our own actions. Credibility to a project manager is more important than technical capabilities. Without it one is incapable of achieving any sort of progress or success, no matter how technically astute one is. We must pay attention to the small details of our own work: promptly returning, or at least acknowledging, phone calls and messages; validating that project information we publish is fact-based; digging into issues to determine the root cause and not focusing on hearsay; making sure there are no typos, poor punctuation, or improper grammar in our materials; taking time to reread an item one last time before we send it to others; being prepared at meetings with our action-item updates or other required inputs; being on time for meetings; remembering to extend simple courtesies to all people with whom we deal (regardless of organizational status); always striving to be objective (this is tough sometimes); and following through on our commitments and promises—even the simple ones.

We project managers must set the example for others by being reliable and credible ourselves. In today's work environment, which can get overwhelming, it may seem acceptable to let the little things slide. When I find myself in that mode I step back and remind myself of what I think is a great and simple credo by which to live and work. In fact, I would like to call it the Project Participation Credo: "Say what you'll do—do what you say." It is important that we pay heed to this credo in the myriad of little things and daily activities in which we participate on all our projects. By doing so, we will have a big impact on project success and reap huge rewards professionally and personally by building our credibility fortress on an unshakable foundation—brick by brick by brick.

Walking the Talk

John Sullivan, PMP

PM Network 16 (November 1999)

During my first job my manager sat our team members down and told us that we'd need to work overtime to meet our deadline and that this meant working through lunch. We left the pep talk and returned to our desks while our manager and his assistant went to lunch.

Inconsistent behavior—acting differently from what is being communicated—is one of the quickest ways for a leader to lose trust. In a 1997 survey by Manchester Consulting, most of the executives polled said that it took an average of seven months for employees to build their trust in a leader, but less than half that time for them to lose it.

"Trust is built by a succession of behaviors, not just words," says John Mariotti, CEO of The Enterprise Group and author of *The Power of Partnerships* (1996) and *The Shape Shifters* (1997). "The old cliché 'walk the talk' is a good one. Behaviors speak much more loudly than words—and these are what build trust."

The prerequisite for trust is honesty, but honest intentions may not be enough when you don't know what is expected of you. The challenge is to find out what your bosses really want. Building trust requires a manager to first have a thorough understanding of senior management's expectations, as well as the company's objectives and mission. Mariotti says that you can start building trust with your team members "by leveling with them and telling them as much as you are sure of and by asking them to work with you while you decipher the rest and warning them that there could be some rapid changes as interpretations change."

Managers need the team to understand how difficult it is to decipher expectations. Sometimes interpretations can be completely wrong. For example, many companies say, "We value education" (check the recruiting material), but then won't allow someone to take a daytime class. When the only reason for this is because "it's company policy," how do you as a manager explain it?

"Sometimes you can't, because there is no easy answer to give," says Mariotti. "I'm sorry, I just can't explain (or justify) that, is all one can say."

But interpretations of company policy can be used to your advantage. Every manager has some flexibility on the enforcement of rules and can use that flexibility to build trust. It may be against policy to take daytime courses, but you can probably allow a team member to come in early in order to make a 4 P.M. class. However, before using your own interpretations to benefit your team, realize that interpreting a policy differently means taking a risk and, once you make an interpretation, you have set a precedent and must consistently follow it.

Another boss of mine always told us when the company was considering layoffs, even though this was against the rules. He did this at great personal risk, but it increased our respect for him. But once he did this, he had to consistently do it. He did, notifying us several times over the years of pending layoffs. Our role in this was to keep the information confidential, and we did.

This is the paradox of trust: to be trusted you must first trust others. In our case, smaller exchanges of trust were in place before each of the layoff warnings. The boss had built a relationship with us in many ways, mostly by allowing us to flex our schedules to attend to personal needs on company time, an interpretation he used to his advantage. Our part of the bargain was not only to get our work done on time but also to do it according to his high standards. Having earned our trust in smaller ways, he knew that he could trust us when it really counted.

Like my old boss, you may one day be caught in the managerial gap between personal values and corporate policy. That's when you'll reap the benefits of being consistent. You'll not only be able to get through the situation, but you'll also get to keep your self-respect.

Section 5

Team Development:
Individual and Group Skills

All Project Members Should Be Treated *Equal!*

Neal Whitten, PMP

PM Network 19 (November 1999)

What if a project is made up of client personnel, vendors, and contractors, in addition to the company's personnel? How should the project manager relate to each of these diverse groups?

This is a common problem on many projects; yet the answer is simple: Once people are assigned to a project, regardless of where they hail from, they must all be treated the same. *No exceptions!*

Figure 1 shows a project that consists of all of these groups. For the purpose of illustration, each team is led by a team leader and is made up of a different group of project members: client personnel, vendor personnel, contractors, and company personnel. Note that, although not depicted in this example, it is possible for a team to consist of a mixture of people from these different groups.

Once the project members have been assigned to the project, the project manager should not focus on their origins. The focus must be on the project, the commitments from each team, and on the corresponding actions that each project member performs toward achieving her assigned tasks. The project manager sees everyone as a project member and will work with each person and group as if she were personnel from the same project team because *she is!*

Each team is expected to have plans, commit to those plans, and track according to those plans. If any team is in trouble or headed that way, the project manager initiates the attention required to help the team get back on plan. Every team is held just as accountable for their commitments, as with any other team.

I commonly see project managers treat the client's personnel assigned to the project with kid gloves, quick to cut them slack at every turn. I often see vendors treated as if they are a black box that cannot be tampered with, their whims easily accepted as cast in stone, with no or little chance of altering. I see contractors

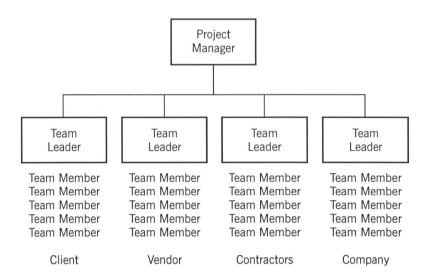

Figure 1. A Sample Project

treated as second-class members of the team, and project information is often withheld from them—information that they need to fully function as members of the project. And I often see company employees treated harshly because of the view that they are the most accessible project members and, therefore, the most easily manipulated.

A project's success is dependent upon the success of each and every project member. An effective project manager recognizes this and works consistently, firmly, and unbiasedly across all members of a project to ensure that the project completes successfully.

Project Teams:
What Have We Learned?

H. Dudley Dewhirst

PM Network 33 (April 1998)

Teams are central to project management: that's been true as long as there have been projects. However, in recent years, organizations in the nonproject world have "discovered" teams. Out of this experience, managers, consultants, and academics developed a wealth of ideas about what makes teams work. Some of it is "old wine in new bottles," but much of it sheds new light on team management issues.

In conventional organizations, teams produce dramatic increases in productivity, improved customer satisfaction, lower error rates, reduced scrap, more rapid delivery, and higher market shares. Project teams develop successful new products and create innovative new services, often in an incredibly short time.

This in itself isn't surprising. What's really intriguing is that some teams do this so incredibly well and so incredibly fast. Teams like these have the potential to change the mathematics of work. For these high-performance teams, the productivity math is $2 + 2 = 6$. Unfortunately, for other teams, the math is more like $2 + 2 = 3$ or less.

The differences between high- and low-productivity teams can be explored by examining the answers to four basic questions: When do you really need a team? What are the different levels of teamwork? What makes teams work? How can I implement and manage a team?

When Do You Really Need a Team?

Because teams require an investment of managerial work and organizational support, it's fair to ask when a team is needed and why. Many projects can be accomplished by a group of individuals that are a team in name only. They can

Characteristics of Project	Team Is Vital to Success	Team Is Not Necessary
Task Interdependence	Individual specialists must jointly make project decisions.	Individual specialists can do their work in relative isolation.
Schedule Criticality	Project has tight time schedule—no slack.	Time is not critical.
Uncertainty	Project is unique and/or has many uncertain elements.	Project is routine—very similar to earlier projects.
Size	Large.	Small.
Scope of Disciplines	Many different disciplines required.	Project limited to few disciplines.
Time Frame	Long.	Short.
Project Importance	High.	Less important.

Table 1. To Team or Not to Team?

succeed because of the nature of the work and the independence of each individual's work from that of other specialists.

Table 1 contrasts characteristics of projects that need a team approach with projects for which the costs of organizing, developing, and building a team may outweigh the benefits.

Many organizations and managers have adopted an all-or-nothing approach to using teams. That is, either all projects require a tightly organized, highly cohesive, and interactive team, or none of them do. Managers need to make distinctions between projects and invest heavily in developing teams for projects that really need high levels of teamwork.

What Are the Different Levels of Teamwork?

To say that the word *team* is used loosely is a gross understatement. Here are four variations in what might be called the "teamness" of a group working on a project.

1. *Star Teams.* According to Katzenback and Smith, in *The Wisdom of Teams*, a star team is "a small group of people with complementary skills committed to a common purpose, with shared performance goals and a common approach, holding themselves mutually accountable" (1993).

The size element is an important consideration. The size that best facilitates team effectiveness is between four and twelve. Above that number, the closeness, ease of communication, and ability of every member to be a real contributor decline, although teams of twenty-five or more members can be effective in some instances.

Naturally, the team must have a mix of skills that fits the task requirements and complements one another. Notice that all the remaining criteria are about the sharing of purpose, goals, approach, and accountability. Team members understand what needs to be done, agree on how to do it, are focused on accomplishing the goal, and have taken ownership of the project.

I've asked dozens of project managers which single criterion is the most difficult to meet. They agree on the last one, "holding themselves mutually accountable."

When a star team comes together, great things usually happen—2 + 2 = 6 or more.

2. *Effective Teams.* Effective teams result when teams don't quite achieve star status. Organizational constraints often prevent proper implementation, development, and support of the team. Project organizations are, like all organizations, imperfect. Even with good support and leadership, many teams do well, but are not great. Perhaps several team members don't get along well. Or maybe some members don't fully develop ownership of team purpose and goals. But effective teams, while they may struggle, do get the job done. For them, 2 + 2 = 4 or 5.

3. *Pseudo Teams.* Pseudo teams result when team members simply do not jell into a cohesive team. These teams would get a grade of "C" at best on each of the characteristics of the star team. There are many reasons why this can occur—lack of leadership, poor chartering, and poor management. Two factors are at play in pseudo teams. First, the team wastes time and effort in "playing at" being a team. Most important, the coordination and cooperation between team members doesn't occur. False starts, rework, and interpersonal conflict result in a productivity sum of 2 + 2 = 3 or less.

4. *Name-Only Teams.* A name-only team, or "NOT," is a group of individuals working largely independently of one another. There is nothing inherently wrong with a NOT. Many project "teams" are really NOTs, in the sense that individuals complete portions of a project on their own, with minimum interaction and coordination with others. If the characteristics of the project in question largely correspond to those in the "Team Is Not Necessary" column in Table 1, a NOT is an effective way of managing the project. In this instance 2 + 2 = 4.

On the other hand, if the project characteristics correspond to those in the "Team Is Vital to Success" column, then the math changes to 2 + 2 = 3 or less.

What Makes Teams Work?

Just what is required for star teams and effective teams to develop in project organizations?

Performance impact: Quantity and quality of output and efficiency. Obviously, teams have to produce or the work of their formation and management isn't worth the investment.

Effective working relations among team members. This doesn't mean that team members necessarily must like each other. In fact, team members can like each other too much. Team members must respect each other, since mutual respect is essential for effective working relationships.

Effective working relationships, influence, and reputation for competence with those outside the team. This is often overlooked. The team needs to obtain resources, information, and support from outside its boundaries. In addition, it must be able to influence organizational decisions.

To achieve these outcomes, teams need cohesion, positive norms, capability, and motivation.

Cohesion is the social glue that holds a group or team together. It results from a team member's desire to be accepted and respected by the other team members and to remain a member of the team.

Teams develop informal standards concerning acceptable member behavior. These standards, or *norms*, evolve through experience as the team develops. Both informal leaders within the team and managers inside and outside the team can influence the norms, but neither can exercise complete control. Norms are a group phenomenon.

Teams must have the *capability* (skills and knowledge) to carry out their tasks. It is not that teams have complete mastery at the start. Rather, members must have enough basic skills and knowledge so they can learn how to do what is required.

Team members must be *motivated* to succeed as a team. That's different from succeeding as an individual. We know that team motivation can be enhanced by the challenge of new and different projects, recognition, and responsibility—the intrinsic motivators. There is also a novelty effect. "It's new, different, and fun—I'll give it a shot." But, there is more.

Individuals differ in inherent motives. Some are more likely than others to be motivated to succeed as a team. Some people do better in teams, others as individuals. David McClelland's categorization of needs as achievement, affiliation, and power helps us to understand this point (1953). People with high affiliation needs are more likely motivated in a team situation. For example, my wife works harder at playing doubles tennis than at singles because of her high affiliation needs. My daughter, with lower affiliation needs, hates doubles, and works much harder at singles.

How to Develop Star Teams

Now that we have described the different variations of team capability and reviewed what is required for team success, we can turn to implementation guidelines. These guidelines describe the ideal. If followed, a star team is the likely result. However, situations and constraints may preclude following all the guidelines. Do as much as you can. Even if a star team doesn't result, the effort is worth it. If an effective team can be developed, you are still a winner.

Staffing the Team

Team members should be selected on the basis of technical competence and the ability to work as a team player. Careful selection of team members is important but often overlooked. Here are some suggestions:

Volunteers are better than draftees. The act of volunteering indicates both motivation and interest (although perhaps not competence). One method used with success is to approach potential members with the desired competence and describe the problem or task. Then ask if they will sign on.

Consider the roles members are likely to play on the team. Research on teams by David Barry suggests that effective teams need four roles to be fulfilled (1991):

- Envisioner—visualizes what might be possible, sees the big picture, the grand scheme.
- Organizer—concerned with organizing, setting the agenda and deadlines, coordinating activities, pushing for closure and completion.
- Social leader—provides social skills, jokes to relieve tension, defuses conflict, keeps everyone involved.
- Spanner—seeks and maintains contacts outside the team boundaries, gathers information, resources, and other help for the team.

Team members might fulfill more than one role, but all are needed. One potential landmine is conflict over roles. Barry cites team failures resulting from such conflict: for example, two strong-willed envisioners, neither a good team player, in a team with no strong organizer (1991).

Don't add low-contribution members. Team members with little potential to contribute lead to trouble. Such members slow teams down and often waste time with naive attempts to help or lead. That is not to say that technicians or mechanics can't be on a team with Ph.D.s. It is the potential contribution that counts.

Diversity helps. Although people with different characteristics (age, sex, education, life experiences, values) make it more difficult for a team to become cohesive, teams with diversity will be more creative if they jell. All-alike teams often like each other too much; thus, they tend to close too fast on decisions and are in danger of *groupthink*.

Managing the Start

Many teams fail because of poorly managed starts. New teams are like babies—very fragile, and they go through developmental stages:

- Forming—confused, wandering discussions, tentative attachment to team, determining tasks, mix of optimism and suspicion.
- Storming—conflict, defensiveness, competition among members, concern about extra work, factions.
- Norming—acceptance of team concept, discussion of team dynamics, developing norms, team spirit, relief that it looks like it is going to work.
- Performing—accomplishment, working through team problems, satisfaction, constructive self-change, learning.

Teams develop at different speeds. Some do their team storming late (usually when the chips are down) and some do not develop the norms needed for success. Managers can help by:

- Making the start an important event. Hold an off-site retreat for a day. Break bread together. Get acquainted. Have a big boss come to kick things off. Discuss goals, tasks, and potential difficulties. Have some team building activities.
- Sharing a vision of success. Explain and discuss objectives. Establish importance and urgency of the team's activities.
- Presenting, discussing, developing the charter.
- Providing training in team dynamics and any new skills required.

Chartering the Team

Teams need to be empowered to be effective. Paradoxically, the only way to empower a team is to define the limits to its power. Teams need direction, goals, and boundaries. A charter should:

- Clarify goals and objectives—This is so obvious. Goals need to be articulated, discussed, explored, debated, and negotiated. Sharing of goals, purpose, and accountability is a criterion for a star team. In addition to getting members pointing in the same direction, clear objectives serve to measure success.
- Define reporting relationships—Teams need to know to whom they report, how often reviews will be conducted, and the level of detail required.
- Settle the authority question—Teams need to know what decisions they can make on their own, what decisions need approval, and when they should ask for a review.
- Establish linkage to the client—Developing effective working relationships with the client is key to team success. The charter should define the frequency and scope of client contacts.

It always helps to maximize team participation in the chartering process. Risking greater levels of participation has potential payoffs in enhancing motivation and commitment of team members. If your organization is not chartering its new teams, learn more about it. The best, detailed advice I have seen for developing a charter for project teams can be found in *Project Delivery: A System and Process for Benchmark Performance* (CH2M Hill 1996).

Building the Team

Here are some suggestions for helping the team develop cohesion, influencing the development of norms, and motivation.

Facilitate cohesion and communication by co-locating the team or otherwise promoting interaction. High levels of interaction help the team develop. If co-location isn't possible, provide a meeting place for face-to-face interaction. Provide a trained facilitator to help the team develop norms of open communication, manage meetings, and make decisions effectively.

Discuss and develop agreement on goals. It is surprising how long it takes for members to fully understand and internalize goals. Continued revisiting and focusing on goals is important.

Provide recognition. Small wins are important in the early life of a team. Success throughout the team's life should be broadcast and celebrated.

Advocate the norms you would like to see; you can't exercise total control here, but you do have influence. One way is simply to broadcast and discuss the norms you want. Some norms you may want to consider are openness, willingness to confront differences, timely and full attendance at meetings, mutual respect, and an appreciation for the value of humor and fun.

Measuring Performance

Measuring performance on projects is problematic. I was once captivated by the intellectual elegance of the earned value method. However, I have found very few project managers who actually use it. There are two problems. One is obtaining real-time measures of costs. The second problem is accurately measuring how much work has actually been completed. Unanticipated events make this difficult, especially on projects that are highly uncertain. Modern information systems technology may solve the time delay problems, but uncertainty remains. My advice is to use whatever systems provide reasonably reliable information. No matter what measures are used, some general guidelines apply.

Provide real-time, direct feedback. Information that is late and filtered or interpreted through layers of management is ineffective.

Outcome measures on costs and schedule should be supplemented with softer measures, which focus on process. Such measures might include client satisfaction, attendance at team meetings, team morale, and assessment by managers from performance reviews.

Encourage the team to develop its own measures. Team members are in the best position to see what measures are needed. Most formal performance measurement systems focus on inputs, outputs, and efficiencies. Process measures often provide better information for performance improvement.

Encourage feedback directly from the client where possible and appropriate.

Make dual use of measures: to provide feedback to the team and to enhance the viability of the team to the larger organization.

Managing Performance

If teams have good charters that define objectives, reporting linkages and team decision-making authority, then the best management is the least management. The largest (over 8,000 teams) study of team performance ever done was conducted by Mohrman, Mohrman, and Lawler (1992). They explored relationships among management and team practices and outcomes such as team performance, individual performance, trust in the larger organization, and teamwork. What surprises most managers is that these activities performed by the team itself were more powerful predictors of effectiveness and performance than anything managers did to manage performance. The strongest predictors of performance were self-appraisal by the team, team development of performance norms, feedback by the team members within the team, and team structuring of tasks.

The lesson is clear—Effective teams manage their own performance. Only three guidelines apply: 1) Hold periodic performance reviews with the team. 2) Try to emulate the sports analogy. Why are people on sports teams motivated? Because goals are clearly defined, rules are clear, effort and performance are linked, score-keeping is objective, performance can be compared to a standard, and others see the score—and recognize excellence. 3) Celebrate team events. Meeting milestones, solving difficult technical problems, receiving praise from the client, having good performance reviews, and finishing the project are all causes for celebration. Have a party, pass out awards, have the big boss come by, just do it!

Project teams hold great promise. If you have ever worked on a star team, you know how effective they are and how exhilarating they can be for team members—not only the productivity math, but also the intrinsic motivation, increases geometrically.

References

Barry, David. 1991. *Organizational Dynamics*. Summer.

CH2M Hill. 1996. *Project Delivery: A System and Process for Benchmark Performance*. CH2M Hill.

Katzenback and Smith. 1993. *The Wisdom of Teams*. Harvard Business School Press.

McClelland, David. 1953. *The Achievement Motive*. Appleton Century Crofts.

Mohrman, Mohrman, and Lawler. 1992. The Performance Management of Teams. *Performance, Measurment, Evaluation and Incentives*. Harvard Business School Press.

Shared Vision Creates Strong Project Teams

Benjamin J. Parker; Joan Knutson, Contributing Editor

PM Network 25 (July 2000)

The foundation of a project is built with the vision as a target. That shared vision becomes the goal of the project, further becoming the measure of completion and a point of accomplishment for the team. So why don't companies spend more time and energy on creating their vision—creating the foundation for their future and for all who work toward it?

The *American Heritage Dictionary* defines vision as "unusual competence in discernment or perception; intelligent foresight—a *leader of vision*; the manner in which one sees or conceives of something; a mental image produced by the imagination." Two quotations also come to mind: Ralph Waldo Emerson said, "Nothing great was ever achieved without enthusiasm." And from the *Bible*, the Book of Proverbs says, "Where there is no vision, the people will perish."

Without vision and the criteria that will be used to judge the success of the project, the team will have no guidance and no ultimate target. Without clear understanding of the vision of an organization or project, it is difficult to keep team members enthusiastic about accomplishing the project. And without goals, an outstanding team has no objective, no sense of cause, and will soon degrade into just another group of individuals.

Project planning should include developing a clear and understood vision. An effective vision has several essential components: it should be concise and easy to memorize; it should be repeatable; and it should be important to the entire organization. A clear and shared vision becomes the goal of the project. Meeting the goal provides the team with a sense of accomplishment and success.

Consider this story: During her morning walk, a woman came upon three men cutting stones. Approaching the first man, she very politely asked what he was doing. The man responded, "I am cutting these silly stones! What does it look like I am doing?" The woman, slightly dazed, politely thanked him and walked away. Approaching the next man, she asked the same question. The second man replied, "I am cutting stones that will be used to build a magnificent new museum." The woman politely thanked him and walked away. She approached the next man and again asked the same question. The third man replied, "I am cutting stones that will be used to construct a magnificent new museum. The museum will house many things, from art to the remains of dinosaurs. This museum is funded by many philanthropies which recognize the need to preserve natural history." The woman, dazzled with the man's response, thanked him and continued on her walk.

This story illustrates how a person's vision affects understanding of the task at hand. Becoming bogged down in the details is very easy. Like the first man, many people find themselves simply going to work. We forget that our role in the business is important to the success of the entire organization. The third man clearly understood his role in the entire project. He understood how important his role was to the success of the museum.

During the height of America's "Space Race," a well-known company bought advertising space in several popular magazines. The advertisement showed a man standing in front of a large bank of computer monitors, each with a very busy technician in front of it. He was holding a broom and pushing a cart filled with janitorial supplies. The advertisement asked the man what his role in the Space Race was. The ad continued with the man stating that he was a member of the team responsible for putting a man on the moon.

The point of the advertisement was not to promote a janitorial service, but rather to remind the reader that all members of the team are important. From the janitor to the CEO, all associates have a role in the success of the entire project.

Who is responsible for communicating the vision? Some would say the executives. Others might say their supervisors. The correct answer is *everyone*. The vision should be developed in cooperation with the team members and all essential stakeholders. A vision developed without the full participation of the entire team will not be fully shared. A project team without vision will quickly degrade to a random grouping of people attending the same conference calls. A solidly defined and well-understood vision is the basic starting point for all that happens within the project.

How to Run an Effective Meeting

Neal Whitten, PMP

PM Network 19 (June 1999)

Meetings, meetings, and more meetings. Aren't we ever going to get some real work done around this place? How many times have you have heard this? Perhaps you've said it yourself a time or two. It has been my experience that most meetings are poorly planned and conducted and, frankly, waste a significant amount of time.

Let's look at a short list of meeting guidelines that can correct this common but pervasive problem.

Plan the meeting. Make sure that the attendees critical to the meeting's success are properly informed and have committed to attend. Reschedule the meeting if the required attendees cannot participate and the meeting cannot be sufficiently productive. Inform attendees of the meeting objectives so that they can come to the meeting with the proper mindset and come prepared. Of course, disclose the meeting date, time, and location.

Start on time. Always begin meetings on time. Don't review progress for latecomers during the meeting. Consider scheduling meetings to start precisely ten minutes after the hour so that attendees can arrive on time from prior meetings.

Identify the meeting leader. All attendees need to know who is in charge of the meeting. Everyone looks toward this person to demonstrate the needed leadership throughout the meeting.

State the meeting objectives. Clarifying the scope of the meeting at the beginning will help the meeting attendees remain focused and productive.

Assign a person to take the minutes. The meeting leader must not take the minutes. This action causes the meeting leader to lose concentration and the ability to be fully engaged in driving the meeting. It also negatively affects the progress and pace of the meeting. The minute taker preferably is a person who is not, otherwise, an essential participant.

Keep the meeting on track. The meeting leader ensures that the meeting begins and remains on track to achieving its objectives. Overly lengthy discussions, tangential topics, and scope creep are discouraged and the appropriate actions are taken to refocus the meeting attendees.

Enforce common respect for all participants. The meeting leader creates and enforces a productive and respectful meeting environment. The meeting's success is dependent on the free flow of information and ideas, as well as the full participation of the attendees. Problems are attacked, not people.

Summarize the meeting achievements. When the meeting objectives have been met, the key points and assignments are briefly summarized. This action helps the attendees to be clear on the meeting outcomes and allows them to immediately begin taking the appropriate actions while the meeting minutes are being prepared.

Distribute the meeting minutes within one workday. Either the minute taker or the meeting leader prepares and distributes the minutes within one workday of the meeting. In either case, however, the meeting leader is ultimately responsible for the content of the minutes and ensuring timely distribution.

End the meeting on or before its scheduled end time. The meeting ends on time to accommodate the other commitments of the attendees. The best-run meetings will almost always end earlier than scheduled. Consider ending the meeting ten minutes early to accommodate attendees arriving to their next meeting on time. If the meeting requires more time than was scheduled and the meeting cannot be continued immediately, then give attendees a heads-up as to its likely rescheduled date and time. End the meeting on time.

The meeting leader is responsible for following these or similar guidelines. Attendees rightfully look to the meeting leader to run effective meetings. Posting these guidelines in all meeting rooms can help to educate and remind meeting participants what they should expect and demand when they give up so much of their limited time to meetings. There is a direct relationship between effectively run meetings and the overall effectiveness of the related organization, project, or team.

Leadership in Project Life Cycle and Team Character Development

Timothy J. Kloppenborg, PMP, and Joseph A. Petrick

Project Management Journal 8 (June 1999)

Successful project leaders are becoming aware of associated links between project life-cycle stage completions and the necessary group virtues that facilitate each project stage. The aggregate set of these virtues shapes the group character of the project team, i.e., their collective readiness to act ethically. At the same time that project leaders are shepherding a project through the life-cycle stages to completion, their professional responsibilities are implicitly expanding to include the identification and reinforcement of the associated sets of team virtues necessary for the success of each stage along the way. The lack of development of team virtues at one stage may well preclude the satisfactory advancement or completion of future project life-cycle stages because the team is not predisposed to complete the prior stage(s) with integrity (Kloppenborg and Petrick 1997).

In this article we identify specific team virtues that are appropriate for the typical activities and closure documents of each project life-cycle stage. After clarifying the theoretical need for team character development, we identify team character development competencies needed by project leaders at each of the project life-cycle stages. We conclude by advocating the simultaneous development of both life-cycle technical competency and team character "behavioral" competency to improve successful project leadership.

Theoretical Basis for Team Character Development

In group dynamics and organizational learning theories, Argyris (1993) and Dixon (1994) note that project teams often "get stuck" in defensive routines that inhibit effective learning and may "remain stuck" unless these dysfunctional behaviors are changed. More specifically, such self-fueling, counterproductive group dynamic processes jeopardize projects in the following ways:

- Issues that are perceived as embarrassing or threatening in projects become undiscussable or are dismissed by being attributed to organizational politics.
- Sensitive project issues are bypassed or covered up to protect project members while inhibiting organizational learning.
- Measures that excuse or maintain the original bypassing and cover-ups are employed, such as blaming others and distancing oneself from responsibility.
- Adverse consequences of actions that harm projects prevail, such as people not completing tasks on time, arriving late and leaving early, missing meetings, or discussing only boring, safe topics. The end result is the gradual dissolution of any effective team collaboration (Senge 1990).

Teams that repeatedly accept excuses for substandard behaviors and results, and do not hold themselves accountable for substandard collective performance earn a reputation for being associated with failed or mediocre projects (Nielsen 1996). Teams can become defensive about their performance and fail to develop the technical project management skills and collective character competencies that could turn them around. These dysfunctional group dynamics can be successfully corrected by enhancing technical competency through the disciplined use of stage-specific project life-cycle closure documents and by developing "behavioral" competence through the practice of intellectual, social, emotional, moral, and political virtues at appropriate stages in the project life cycle.

Successful project completion is contingent upon members working together effectively as a project team. When group dysfunctional behaviors prevail, however, schedules slip, costs overrun, output quality diminishes, and, in extreme cases, projects fail.

Project Life-Cycle Stages

In today's hypercompetitive business environment, professional project managers feel pressured to rapidly complete projects. The disciplined use of a project life-cycle model may help project managers overcome two key technical problems: 1) late identification or omission of key project components (such as risks, tasks, features, resource needs, personnel roles, and responsibilities), and 2) continued investment in a failing project.

While there are different models of project life-cycle stages, we have adopted a standard, generic four-stage model that includes the following: conceptual planning, process organizing, implementing and controlling, and evaluating and system improving. Completion of each stage requires generating and securing approval of stage-specific closure documents (Martin and Tate 1997). Project leaders are expected to facilitate the successful completion of each stage with its attendant activities and closure documents (Adams and Caldentey 1998; Greer 1996; Project Management Insitute 2000). A variety of leadership and management skills are needed to guide a project through each project stage (Verma 1996).

First Stage: Project Conceptual Planning

The first stage of project conceptual planning identifies the needs and desires of the customer—the user of the project deliverables. This will be the basis for determining not only the customer's criteria for acceptance of the final deliverables, i.e., one of the project's success measures, but also the starting point for planning and performing future activities. The company's major business objectives and strategies need to be identified and understood so that project goals can be associated with them. A high-level executive in the organization often serves as a champion for the project. This champion can be a resource, coach, advocate, and sounding board for the project manager. The champion should help identify priorities and constraints for the project. All of these measures are important so that project personnel can make informed decisions that are consistent with the needs of the organization.

It is now appropriate for the planning team to identify risks associated with each final deliverable. At this time, the project team can make ballpark estimates of time, cost, and performance expectations. These will be used to determine if the project is feasible and should continue, or impractical and should be discontinued. The closure document for this stage is the project charter, which includes all of the elements thus far mentioned. The purpose of the charter is to achieve among all stakeholders (champion, project manager, project team members, customers, and functional managers) a common understanding of what is to be included in the project and what is to be excluded. By defining these essential elements now, the project team will have a guide to create the more detailed plans defining requirements, schedules, and costs, and increase the probability of delivering an output to the customers that meets or exceeds their expectations.

Second Stage: Project Process Organizing

Subsequent to conceptual planning, two main types of activities are accomplished in the second stage: those dealing with detail planning and those dealing with the project team. The results from the first stage are the working inputs for this stage. The detailed cost, schedule, and activity plans can only be developed with the information provided in the charter. The detailed activity plans are the first to be identified. Project team members will often meet to jointly plan at a crude level of detail what must be included so that no major activities are left out. Then members individually or in smaller groups will often flesh out the details of necessary work in their respective areas. These detailed activity plans are then used to identify schedule, cost, and resource plans in corresponding detail.

The second main set of activities in this phase deals with the formation and development of the project team. The team must be selected on the basis of knowledge, skills, and attitudes appropriate for necessary project completion. The project manager needs to coordinate with the champion and the functional managers on project team selection and development. Roles and responsibilities for each team member must be delineated. In addition, all team members need to commit to the overall goals of the project, to their individual roles and responsibilities, and to informal standards for working together (Dewhirst 1998). The output of this phase should be a detailed project plan and a dedicated project team that are directed toward successful project implementation and control.

Third Stage: Project Implementing and Controlling

The main activities of this stage include securing the necessary resources to perform the project work, executing the activities identified in the project planning, monitoring and reporting on project progress, and replanning as needed. This is generally the longest stage of the project both in terms of duration and effort. Additional resources may be procured both from outside and within the organization to enhance the quality and timing of implementation activities.

Progress needs to be monitored and reported on a regular basis. To adequately monitor progress, useful and necessary information needs to be disseminated to various project constituents. Accurate measures need to be developed to track progress. A change control process needs to be used to handle requests for change. Essential changes should be approved and the project should be replanned accordingly. Optional changes may or may not be accepted depending on the constraints and priorities established during the project conceptual planning. The culmination of this stage occurs when the customer formally accepts the output from the project.

Fourth Stage: Project Evaluating and System Improving

This is a valuable yet underused project stage. Many project team members are tired and behind in other work, so when the customer accepts the project output they feel they can disengage. This is a big mistake since this phase is a wonderful opportunity for evaluating and improving the organization's project management system. The evaluation should include the processes used in the project, the outputs from the project, and the team members and other individuals who performed the work. Lessons learned should be developed so that both the project management system and people can be improved. These lessons can be incorporated, both in a rather extended version in the final project evaluation report and in an abbreviated version that is circulated widely within the company. Care must be exercised when deciding which lessons should be shared and at what level of detail with various people. The goal is to give concise ideas to people who are likely to read and consider them, but not burden anyone with large reports they are unlikely to read. The closure document for this phase is the final evaluation report, sometimes called the project history.

While most project managers are familiar with the project life-cycle stages, the associated stages of team character development, which are necessary to overcome dysfunctional group dynamics that impede project success, are not as widely understood.

Team Character Development Stages

One way to strengthen the collective capacity of team members to complete the project life cycle successfully is to regard projects as opportunities for team character development. In this respect, successful projects not only facilitate organizational decisions and build relationships and role competencies, but also necessitate and develop team character (Gadeken 1998).

Group Character and Virtue Development in Successful Projects

Team character is the collective set of virtues and pattern of intentions that dispose members to be ready to act ethically (Petrick and Quinn 1997). Team character expands and shrinks with the exercise of virtue and the avoidance of vice in projects. Virtue is the disposition to desire an action that is favorable, either for the well-being of society/world or for the flourishing of the agent for his own stake (Brandt 1988). Virtues are cultivated through examples and regular exercise so that honorable intentions and good acts become second nature to virtuous teams.

Organizations can shape and support team character development by institutionalizing organizational ethics-development programs (Petrick and Quinn 1997). These programs, in addition to having a written statement of values and a code of ethical conduct, specify moral standards in recruitment, performance appraisal, whistle-blowing, and reward subsystems, and provide ongoing ethics training and leadership integrity development for all project participants. Individuals and teams that exhibit exemplary ethical conduct are commended while unethical conduct is swiftly and fairly punished, so that everyone in the organization knows that being a virtuous team member pays off. In morally supportive organizational cultures, therefore, virtuous teams are collectively ready to act ethically; nonvirtuous teams are reluctant to oppose them or resist ethics initiatives within their organizational domain (Moberg 1997; Petrick and Quinn 1997).

The project life cycle creates a powerful operational opportunity for expanding team character through the exercise of specific virtues at appropriate intervals. Each project life-cycle stage benefits from a critical mass of specific virtues that drive the successful accomplishment of that project stage:

- In the planning stage, the intellectual virtue to anticipate important project opportunities and constraints is crucial at the outset to focus energy on a preferred future.
- In the organizing stage, the team capacity for mutual respect and trust, passionate project commitment, learning collaboration, and sincere emulation require socially and emotionally virtuous team norms.
- In the implementing and controlling stage, honest feedback, courageous perseverance, and prudent commitment summon the moral resources of the team to overcome obstacles and execute the project.
- In the evaluating and system-improving stage, the team capacity to fairly and inclusively share the burdens of evaluating results and improving future projects requires political citizenship and organizational justice.

While a case could be made for the usefulness of any virtue at any stage, because of the interdependence of virtues, we believe certain team character capacities are leveraged more effectively at appropriate intervals by the practice of specific sets of virtues. Successful projects can be envisioned as occasions for team character development through the exercise of appropriate intellectual, social, emotional, moral, and political virtues at each of the four project life-cycle stages, as depicted in Table 1.

Intellectual Virtues in Project Conceptual Planning

As shown in Table 1, the key intellectual virtues that drive project conceptual planning are imagination, knowledge, and foresight. Intellectual virtue consists of knowing and appreciating what is ethically desirable. Managers with intellectual virtue vividly imagine a preferred future, prioritize objectives, and tell the story of their project in a compelling manner. They envision a desired project outcome; they know how to strategically develop, systematically organize, and factually base that shared vision; and they have the operational foresight to tactically address anticipated constraints and risks. Such managers build team character by providing others with the collective stimulation of a better future, a better project charter, and a more vividly imagined project outcome (Senge 1990).

On the other hand, the nonvirtuous team's range of envisioned, ethical options becomes narrow; their ignorance of feasible alternatives restricts their freedom to act creatively and their practical wisdom degenerates over time. Intellectually virtuous project managers and teams that take responsibility for their own intellectual virtue cultivation (through ongoing self-discipline, reflection, and education), are tolerant and open to diverse respondents, serve as role

Project Life-Cycle Stage	Team Character Traits	Typical Activities	Closure Documents
Planning Conceptual Planning	Intellectual Virtues • Imagination • Knowledge • Foresight	• Identify final deliverables, goals, constraints, priorities, and risks. • Determine overall feasibility.	Charter Approved
Project Process Organizing	Social Virtues • Cooperation • Respect • Trust Emotional Virtues • Expressiveness • Commitment • Emulation	• Detail activities, cost, and schedule. • Select team, train, and develop commitment.	Project Plan Approved
Project Implementing and Controlling	Moral Virtues • Honesty • Courage • Prudence	• Procure resources, complete project activities, monitor progress, replan as needed.	Project Output Accepted
Project Evaluating and System Improving	Political Virtues • Justice • Inclusiveness • Citizenship	• Evaluate project process, results, and personnel. • Reassign workers and other resources. • Improve system and people through lessons learned.	Evaluation Report Approved

Table 1. Project Life-Cycle Stages and Team Character Traits

models in planning effective projects, and enhance the collective cognitive readiness to act ethically (Petrick and Quinn 1997).

Social and Emotional Virtues in Project Process Organizing

In Table 1, the key social virtues that energize process organizing are cooperation, respect, and trust (Jones and George 1998). Social virtue consists of the spontaneous enjoyment of the company of good people, demonstrated by congenially respecting and trusting others. Socially virtuous project managers facilitate cooperative, rather than competitive, relations among team members by ensuring inclusive input into the detailed project planning process. In addition, socially virtuous project managers demonstrate their respect for others by a spontaneous, cheerful, considerate manner and create a playful climate where good-natured humor helps diverse individuals feel included in an effective and satisfying project team. Socially virtuous managers reward team members by showing them trust, thereby creating an atmosphere in which better project plans can be developed and more enjoyable, effective teamwork can prevail (Whitener, Bradt, Korsgaard, and Werner 1998).

Socially virtuous project managers and teams that encourage collaboration and good-natured humor create the social atmosphere to act ethically in project undertakings. Social virtues prevent managers and teams from engaging in patterns of discussion that undermine collective learning through disrespectful and untrustworthy exchanges (Senge 1990). For example, a project manager faced with her personal shortcomings in a meeting gains a sense of perspective and builds congenial coworker relations by being able to laugh at herself while addressing the character flaw that needs attention.

Furthermore, the key emotional virtues that sustain the second stage of the project life cycle are expressiveness, commitment, and emulation. Emotional virtue consists of feeling and expressing joy when acting ethically or regularly experiencing commendable passions. Emotionally virtuous project managers keep people informed and involved in making decisions that affect them. They express themselves candidly and provide opportunities for team members to express feelings and receive interpersonal validation and emotional reassurance (Goleman 1998). They demonstrate and inspire passionate commitment to project processes and outcomes; their focused devotion overcomes lukewarm inertia and their emotional enthusiasm is contagious. In short, emotionally virtuous managers create and sustain an atmosphere where employees can intrinsically enjoy their work (Senge 1990).

Emotionally virtuous project managers communicate sincerely rather than sarcastically or cynically. Their genuine appreciation and inclusion of others dispels group cynicism in project activities (Dean, Brandes and Dharwodkar 1998). In addition, they stand up for emotional emulation, not resentment. Emulation is the emotional process of being positively motivated by another's success to do one's personal best. A project team whose members revel in each other's success will be energized to execute successfully the project plans they jointly develop. It is the opposite of collective resentment. Resentful project managers and teams begrudge the success and achievements of others and spitefully impede project progress (Sheaffer 1988).

Project managers who are envious of the success of others and tolerate vocal group resentment of others in projects, rather than collegial emulation and team commitment, erode the collective emotional energy to act ethically in projects. On the other hand, project managers who coordinate processes in ways that celebrate rather than denigrate individual accomplishment create a supportive emotional climate for project organizing excellence.

Moral Virtues in Implementing and Controlling Projects

The key moral virtues that drive implementing and controlling projects are honesty, courage, and prudence. Moral virtue consists of resolutely heeding the call of conscience with a discerning sense of right and wrong. Moral project managers honestly confront the truth regarding project progress, courageously face issues, and are prudent work partners (Murphy 1993). Their honesty accurately reports problems in time to make necessary changes, reinforces the norm of project accountablility, and precludes shortcuts that could endanger long-range project success (Hosmer 1995; Mayer, Davis, and Schoorman 1995; Moberg 1997). Courageous managers persistently overcome obstacles. They do not cower before superiors when confronting project difficulties, do not seek favor with employees by belittling upper management, do not shrink from confronting employees with constructive criticism in an open manner, and do not cave in to pressures when the going gets tough in project implementation and control (Petrick and Quinn 1997).

Political Virtues In Project Evaluation and System Improvement

Finally, in Table 1, the key political virtues that sustain project evaluation and system improvement are justice, inclusiveness, and citizenship. Political virtue consists of the responsible acquisition, use, and sharing of power to achieve worthy ends. Politically virtuous project managers and teams have a passion for justice and fairness (Greenberg 1996; Solomon 1990). Individuals who carry out delegated project assignments are recognized and rewarded, avoiding any hint of favoritism or inequity. In addition, politically virtuous project managers delegate inclusively and avoid in-group cliquish behavior or other forms of political favoritism (Lumsden and Lumsden 1997). All project participants are encouraged to identify and candidly share lessons learned from project activities. Finally, these politically virtuous managers challenge group members as organizational citizens to participate and share the burdens of project responsibilities and to enthusiastically persuade other organization members to utilize lessons learned from completed projects. Politically virtuous project managers and teams limit bickering, prohibit "freeloaders," and control abusive participants. They abide by good citizenship standards of participation in projects, fulfill project obligations, and widely share the lessons learned to promote moral progress and organizational learning (Dixon 1994).

Conclusion

We have shown that responsible project leadership today entails both team technical competency and team character development competency. The lack of project team character development can preclude successful project completion by implicitly allowing dysfunctional, nonvirtuous conduct to become a team "behavioral" norm. Substandard performance, insensitivity to project problems, defensive shirking of responsibility, not completing tasks on time, people arriving late and leaving early, and the gradual erosion of team collaboration are some of the adverse impacts of weak team character. Project leaders and teams that routinely accept excuses for substandard technical performance and weak team character development develop reputations for being linked with failed or mediocre projects.

To address these dual project leadership competencies, we accentuated the associated links between the disciplined use of project life-cycle stage completion documents and the necessary team virtues that facilitate each project stage. The first project life-cycle stage, conceptual planning, should result in an approved team charter and is facilitated by project participants that demonstrate the intellectual virtues of imagination, knowledge, and foresight. The second project life-cycle stage, process organizing, results in an approved project plan; the successful completion of this stage is facilitated by project participants that demonstrate the social virtues of cooperation, respect, and trust, and also the emotional virtues of expressiveness, commitment, and emulation. The third project life-cycle stage, implementing and controlling, should result in an accepted project output; project participants that demonstrate the moral virtues of honesty, courage, and prudence facilitate the successful completion of this stage. The fourth project life-cycle stage, evaluating and system improving, should result in an approved evaluation report; project participants that demonstrate the political virtues of justice, inclusiveness, and citizenship facilitate the successful completion of this stage.

We regard the simultaneous development of project life-cycle technical competency and team character development—behavioral competency—as new challenges for professional project leaders today. We hope the structured blueprint for increasing awareness and understanding of these associated links will contribute to more professional and successful future project leadership.

References

Adams, J. R., and M. E. Caldentey. 1998. A Project-Management Model. In D. Cleland. *Field Guide to Project Management:* 40–60. New York: Van Nostrand Reinhold.

Argyris, C. 1993. *Knowledge for Action: A Guide to Overcoming Barriers to Organizational Change.* San Francisco, CA: Jossey-Bass.

Brandt, R. B. 1988. The Structure of Virtue. In P. A. French. Ed. T. E. Vehling and H. K. Wettstein. *Midwest Studies in Philosophy: Ethical Theory, Character and Virtue:* 42–60. Notre Dame, IN: University of Notre Dame Press.

Dean, J., P. Brandes, and R. Dharwodkar. 1998. Organizational Cynicism. *Academy of Management Review* 23, 2: 341–52.

Dewhirst, H. D. 1998. Project Teams: What Have We Learned? *PM Network*, 12: 33–36.

Dixon, Nancy. 1994. *The Organizational Learning Cycle.* Maidenhead, UK: McGraw-Hill.

Gadeken, O. C. 1998. Ethics and the Project Manager. *Proceedings of the 29th Annual Seminars & Symposium.* Long Beach, CA.

Goleman, D. 1998. *Working With Emotional Intelligence.* New York: Bantam Books.

Greenberg, J. 1996. *The Quest for Justice on the Job: Essays and Experiments.* Thousand Oaks, CA: Sage.

Greer, Michael. 1996. *The Project Manager's Partner.* Amherst, MA: HRD Press.

Hosmer, L. T. 1995. Trust: The Connecting Link Between Organizational Theory and Philosophical Ethics. *Academy of Management Review*, 20: 379–403.

Jones, G. R., and J. M. George. 1998. The Experience and Evolution of Trust: Implications for Cooperation and Teamwork. *Academy of Management Review* 23, 3: 531–46.

Kloppenborg, T. J., and J. A. Petrick. 1997. Meeting Management and Group Character Development. *Journal of Managerial Issues* 11, 2.

Lumsden, G., and D. Lumsden. 1997. *Communicating in Groups and Teams: Shaping Leadership*, 2d ed. Belmont, CA: Wadsworth Publishing.

Martin, P., and K. Tate. 1997. *Project Management Memory Jogger*. Methuen, MA: GOAL/QPC.

Mayer, R. C., J. H. Davis, and F. D. Schoorman. 1995. An Integrative Model of Organizational Trust. *Academy of Management Review* 20: 709–34.

Moberg, D. 1997. Virtuous Peers in Work Organizations. *Business Ethics Quarterly* 7, 1: 67–85.

Murphy, K. R. 1993. *Honesty in the Workplace*. Belmont, CA: Brooks/Cole Publishing.

Nielsen, R. P. 1996. *The Politics of Ethics*. New York: Oxford University Press.

Petrick, J. A., and F. Quinn. 1997. *Management Ethics: Integrity at Work*. Thousand Oaks, CA: Sage.

Project Management Insititue. 2000. *A Guide to the Project Management Body of Knowledge (PMBOK® Guide) – 2000 Edition*. Newtown Square, PA: Project Management Institute.

Senge, P. M. 1990. *The Fifth Discipline: The Art and Practice of the Learning Organization*. New York: Doubleday.

Sheaffer, R. C. 1988. *Resentment Against Achievement*. Buffalo, NY: Prometheus.

Solomon, R. C. 1990. *A Passion for Justice*. Reading, MA: Addison-Wesley.

Verma, V. K. 1996. *Human Resource Skills for the Project Manager*. Upper Darby, PA: Project Management Institute.

Whitener, E. M., S. E. Bradt, M. A. Korsgaard, and J. M. Werner. 1998. Managers as Initiators of Trust: An Exchange Relationship Framework for Understanding Managers Trustworthy Behavior. *Academy of Management Review* 23, 3: 513–30.

Learning with Style

John Sullivan

PM Network 17 (August 1997)

Projects don't work without people, and people don't work without instructions. You have to tell them what you want. If you've ever tried to explain a task to your staff members from start to finish and returned to your chair feeling like they just didn't understand you, your intuition is probably correct.

You've run head on into "learning styles." Unlike so many other "styles" (leadership, personality, and so on) there are, thank goodness, only two types of learning styles (at least for the purposes of this article): "part-to-whole" and "whole-to-part."

Whole-to-part people have more of a global approach to learning. They like to go right to the end, get the big picture, and get on with it. About 75 percent of people use this learning style. By contrast, the part-to-whole learning style is sequential, like learning in a straight line. People who learn this way like to stay in order and go step by step. Even though only about 25 percent of people use this style, this is the approach traditionally taught in schools.

Most training and delegation of work is done sequentially—"this is step one, this is step two, and so on." That's great for part-to-whole thinkers. But since approximately 75 percent of the population use the whole-to-part learning style, it's better (at least statistically) to say, "This is what the job will look like when it's done. Now, let's look at how to accomplish this."

"For whole-to-part people, the most efficient way to learn is to have a goal and to seek information to meet that goal," says educational consultant Ann Anzalone. "For these people, there is too much information available, and it's impossible to keep up with it all." The part-to-whole people want to learn the traditional way: from beginning to end. Anzalone is quick to add that neither way is better. She stresses the fact that these are learning *styles*, ways of processing information.

Tailoring your approach to a particular learning style can make your communications more effective. While formal tests remain the best way to assess learning style, there are rules of thumb you can use to help determine how people learn.

Whole-to-part people seek the overall picture and are more "pattern oriented." They often say things like "What's the point?" or "What's the bottom line?" They may read the last page of a report first, to get to the conclusions or recommendations section. Because they are usually "seeking" things, a cluttered desk can sometimes be a clue to whole-to-part behavior.

Most part-to-whole people value order, so that their desks are probably clean. Their verbal communications usually contain a lot of details, and they are more likely to read a report from the beginning to the end.

One of Anzalone's clients is GZK, Inc., a franchiser of fast-food restaurants. "We've always taught part-to-whole style, step-by-step," said Steve Judge, GZK's training manager. "Today, most employees are interested in the 'bottom line.'"

GZK tried a different approach with a new cashier by explaining the job to her in reverse order. They stated the desired outcome first—to serve customers and keep them happy—then explained the keys and buttons on the cash register. The result: she did much better than most new hires. Instead of ignoring customers and concentrating on ringing up the order, she explained to customers that she was new and asked for their patience. She was taught to serve the customer, and part of that job included running the cash register.

In addition to happier customers, Judge believes that there is another benefit to this technique—a more interested employee. "Employees go to work to succeed—and that's really critical to the psyche of the new person," Judge says. With this kind of instruction, people know what a good job is so that they recognize their efforts when they do a good job. GZK is considering adopting this technique in its training manuals.

Keep in mind that this is only one piece of the management puzzle. Other parts include personality, learning style, and intelligence. "All of these come together to make the whole," says Anzalone. "You want to make the pieces fit as well as possible." Learning style is an important piece of the puzzle because, says Anzalone, "It is the key for understanding. Part-to-whole people have some flexibility in their learning; whole-to-part people have to learn *their* way. They *have* to have a focus; they *have* to know the end."

Look at your project team, and try to determine who uses what learning style. Next time you delegate some work, adjust your instructions to fit the team member's style. Communicating the day-to-day tasks more effectively can help improve the overall project execution. Who knows? You just may find yourself being understood.

Mentoring in the Project Environment

Joanne Gumaer

Proceedings of the 30th Annual Project Mangement Institute 1999 Seminars & Symposium

Organizations need to complete projects faster, cheaper, and better in order to survive in a competitive world. This pace of change demands that project teams gain the capacity to learn continuously and quickly. Mentoring supports much of what is currently known about how individuals learn, including the importance of experiential, situated learning.

Today the emphasis of skill development is on knowledge plus competencies. Traditional classroom training provides the knowledge, and a formal mentoring program provides the development of competencies. Training plus mentoring plus experience leads to continuous professional development.

The project environment provides several challenges to implementing a mentoring program. Short-term relationships with team members, aggressive timelines, and disparate teams are all common to the project environment. These factors present a challenge to the project manager to provide an effective mentoring program.

This article describes a brief overview of mentoring and its benefits and five mentoring programs tailored to the project environment.

Mentoring through the Ages

The concept of mentoring was first documented in Greek mythology, in Homer's tale of Odysseus. Odysseus entrusted his son, Telemachus, to his trusted counselor, Mentor, when he set out on his odyssey. The old man, Mentor, became the surrogate father, guardian, and teacher of Telemachus, the young mentee. Thus,

Figure 1. Continuous Professional Development Formula

the description of a mentor is a role model or leader who is willing to nurture the growth and development of an individual with less experience by sharing knowledge and insights that have been learned through experience.

Throughout history, there are numerous examples from different cultures in which a wise person or instructor coached, mentored, and empowered junior members. This practice continues today in many professions. Today the education, library, and community services have the most documented work on formalized mentoring programs. This article borrows on their processes and adapts them to the project environment.

Definitions of Mentoring

There is no Guide to the Body of Knowledge in Mentoring as there is for project management. Therefore, the definition of mentoring varies, depending upon the situation. Following are several commonly accepted definitions of mentoring.

The dictionary definition is a wise and trusted counselor or teacher. In the religious community, the term is interpreted as a personal guide or teacher in spiritual and philosophical matters. According to the business community, the term is thought to mean a recognized leader in a field who serves as a personal coach or guide in professional and business competencies. In the academic community, the term is interpreted as an acknowledged and influential advocate of a movement or idea, who serves as a personal guide or teacher in developing disciples of the movement or idea.

While the term takes on a different meaning depending upon the environment, the common element is that the mentor is respected and trusted for her expertise.

Benefits of Mentoring

Mentoring benefits all parties involved, including the organization, the mentored individual, and the mentor. Summarized are the key benefits of a formal mentoring program.

Benefits to the Organization

There are many advantages for an organization that has a formal mentoring program. However, the most effective mentoring programs occur when the program is part of an overall organizational commitment to learning and quality.

Staff morale is increased as a result of the flow of communications between senior management and junior personnel; talent is discovered; talented and motivated staff members are retained; and a stable base to use during periods of major organizational and career change is established.

Leaders and leadership qualities are developed as a result of real learning and behavior change, a fostering of shared values and teamwork, and improved management through development of interpersonal and technical skills. Increased business productivity occurs due to creating personal performance goals in line with corporate objectives. Creativity and innovation are encouraged from developing trust and empowering mentees. The development of project managers is accelerated through removing obstacles to successful project management by predicting and managing personal and organizational regression.

Benefits to the Mentee

Mentoring by senior colleagues has effectively facilitated the personal, intellectual, and career development of junior members. At the individual level, the benefits of being mentored vary widely, depending on the particular needs, aspirations, and situation of the mentee. Following is a list of the common benefits to the mentee from a review of the literature on mentoring programs.

- Gaining the confidence to lead and champion the project.
- Having improved people-management skills.
- Having improved listening, challenging, and empathizing skills.
- Gaining the confidence to set and achieve increasing performance goals.
- Having someone to whom you can talk openly.
- Having a wider perspective on the impact of an individual's management style.
- Being less ruled by feelings and more able to cope with difficult situations.
- Having the courage to be more radical and to more strongly sell ideas.
- Opening up additional ways of thinking.
- Being more mindful of the need to deal with the underlying problems, not just the symptoms.

Benefits to the Mentors

The mentors themselves benefit from the perpetuation of the project management culture, the satisfaction of contributing to the success of others, and the enhanced potential for collaboration with junior colleagues.

Five Mentoring Programs Tailored to Project Management

Each mentoring program meets different needs. Some focus on academics and career guidance, some provide role models, and some provide extra support and guidance concerning resolving day-to-day problems. Each is appropriate for a different situation. This diversity of programs provides options not only for mentees, but also for mentors, depending on the particular needs, interests, and commitments.

The following highlights five different program types, illustrating each with adaptations to the project management environment.

Traditional Programs

A senior project manager is assigned to a new project manager as a mentor. This generally is a long-term relationship of at least a year, during which the mentor is a role model and source of professional development for the mentee. This method is suitable for long-term projects of one or more years in length. The mentee and the mentor meet formally twice a month for the life of the project. In the initial meeting, a learning plan is developed. During this meeting, learning needs are identified and prioritized. Then the appropriate learning activities for the learning style of the mentee are determined. The mentee and mentor determine the objective and the format for each meeting and when and how frequently the learning plan is evaluated. The key to success for this program is setting a high priority on mentoring by both the mentor and mentee.

Short-Term Focused Activity

Programs in this category focus on a particular goal or topic, such as schedule development or team building. A specific time phase of no more than six months is set to accomplish the goal. Choose this method for short-term projects in which team members go their separate ways at the end of the project. Also short-term mentoring is beneficial when a team member is highly skilled technically and desires to gain a specific nontechnical skill. Each mentee is matched with a mentor who is skilled in the focused activity. Together they agree on a schedule of meetings and learning activities appropriate to the specific skill. This is an excellent method for developing weak areas or filling in skill gaps.

Group Mentoring

A senior project manager is assigned to two or more junior team members. The group focuses on developing project management skills by learning from a mentor and from one another. This technique can be adapted to either a long-term mentoring or a short-term focused-activity mentoring program. The mentor and mentees meet to determine the format and type of mentoring. Additionally, they identify which project management learning needs on which to focus. The next step is to set a schedule of learning activities and meetings to review how the skills are put into practice. This method works best when the mentees have similar project management competencies. The learning occurs from the mentor's expertise and from the mentees sharing their lessons learned with each other.

Peer Mentoring

Each team member takes a turn to mentor the others in the group. Each project team member chooses a particular skill to mentor the others, and then the team members put the skill into practice after the session. Each session follows a disciplined approach. The session begins with a debriefing in which the team members share what they did to apply the skill from the previous session. Then the team mentor introduces the new topic and learning objectives, followed by a review of the material, examples, and an exercise. Then each team member shares with the group how he will implement the skill. In closing, the session is evaluated, and feedback is given to the mentor. Prior to implementing this program, the project team receives training from a skilled facilitator on how to identify the skills to develop and how to train the team in lesson-plan development and delivery.

This program generally lasts for the duration of the project. This is a great for team building and project management skill development.

Team Mentoring

Team mentoring occurs when two or more senior project managers are assigned to a mentee. The mentors and the mentee determine the mentoring goal and the roles and responsibilities of each member. This method is particularly beneficial for developing a project manager to manage culturally diverse teams or to manage global projects. In that situation, the project managers assigned to the mentee would have different cultural backgrounds.

Summary

Whatever method or methods of mentoring an organization chooses, the process of implementing the program is the same. A formal mentoring process with clear policies is the key to successfully implementing a project management-mentoring program.

The formal mentoring program provides a structured approach to selecting, training, and supporting mentors. It also allows for evaluation of the program and continuous improvement of project management. Additionally, there is a platform upon which mentors can be recognized. Typically, the mentoring program can be initiated through a project office or the training and development department.

Whether a team member is full time or part time with other functional duties, the time spent on project management activities requires a unique set of skills, competencies, and political discernment. Observing a trusted senior person gives the mentee a safe place to try out ideas, skills, and roles with minimal risk. The knowledge acquired is constantly reinterpreted and developed through practice on real-world project activities.

Establishing an Internal Mentorship Program

Joan Knutson and George Kimmell

PM Network 23 (January 2000)

Project management mentoring is not your stereotypical organizational mentor/mentee relationship. Mentors are seasoned project management professionals assigned to project teams in order to coach the project leader and the project team.

Project mentors had the opportunity to work with the corporate information services (CIS) department at Reynolds Metals Company (RMC) in Richmond, Virginia, to establish and roll out an internal mentorship program. At RMC, the client's mandate was to accelerate the application of the project management discipline within its department. This would be accomplished by introducing a standardized project management process and by supporting the project community during the learning curve associated with assimilating the new process with a cadre of mentors.

The job of mentor, as described in the case study, was to act as coach for the assigned project leader(s). As coach, the mentor was asked to raise awareness so that project leaders and team members could become more knowledgeable concerning the project management process; help the project leader assess his own skills and competencies and work on appropriate improvement plans; allow the project leader being mentored to own his own discovery, analysis, and actions; and communicate effectively by actively listening and providing constructive advice and feedback.

First, the mentor cadre set seven goals: improve mentoring skills; develop techniques to handle specific interventions; identify individual skill gaps, and determine how they can be filled; improve ability to deal with cultural roadblocks; continue to transfer knowledge from the mentor to the project leader;

improve ability to facilitate specific events such as a project launch; and continue to develop interpersonal skills.

The mentor cadre then conducted a risk analysis and identified the following possible risks:

- People working on projects would complain that they didn't have time to do project management the right way.
- People might perceive that having a mentor indicated that the project leader was considered incompetent of managing the project alone.
- The mentoring process might be seen as just another "flavor of the month"; or worse, the mentor might be construed as a spy sent to inform management of all the bad things that were happening on the project.
- The mentor might be enticed to take over the actual work rather than remaining the coach.

Being forewarned is being forearmed. Because the mentors were on the lookout for these problems, they were in most cases able to avoid them, or at least mitigate their negative effect to the mentorship program.

All in all, the initiative was a success. I had the opportunity to conduct the end of the first year debriefing with both the mentor team and top management. Both groups unilaterally agreed that the initiative had been worthwhile. And more importantly, management was willing to continue to fund the effort, and the mentors were willing to continue to contribute to the initiative. Congratulations, RMC, for a pioneering effort in the project management discipline.

RMC Case Study

In August 1998, the chief information officer of RMC commissioned a project to renew emphasis on project management in the company's CIS department. A project management team was formed to address this charter. A series of focus groups were held for people throughout the 250-person organization. Participants in the focus groups included managers and project management "practitioners"—in other words, project team members, the people who lead and work on information systems and information technology project teams every day.

There was a great deal of interest on the part of the participants regarding the project management initiative in CIS. The results of the focus group clearly identified several significant points that the project management team would need to deal with:

- The need to build customer confidence through a series of successful projects delivered, using standard project management practices and procedures.
- The need for continuous top-management support and an emphasis on project management.
- The need of CIS managers and practitioners for information-on-demand about project management processes.

The CIS project management team selected project mentors to partner with it in this effort. We had to make or buy a project management process and train the critical mass of the project practitioners on that process. We chose to buy an already developed and tested process. CIS adopted the ten-step project management process in our project mentor's course as the standard, repeatable process to be used on all CIS projects.

The project mentor delivered its *process* course. As often as possible, the project management training was delivered to project teams as they were being formed to work on new projects. The training provided a process baseline for the team to use in managing the project and served as both a team-building event and project launch pad.

Now that the foundation was laid, in the form of a critical mass of project practitioners trained, relative to a repeatable process, we were able to address each of the issues listed above.

Customer Confidence

The project teams emerged from the three-day training course with most, if not all, of the project initiation and definition activities completed and ready for the project customer's review. Customers also were invited to attend the training course with their project team, and when they were able to do so, the project and product end results were extremely good.

The team training for each class was reinforced by having the instructor return several weeks later to reinforce the key points in a real-world, "case–study" environment. Referencing projects they had begun, the students could then ask questions about the project management processes that they had been applying.

Customers became more involved in the process and began to see the value of a consistent project management planning and control methodology. Projects were better at meeting the project management parameters of time, cost, and quality. Most importantly, customers were being kept informed of the status and of any significant problems in time to make better business decisions.

Continuous Top-Management Support and Emphasis on Project Management

Initially, management also participated in an executive briefing during which it set the direction and tone for the entire project management initiative, as well as for the mentorship program.

The CIO and his direct reports repeatedly demonstrated top-down management support of the initiative by requesting information in the form of project status reports and briefings. Management also made a concentrated effort to recognize the accomplishments resulting from the renewed emphasis on project management policies and procedures.

CIS Managers and Practitioners Need for Information-on-Demand about the Project Management Process

The challenge was how to deliver information on demand. The concept proposed was to have people with strong project management credentials available to the project teams whenever the team had questions about project management or about the adopted project management process.

A small team of mentors was assembled from within CIS. A conscious effort was made to ensure representation from each of the CIS directorates. This small team grew to about twelve people and was referred to as the mentor cadre and was tasked not to lead projects, but to help others develop and strengthen their project management skills.

These mentors were assigned specific projects. They were not the project leaders, nor were they official project team members. They acted as "shadow consultants" to the project manager, previewed management briefings, attended project team meetings as a second set of eyes and ears for the project manager, and reviewed status reports to help the project manager sight any possible warning signals.

In order to prepare the mentor cadre for the task at hand, the project management team and its vendor partner created five coaching sessions for the mentors. These sessions focused on skills required for facilitating and coaching; launching a project; building team rapport and sustained morale; reviewing projects midpoint; and intervening in order to address traditional project problems. These sessions and additional coaching, both from within and from the project mentor, helped the mentor cadre rise to the occasion and support its assigned teams.

Results

After almost a year, the following results were isolated through a second series of focus groups. Approximately sixty people were trained in the project management process. These people had worked on some forty-eight projects, twenty-five of which had used the project management process. Twelve people had participated in the mentorship cadre and had worked with thirty-three project teams. Relative to a question concerning what worked well, over one-third of participants cited the mentorship program as a major contributor to improved project management productivity.

Also, in response to the question, "What are the major activities of project management?", the balance shifted during the year. At the beginning of the initiative, respondents had placed heavier weighting on controlling the project, while at the end of the first year the emphasis moved to planning. (I would like to suggest that this redirection of focus up-front was in large part due to the guidance and coaching of the mentor cadre.)

As we look to the future, the long learning curve for the project leaders is being overcome. The mentor cadre had a motto: "We are not here to fish; we are here to teach people how to fish." Project leaders, who are routinely applying the new project management processes and skills, are improving their competencies and are requiring less mentoring. As a result, beginning 1 September 1999, the project leaders reached a competency level so that all projects in CIS have been required to apply the ten-step project management process. We owe much of this fast ramp-up and increased project success to the mentorship program.

If This Is a Team, How Come We Never Practice?

Karl W. Croswhite, PMP

*Proceedings of the 28ᵗʰ Annual Project Management Institute
1997 Seminars & Symposium*

American industry is enthusiastically adopting the concept of integrated, cross-functional product teams. In this article we will discuss how industry has arrived at the need to execute projects in a team environment. We will look at the major reasons that projects fail and why the establishment of teams does not eliminate these failures. We will examine the effect of organizational structure on the efficacy of teams, and we will look at the role that project management should play in correcting these deficiencies.

Are We Really on Teams?

We all know the value of teamwork. Our leaders constantly encourage us to work together. The worst possible reputation a person can have is that she is not a team player. But how valid is this analogy? How many of you are on a team? When was the last time your team held a practice? Do you have a playbook that describes the processes that you will follow to achieve success? Does it describe the roles and responsibilities of the players on the team? Who is your coach? Do you have all of the necessary players on your team? If you were responsible for organizing a practice for your team, what sort of activities would you include? Let's see if we can find the answers we need, assemble our team, and practice in a manner that will enable us to win.

Ground Rules and Assumptions

For ease and clarity of discussion, let us make the following assumptions:

- The terms *project management, project,* and *program* are as defined in *A Guide to the Project Management Body of Knowledge (PMBOK® Guide) –* 2000 Edition.
- The enterprises we are discussing have multiple product divisions, each of which is executing multiple programs.
- The enterprises we are discussing generate their revenue through the successful execution of projects.
- The enterprises we are discussing wish to operate in a team environment.
- Our ultimate goal is to create an environment that will foster team success.

Why Do Projects Fail?

Since the game we are playing is the accomplishment of projects, we need to understand what causes teams to lose. There have been numerous studies done on this subject. Most of our companies do some form of post-proposal or post-project analysis. We have produced volumes and volumes of "lessons learned," and the findings are remarkably similar. Projects fail for the following reasons:

- Lack of planning.
- Lack of executive management support.
- Incomplete requirements.
- Changing requirements.
- Lack of user (customer) involvement.
- Inadequate resources.

It is important to note that projects are not failing due to inadequate technical expertise. They are not failing due to inadequate tools or systems. They are failing due to bad management. They are failing because we let them fail.

Why Teams?

To understand how we can establish the necessary environment for successful teams, we must first answer two basic questions.

1. What is the reason for moving to a team approach?
2. What is the primary purpose or function of a team?

To answer the first question we have to examine the environment from which the team concept emerged.

Most of our companies were originally structured as functional hierarchies. All of the thinking was done at the top, and direction flowed down through functional chains of command to people actually performing tasks that contributed to the production of a product or service. Project management existed only as the byproduct of the general management of the business. As the business grew, a need developed to focus attention upon specific product lines or market segments individually, thus creating product divisions within the overall

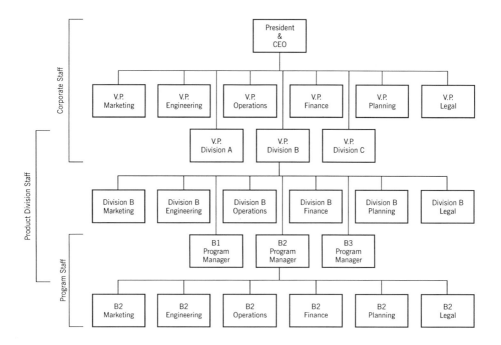

Figure 1. The Functional Hierarchy

enterprise. These divisions adopted an organizational structure that mirrored that of the existing enterprise with each of the functions reporting in a dedicated "hard-line" relationship to the division manager, thereby adding a layer of overhead function and cost. They constitute a complete enterprise within the enterprise. Again, project management exists only as the sum of the management of the functional departments.

As these product divisions developed multiple customers and contracts, the same need developed to be able to focus attention on each of them individually, and the same evolution was repeated. People performing a specific type of task report to a functional manager, who reports to the project manager. This time the result is what is defined as a "projectized" organization structure. Unfortunately, it also has the effect of adding another layer of overhead cost and organizational burden. The project manager reports to the division manager who reports to the president of the company, and each maintains a staff to execute the overhead tasks at each level in the enterprise. The resulting organization is shown in Figure 1.

Unfortunately, some of us are still functioning in this structure. I say "unfortunately," but many will say that there is nothing unfortunate about it. Many companies have been very successful in following this evolutionary pattern, have been in existence a long time, and have provided a very good return to their stockholders. I can't argue that. But I can argue that even though a company may have a long history of successful projects, producing high-quality products, this traditional approach to working projects has inherent inefficiencies built into it that will not be affordable in the coming century. It forces our experts to communicate in series and generally by paper. This is a slow process that limits, and even precludes, interaction between functional organizations. As a result, many mistakes are made which necessitate costly rework. This approach also tends to compartmentalize activities, making processes more resistant to changes and organizations less sympathetic to the needs of other organizations.

To remain competitive, we have to find a way to satisfy our customers' requirements while minimizing our costs and reducing our product cycle times. This is where the concept of teams comes in. Integrated, cross-functional product teams are seen as a means to reduce project flow and costs and improve communication. The assertion is that project flow times can be reduced because decisions that were once made sequentially can now be made concurrently. Furthermore, these decisions are based upon a life-cycle perspective, which should minimize the number and degree of changes during the project. Overall project cost should be reduced as a result of fewer and less drastic design and engineering changes, better coordination with manufacturing, and so forth. Finally, by removing most of the physical barriers that have stifled communication in the past, there should be freer and more open discussion between all represented functions. There is also a significant reduction in overhead costs *if* the overall organizational structure of the enterprise is reengineered to fit the team approach to the execution of projects.

What Is the Function of the Team?

Now that we understand why we are pursuing the team approach, we need to answer the second question: What is the primary purpose or function of the team?

The purpose of the team is to execute all of the tasks necessary to produce the product for which it is responsible. That is to say that the team must develop specifications, design, develop, test, produce, and deliver the product that satisfies the customers' requirements. There is nothing new or unique here. This same statement is just as accurate when applied to a project operating in a projectized functional organization or in a strict functional hierarchy. So what is unique about a team?

The unique aspect of the team is that it also has the responsibility of planning and managing its work and processes. The team is responsible for defining the scope of its work, defining the tasks required to execute that scope, scheduling the execution of those tasks, assigning budget to those tasks, assessing and planning the mitigation of risk, and then monitoring and reporting their progress. In other words, the team has responsibility for scope management, time management, cost management, quality management, risk management, procurement management, communications management, and, to some degree, human resources management. The team is responsible for project management.

Why Teams Do Not Perform Successfully

In 1994 Paul Osterman, an economist at MIT, conducted a national survey of innovative work practices. He found that more than half of the companies surveyed were using teams, and that approximately 40 percent of those companies reported having more than half of the organization working in teams. The effect of teaming, if you read the literature aimed at the managerial audience, would indicate that the results are excellent: teams outperform individuals, and self-directed teams perform best of all.

But the results are really not that clear. Research on team performance shows that teams usually *do not* perform as well as the sum of their members' individual efforts. It seems that there is really no empirical data that teams are more efficient. In fact, when interacting teams are compared to "nominal" groups (i.e., groups that never meet, whose output is constructed by combining the separate contributions of those who would have been team members), nominal groups actually perform better. This is illustrated by Ivan Steiner's equation AP = PP − PL. That is, the *actual* productivity of a group equals its' *potential* productivity (what the team is theoretically capable of, given the resources brought by the members) minus what he calls *process losses,* such as coordination and motivational problems (Steiner 1972).

We have seen the reasons why projects fail. We have seen the reasoning behind the implementation of project teams and the unique responsibility that teams have. We know that teams, for the most part, do not execute projects successfully. Why? The reason that teams do not overcome these failure modes is that they are not structured to do so. Or maybe I should say that the structure in which the team exists does not enable them to do so.

The Effect of Organizational Structure on Teams

"Different people in the same structure tend to produce qualitatively similar results. When there are problems, or performance fails to live up to what is intended, it is easy to find someone or something to blame. But, more often than we realize, systems cause their own crises, not external forces or individuals' mistakes" (Senge 1990).

As we can see from our earlier description of the company, division, and project structure, the only thing that is really changed in the team environment is the way in which functional organizations interact. The team may be able to execute some series of processes more rapidly by increasing the concurrency of tasks, but the processes haven't really changed, and the team has not added the catalyst that is required for success. Since we have not really changed the overall structure in which the team operates, it should not be surprising that our results are unchanged.

In some implementations, it is intended that the leadership role be transferred from function to function as the project progresses. At the outset a systems engineer would lead the team since the most immediate product would be requirements and specifications. The leadership role would then pass to a design engineer since the next major product would be drawings. From here, leadership would pass to manufacturing engineering and so on. From the perspective of the traditional functional hierarchy this may seem like a significant improvement, but there is a problem with this idea.

This approach actually perpetuates one of the paradigms we are trying to eliminate: functional stove pipes! Systems engineering leads until the requirements and specifications are complete and then hands off to design. "Good luck!" Design hands off to manufacturing, "Here are the drawings; sorry they're late. You can make it up, can't you? What's the matter? Aren't you a team player?" This is the same old toss-it-over-the-fence attitude that has been hurting us for years, the nagging groin injury of project performance.

If this was a design team and engineering was in charge, it would make sense. If it was a production team and manufacturing was in charge, it would make sense. If it was a subcontracts management team and procurement was in charge, it would make sense. But an integrated product team is none of those things. It is *all* of those things with the additional unique task of project management. In fact, project management is the only function of the team that remains constant throughout the life cycle of the project. We need to create an offensive coordinator for our team, whose role is to lead the integration of the functions of the other players. I would suggest that it would be logical for this leader to come from a project management functional organization.

Required Structural Changes

In most of our companies there is no project management organization. Some of us have a small group of individuals somewhere, addressing project management processes and tools, but this is usually a group contained within some other functional organization (probably IT), distanced from the arena of day-to-day project execution. More typically, scope management gets handled by a contract's organization, time management is done by some sort of planning/scheduling organization, cost is done by some form of estimating/accounting group, and so on. These functions are usually included in the category of "support organizations" and are not part of the core team. What is required to create teams that can avoid project failures is a reengineering of our basic organizational structure.

Since our assumptions say that we want to create an environment that will foster team success, let us look at our existing structure to see what does or does not contribute to team success. We could approach this from either perspective, but let's go from the top down.

Let's go back to Figure 1. At the corporate level, is there anything that is not required for the success of the team? I suppose that some items could be debated. However, most of the staff functions illustrated here are necessary for the successful functioning of the enterprise, and there would be no teams if there were no enterprise. As for the functional organizations, I suppose you could argue that functionals are only necessary when they exist on teams. I would suggest that this argument does not hold up. The functional organization at the highest level exists to provide members to the teams and to provide the processes, tools, and training required by the team members to perform their task.

So do we leave the corporate level structure as is? I don't think so. There needs to be one functional organization added.

The Missing Link

To complete the foundation for our new structure we need to create one new organization: project management. To create this new function we will combine pieces of several already existing functions. From contracts we'll take that portion of the effort that pertains to defining and controlling scope. We will leave those aspects of the effort that pertain to the legalities of contracting. From finance we will take those things that pertain to budgeting and cost control at the team/project/program level and leave those things that relate to overhead, taxes, payroll, and financial accounting in general. From planning we will take all aspects of planning at the team/project/program level and leave those things that pertain to planning at the strategic level. From operations (procurement) we will take subcontract management.

Finally, from all functional organizations we will take those people who aspire to a career in project management. This is in addition to all of the people who perform the tasks listed earlier. If an engineer (planner, buyer, cost analyst) is selected for, and agrees to accept, an assignment as a team leader, he would be transferred (hard line) to the project management organization. From that point forward his performance would be measured on how well he performed the function of project manager (at whatever level) and not on his original technical specialty.

So what do we do at the product-division level in our restructured organization? This may be the most difficult question to answer. I would argue that there is really no unique function at this level. I would then argue that, in an enterprise of any magnitude, this level is necessary—if only to provide for a reasonable span of control in the management structure. For the time being I would say that the decision to remove or retain a division-level organizational structure is dependent upon the size of the overall enterprise. If we do decide to retain it, it will be structured differently from the organization shown in Figure 1. Rather than having a division manager who reports to the president, there will be a division project manager who reports to the vice president of project management at the company level. Since all of the program/project managers report to this position, this is the means by which we will accomplish the vertical integration of the project management processes. Since our program-level structure already has a project manager, there is nothing we need to change here.

As previously discussed, the only change we need to make at the team level is that the team leader is now a hard-line member of the project management functional organization. The rest of the team members report in a matrix structure: hard line to their functional manager and soft line to the team leader. The resulting organizational structure is referred to as a "strong matrix organization" and is illustrated in Figure 2. This matrixed team organization is what will enable us to accomplish the horizontal integration of processes necessary to release the potential productivity of the team.

What about Practice?

Now that we have reengineered our organizational structure to enable the teams to perform their primary functions, what else do we have to do to maximize their performance?

Well, I would suggest that the first thing is to make sure that the priorities of the entire organization (enterprise) are in alignment. The entire enterprise needs to be aligned to provide maximum support to the team. The demand for support should be from the bottom up, not, as is so often the case, from the top down.

Just as there are many members of a sports team who never take the field, there are many members of our enterprises who will not be on our teams. In business we have the company president and corporate staff, the functional managers, the training staff, and many more. What are their prime functions?

As with professional sports teams, our business teams should be formed far in advance of the game. Even in an all-star game, the team members are brought together to practice for some time before they are expected to perform. Doesn't it seem strange that our teams usually aren't formed until the last possible instant before the game and, in some instances, aren't even completed until the game is in progress? I wonder how many coaches would wait until fourth down before they hired a punter?

Recent research has identified three times in the life of a team when members are likely to be especially open to coaching interventions: the beginning, when

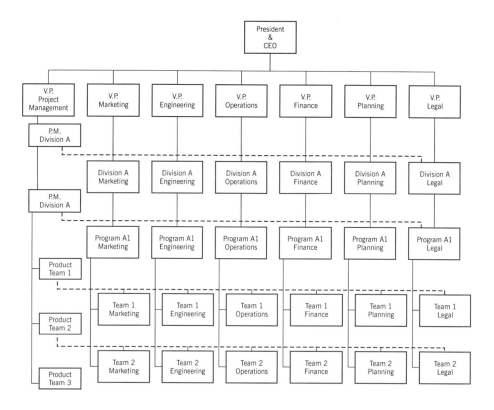

Figure 2. The Strong Matrix Organization

a group is just forming; the midpoint, when the group is halfway through the work; and the end, when a piece of work has been finished (Hackman 1996).

Professional teams conduct preseason training camps. Wouldn't it be a good idea for us to have a preproject training session? This would provide the opportunity to finalize the composition of the team. It would also provide the environment in which the team could study the playbook, clarify the expectations for each player, and participate in developmental exercises to perfect timing and execution. Like athletic teams, business teams need to learn continually from their actions and to adjust them on an ongoing basis. Practice, practice, practice.

References
Senge, Peter. 1990. *The Fifth Discipline*. New York: Doubleday.

Section 6

Resolving Conflict

Is Everybody Happy?

Kenneth E. Atwater, PMP

PM Network 60 (November 1999)

As any seasoned project manager knows, the answer to the question, "Is everybody happy?" is a resounding, "NO!" Well, not all at the same time, anyway. Every project manager has to deal with the triple constraint of balancing time, cost, and quality. (Some refer to schedule, budget, and performance, which are essentially the same things.)

As professionals we use many tools to keep things in balance. We develop detailed schedules with the most powerful project management software available. Reports are generated showing the critical path, total float, and free float. Earned value calculations are developed to make sure that the project stays on budget as well as for trends forecasting. We may even add a Monte Carlo simulation analysis of the schedule in order to predict with certitude the probability of meeting a specified schedule date. A quality plan is developed to make sure that the project product or service meets specified criteria. Quality stage-gates are incorporated into the project plan from the very beginning.

This article is about the other triple constraint that the project manager must balance: client, project team, and employer expectations. This triple constraint is just as critical to project success, but the quantitative tools are largely unavailable. Balancing client, project team, and employer expectations is made more difficult because they are constantly changing. I worked on one project where this was called creative tension. On other projects it was referred to as a physical discomfort in the lower part of the human anatomy. Since there are few formal tools, the project manager must rely on his people and communications skills. As a consultant, I find myself in this situation on every project. There are some things I have learned that may prove helpful. The recommendations don't apply just to consultants, however. In-house project managers also must satisfy internal clients, their bosses, and the project team.

You Can't Please All the People All the Time

Article 3, Section E, in the Project Management Institute Code of Ethics states that as project management professionals, we will "be honest and realistic in reporting project quality, cost, and time." In short, we will tell the truth. Doing so is bound to upset someone at some point. It is instructive for the project manager to understand this concept when trying to balance the desires of the project team, the client, and her employer. If project managers try to be all things to all people, they will usually end up being nothing to anyone.

The project manager must continue to report the status of the project as accurately as possible. It would be wrong and unethical to couch any status reports based on who is to receive the report or the perceived notion that one of the stakeholders may not like the news and become upset. In fact, consistent and accurate reporting will help set expectations, and in the long run reduce the likelihood that one of the *big three* will be upset, or if so, at least not for an extended period of time. People don't like having other people upset with them, and project managers are no exception. However, project management is fraught with conflict. At some point in any project, the client, project team, or our employer will be less than pleased with how the project is being managed. Professional project managers understand and accept this fact of life; after all, *it is what it is*.

Don't Play One Group Against Another

All the individuals—client, project team, and employer—are key to the overall success of the project. Sometimes in an effort to protect themselves, project managers may play one group against another. For example, a consultant may tell the project team, I agree that the time frames are unreasonable, but that's what the client and our employer want. Ostensibly this is done to demonstrate to the team members that the project manager is on their side. This is wrong! While the project manager may gain short-term accolades from the project team, in the long run he will lose credibility not only with the project team, but also with the client and his employer. If the project manager is concerned about the schedule, it should be addressed directly with those individuals empowered to make a change.

The project manager should be concerned with balancing the needs and desires of all the parties. This can best be done by open and honest communications. Rather than trying to play the project team against the other stakeholders, it would be better to try to get project team members to see the project from the points of view of the client and their employer. By the same token, every reasonable effort should be made to get the client to understand that the project team brings unique and valuable experience to the table regarding the effort required to complete certain tasks. By keeping all parties focused on the common goal of project success, the project manager should be able to avoid this hazard.

All project participants should accept a formal communication plan established at the outset of the project. Such a plan will minimize the inclination to play games because it will serve to keep expectations in focus and show that the project is meeting those expectations.

Know What Makes Them Tick and When

Each of the three parties involved in this balancing act has different desires, or *hot buttons*, during the term of the project. Knowing these desires and acting accordingly can greatly enhance the chances of keeping everyone happy (or at least avoid everyone being unhappy at the same time). The members of the project team usually want challenging assignments, respect for the skills that they bring to the table, and inclusion in decisions that affect their lives. The client or internal customer may be primarily concerned with meeting a given schedule at a given price (not necessarily in that order). If our employer is a consulting company, it usually is seeking a long-term relationship and increased billable hours (again, not necessarily in that order).

When including the project team in decisions, the project manager could challenge the team to think of new ways to perform project tasks in order to stay on schedule and within budget. One of the first things the project manager should do is set realistic goals regarding cost and schedule with the client/internal customer. Once expectations are set, it is important that the client be kept informed of project schedule and costs. Earned value analysis is perhaps the most useful tool a project manager has in her repertoire. If you work for a consulting company, like I do, you must balance billable hours with the goal for a long-term relationship with the client. These two goals are not incompatible. One thing that can be done is to look for other opportunities to provide work for the client. Doing so will begin to establish a long-term relationship. Perhaps billable hours can be adjusted, depending on the length of the assignment.

Get Certified

Credibility is the *sine qua non* of a project manager's skills. The vast majority of a project manager's time is spent communicating with the big three. Most of that time is spent trying to persuade the client, project team members, and our employer to do things that will increase the likelihood that the project will be brought in on time, on budget, and on quality. Since, as project managers, we rarely have authority commensurate with our responsibility, we must rely on other means of persuasion.

Our ability to persuade project participants will be greatly enhanced if we are believed to be experts in our field. Simply having the appellation "project manager" after our names is not enough. The title of project manager has become as ubiquitous in corporate America as Beanie Babies in department stores (and, unfortunately, about as meaningful). Certification is an independent verification that one has obtained a certain level of knowledge of project management principles. Once certified, we must demonstrate how that knowledge is beneficial to all project participants. We must show clearly how the knowledge areas contained in *A Guide to the Project Management Body of Knowledge (PMBOK® Guide)* are applicable and add value to the project management process. It may be necessary to educate project participants on the significance of the project management professional designation. They need to understand the breadth of the written examination as well as the educational requirements. Perhaps the most relevant aspect to clients is the level of experience required to become certified.

You Never Really Arrive

As it is with cost, schedule, and quality, the other triple constraint requires active management throughout the life of the project. Likewise, as project managers, we will be called upon to exercise our judgment and make prudent tradeoffs. Keeping the needs and expectations of all project participants in equipoise is the ultimate goal. Doing so may require the project manager to adopt the rumination of Mr. Spock in one of the *Star Trek* movies: The needs of *man* outweigh the needs of the few.

Balancing client, project teams, and employer expectations is as important as balancing cost, schedule, and quality throughout the life of the project. While formal tools such as earned value and quality gates may not be available, simply understanding that the other triple constraint exists is beneficial to the project manager. Becoming certified and applying the project management principles found in the *PMBOK® Guide*, I believe, are essential to long-term success in the project management profession.

Discovering Bias in Facilitated Teams

Edward A. Ziv

PM Network 97 (September 2000)

A smoothly operating project team can be a thing of beauty—productive, creative, and truly greater than the sum of its parts. There are times, however, when keeping a team together, focused, and productive can be as challenging as climbing Mount Everest ... barefoot ... carrying someone on your shoulders.

Whether you are serving the team as a formal facilitator, a project leader, or simply a team member, it can be frustrating when those around you seem to be fighting the process. Disagreements, of course, are to be expected, as teams are usually designed to have representatives of differing views, experiences, and positions.

The problem isn't that these opinions and feelings exist; it's when team members fail to recognize their own or each other's biases that a molehill can turn into an immovable mountain. So rather than trying to fix these biases, it's imperative that they be brought out into the open.

Who Are You Calling Biased?

Nobody wants to be thought of as biased. It conjures up images of prejudice and closed-mindedness. A bias, however, is simply a deeply held opinion or a subjective view. Biases are normal, a healthy part of life, and we've all got them. They come from many places:

- Our lives; including religion, schooling, friends, relatives, and heritage.
- Overt work influences, more specifically, our perception of the corporate vision and our personal and departmental goals.
- Subtle work influences; which entails the corporate culture, including work experiences and the stories and heroes within our work environment.

Why Should I Care?

Take the case where a new departmental structure is being considered. A team member might be biased for or against the idea because of previous experiences with individuals in the department, a perception that big departments are ineffective, or a memory of what happened the last time the company tried to do something like this. However, what emerges in the actual meetings might be statements such as, "That will never work," or "This will cost too much to implement." It is important when conflict arises or judgments are made that the team address the true issues rather than running around in this smokescreen.

Also, biases can be an impediment to team formation and communication. Recognizing the biases, conflicts, and motivations will facilitate better communication within the group itself and between the group and management.

Not all conflicts have to be resolved and not all motivations have to surface. We're not talking about group therapy here; the team exists to get a *job done*. If a bias gets in the way of this or inhibits comfortable and clear communication, the team may still function, but will carry a "pearl"—an irritating and uncomfortable nugget that won't easily disappear. Like a pearl, layers will be built over time and accommodations made, but the underlying problem will never be resolved.

Recognizing Bias

This is the easy part. Simply look for *stubborn, unsubstantiated*, and *vocabulary* differences—the SUV symptoms.

The first indication that biases exist is when otherwise rational people turn obstinate. If one person stubbornly holds to an opinion in the face of facts, or two people line up on either side of any disagreement, someone is probably carrying baggage. If the disagreement becomes a standoff and both sides dig in for a pitched battle, you're looking at full suitcases and maybe a few carry-on bags.

The second sign of biases emerging on your team are trigger words indicating unsubstantiated beliefs. Listen carefully for these, because with homogenous teams the bias may be shared and may not lead to any conflict. If team members respond to your challenges with ambiguous answers like, "That's the way we do things," or use subjective terms such as big, important, and busy, or words like can't or won't, you're probably looking at a bias.

Let me illustrate. My company was brought in to help complete the conversion to a new computer system. The previous effort had dragged on for two years, and with each customer record taking three months for completion, it became evident that it wasn't going to finish for some time more. When we took over the project, we were told that three different groups were involved in reviewing each record, "Because that's what the customer needs!" The solution was to get members of each of the groups into the meeting and ask each the same questions. As a team, we discovered that this process was originally put in place because of a lack of confidence arising from the *first* conversion, over two years ago. Set free by this revelation, all team members pulled together, debated each other's assumptions, agreed to be flexible in their solution, and in two hours designed a new process that converted the final twenty customers in less than two months.

For the unsubstantiated assertion, the key is in asking open-ended questions, such as, "Why do you say this?" and, "What would happen if we did it this way?"

Bias can also take the form of differing vocabulary or industry-specific jargon. This is easier to deal with than a personal bias because there are usually no feelings or history to overcome. At the same time it can be most frustrating, because two people who until now may have been working well together may suddenly find themselves speaking different languages.

In designing an automated system for a brokerage house, for example, we found ourselves perplexed by the features and detail being requested to support the "end users." The right questions eventually uncovered a language bias that had created the confusion. While "end user" meant data-entry person to the programmers, to the brokers it referred to the executives who were the ultimate recipients of the reports generated by the system.

Differing terminology may put two people on the *same* side of an argument without either realizing it. This occurs so often that we refer to it as vehemently agreeing.

Vocabulary biases are the easiest to address. There is no end to the number of deadlocked situations that have been resolved by someone stepping in and saying, "What do you mean when you say…?" In facilitated sessions, we also use the ubiquitous flip chart to track words with specific meanings, abbreviations, and jargon. Be especially aware of acronyms—does ATM mean the Automated Teller Machine or Asynchronous Transfer Mode? It depends on who is talking and who is listening.

The Solution

One of the most effective ways to rid a team of bias is through discovery and confrontation. Asking open-ended questions such as, "Why do you say this?" and, "What would happen if we did it this way?" will help to bring the bias to light. Confrontation is another effective method. It is especially helpful when the bias comes from attribution. Bringing the person or group being referenced together can verify or disprove the assumption. If the bias rests on unsubstantiated facts, ask for the source.

Biases are beliefs. Just because they tend to be deeply held doesn't make them wrong. It may be that the dissenter is correct. Yet, the team cannot accurately give the issue its due until the feeling itself and the reason behind it are brought clearly into the light.

Resolving Team Conflict

Erik J. Van Slyke

PM Network 85 (June 2000)

Conflict is a regular part of organization life. Whenever people form a team responsible for accomplishing an objective, they are going to have disagreements. Misunderstandings, personality clashes, and differences of opinion are standard fare for team interaction. At best, these conflicts provide an opportunity to learn and a chance for innovation. At worst, they can destroy individuals and bring productivity and effectiveness to a grinding halt.

Since conflict is such a common event that often produces important results, our goal as project leaders and individual team members should not be to eliminate it. Instead we should create an environment that encourages and maintains the positive and productive aspects of conflict. The problem is not so much conflict itself, but how teams deal with it. Not every conflict can be resolved, but we should at least approach all conflict with a mindset to seek constructive resolution.

When we are in conflict with another team member, the first step we often take toward resolution is to offer additional information intended to demonstrate the logic and reasoning that supports our view of a fair solution. When the parties remain unconvinced, we typically try harder to convince them by persuading, arguing, manipulating, sulking, bullying, or withdrawing from the interaction. Very often, this process proves time-consuming and frustrating, and the conflict ends without a satisfactory resolution. In the team environment, what started as one-on-one conflict can also create additional conflicts with teammates who are frustrated with the dispute. All parties walk away from the interaction thinking, "Why don't they listen to me?"

Exactly—listening is the key to constructive conflict resolution. The issue in conflict is not whether the other party listens to us, but rather whether we listen to and understand the other party's perspective. Only after we have listened to the other party will that party listen to us; only after the other party feels understood will that party want to understand and be influenced by us.

By seeking first to identify and understand the needs and interests of the other party, we create an environment that increases the chances of resolving the dispute in a way that is satisfactory to all parties involved. To achieve a true win/win resolution, we must first help the other party identify the criteria that will help that person achieve a win. The trust and relationship bonding that occurs as a result will prepare the other party to listen to our needs.

This collaborative process provides the information and emotional support necessary for collaborative problem solving. By creating a framework or moving beyond competition to cooperation, we can better identify a shared goal—the basis for true teamwork.

Collaboration requires that conflict resolution proceed through a series of steps that creates more effective interaction. Disputing parties must understand that each step is an important ingredient of the relationship-building process that leads to creative, team-based solutions. The steps progress logically and should be departed from only to return to a previous step as a means of enhancing the relationship and increasing understanding.

Prepare for the Interaction

Whether ongoing controversy or a new dispute, a few moments of focused attention prior to interaction will improve our effectiveness. Even if we are highly skilled and experienced in the resolution process, preparation for the current situation will help us remain constructive throughout the interaction.

Preparation gives us the big-picture perspective. It helps us think through the issues of conflict and try to come to an initial understanding of the interests involved for both us and the other party. We should spend almost as much time preparing for the interaction as we expect to spend resolving the conflict. In preparing, consider the following:

- What is the nature of the disagreement?
- What is the position of each party?
- What does each hope to accomplish?
- What will happen if we cannot resolve the issue?
- What information are we lacking to help us fully understand the situation?
- What is the history of the relationship between the disputing parties?
- Who has more power? Where does that power originate?
- Do we each have the authority to make and follow through on commitments?

Initiate the Exchange

Just because one team member has identified a troubling issue does not mean that the other person is aware of the problem. People's orientation to conflict may minimize their desire or ability for confrontation. They may not understand the specific problem, or they may lack conflict-management skills. Whatever the reason, we often have to initiate the exchange. How we communicate our problem will determine whether the confrontation escalates the tensions or keeps the resolution constructive.

The secret of constructive resolution is managing the emotions that can be ignited by the dispute. Conflicts turn into battles because we ignore them. Rather than confronting the other person, we sit on the issue often until we are ready to explode. It is critical that team members are encouraged to initiate the exchange, which involves:

- *Confronting*. Let the other party know that there is an issue to discuss; communicate in a supportive, open-ended manner. When confronting, it is important to communicate the problem and then demonstrate a desire to listen to the other person.
- *Involving*. The reason we listen to conflict is to involve the other party. Involving means asking for that person's perspective, opinion, feedback, and help.
- *Problem Solving*. Listen for the other person's perspectives, needs, and interests, and invite his analysis of the situation.

Facilitate the Relationship

For collaboration to succeed, both parties must be motivated to work together rather than compete. One can initiate the process, but eventually both must be in the collaborative mode in order to resolve the issue.

To facilitate the relationship during conflict, we must demonstrate a willingness to be open, and show that we trust the other person by sharing meaningful personal information. When both parties in conflict communicate openly and honestly, their needs and concerns can be identified. This provides the information required to shift the conflict from a positional dispute to interest-based problem solving. Interestingly, open communication by one person creates open communication by the other. The more we reveal about ourselves, the more the other person will reveal to us.

We also need to strive to create a positive and supportive emotional environment so that others feel good for having interacted with us. This can be accomplished by listening and trying to understand the issues, interests, and needs of the other person.

Interaction should be frequent. Shared interests and needs build a common sense of purpose that makes the objective issues easier to manage, and they strengthen teamwork.

Understand the Interests

Understanding the interests accomplishes two tasks critical to resolving the dispute. First, we learn the underlying interests and needs that are important to the other party, which must be satisfied if constructive resolution is to occur. We identify *why* the other person wants what she wants. Second, we establish the criteria or solutions. We identify *how we will know* if the agreement has fulfilled the interests of those involved. This is when listening skills are more important.

The second aspect of understanding the interests involves identifying the criteria by which the ultimate agreement will be measured. When an objective measurement system is established, both parties are counting the same things. If we hope to facilitate a long-lasting, constructive resolution, we need a tool to make sure that the agreed-upon solutions satisfy both sides.

Examine the Solutions

The search for solutions is the creative part of the collaboration process. Once both parties understand the interests and have established the criteria for solution, they can then generate a variety of possible options to solve the identified problems. A variety of team-based techniques, such as brainstorming or mind mapping, can be used to maximize creative potential and generate a host of ideas. Both parties should ensure that ideas are not criticized or judged as unworkable, too expensive, unrealistic, or too abstract. Third parties can also be invited to the process of generating ideas, as they can provide needed expertise or merely a fresh perspective on the situation.

Reach Consensus

Once options have been identified, all parties involved should evaluate the alternatives. Consensus is achieved when each party in conflict feels that he has been heard and understood by the other, is able to live with the decision or solution, and is willing to commit to his role during implementation.

Mediating Conflict

When team meetings disintegrate into tension-filled shouting matches, project leaders often have to intervene and facilitate the resolution process. As mediators, the goal is not simply to help parties agree, but also to develop and enhance constructive conflict-resolution skills within the team. Managing team conflict constructively involves making sure that interaction is based on a common set of objectives.

Shared Perception of Reality

By building and strengthening shared realities, project leaders create new affiliations that facilitate relationships and increase understanding of individual interests. The result is a shift from us versus them resistance to collaborative efforts based on the acceptance of unique individual creative contribution within the team.

Results-Oriented Operating Agreements

Operating agreements are the rules that guide creative, team-based interaction. These rules help us keep perspective; we recognize that sometimes team conflict does not necessarily feel constructive, but that is part of the larger process. The agreements should clearly identify the results required in order to achieve win/win solutions, as well as the objective, measurable criteria that will be used to assess results. In addition, they should identify how the team will measure the output to determine whether the solution meets expectations.

Clarified Roles and Accountabilities

For operating agreements to foster collaborative success, teams must establish clear delineation of the results expected by each interdependent contributor. Desired outcomes, communication requirements, resource conditions, and expertise should drive these roles. Teams should clarify areas of accountability, but should create some overlap that forces interaction.

Consensus Decision-Making

The consensus-building process manages the emotional elements and personal issues, and helps team members feel understood. Mediators should not decide how to resolve the conflict.

Formalized Conflict-Resolution Process

A formalized process gives the team permission to take a time out from its task orientation to manage conflicts as they occur.

By using listening as the means of guiding conflict from positional disagreement to an exchange of thoughts and ideas, project leaders can create an atmosphere of trust and collaboration. This enhances team interaction and leads to more innovative and effective results. Team members who adopt a collaborative focus learn to seek solutions that will satisfy themselves while simultaneously satisfying others. Team conflicts are then more easily transformed from bickering and competition to opportunities to learn, innovate, and grow.

Dealing with Dissent: The Story of Henry

Bud Baker

PM Network 17 (March 2000)

Henry is a good man. He's uncommonly bright and never fails to give 110 percent effort. He has a strong technical background and is committed to the success of his project. Henry is an ethical man with a well-developed sense of right and wrong.

A perfect team member, right? You'd like a dozen Henry-clones for your own project? Well, read on.

Henry's team was tackling a construction project. The goal of the project was clear, but the means to that end were not. Henry's approach offered substantial labor savings, but entailed high risk. The rest of the team advocated a labor-intensive, low-technology, lower-risk proposal.

The project manager heard both arguments and then sided with the majority: The project would go with the safe, low-risk technology, and thus avoid the risks associated with Henry's recommendation.

Now the fun began. As the project developed, the usual real-world problems began to arise. And at each turn, Henry would try to resurrect his own rejected approach. "It's not too late," he'd remind his team, "for us to change to the *right* way." Henry soon was using arguments that would make Machiavelli blush: "Well, finding a better way is just continuous improvement, isn't it? Isn't that something we all believe in?" He'd even conjure up the hallowed ghost of W. Edwards Deming: "I'm just trying to improve quality. You're not against quality, are you?"

Not surprisingly, Henry's maneuvering did not exactly endear him to his fellow team members. The first half of every staff meeting was spent rehashing Henry's proposal, the same proposal rejected months before. Email among project members became testy; then some authors began to omit Henry from emails altogether. Add to all this the frequent absences of the project manager, whose extensive travel often left the team without a great deal of supervision.

Eventually, the project concluded. Old-fashioned hard work won out over intraproject politics. The client was satisfied, but the damage to project team relationships, especially affecting Henry, will be a long time in healing.

Chances are that you've had a Henry on one of your teams or that you will some day. Keep in mind that Henry has skills that are vital to your project's success, and that, for the most part, his motives are pure—he *really* believes he's doing the right thing. You don't want to stifle his creativity, but you also can't stand the constant distraction, divisiveness, and damage to the morale of the project team.

So here's the question: *What does a project manager do with Henry?*

Fortunately, project managers aren't the first to face this dilemma. Military leaders have had all this worked out since before Julius Caesar ventured beyond the city gates of Rome. And generally, the stakes for the military leader are higher. Imagine Caesar facing the fearsome Gauls while Henry tugs at his sleeve, saying: "Gee, boss, do ya think this is such a great idea?"

The Royal Navy, in the time of Lord Nelson, handled their Henrys quite directly. They had thirty-six Articles of War, which were read to the ship's company every Sunday. (As almost each article decreed that the guilty party be executed, one suspects that the crew paid more attention than is customary in a staff meeting today.) The articles forbade any criticism of the ship's decision-making, under penalty of death.

These days, society takes a somewhat dimmer view of public executions of wayward team members, though most project managers have had days when the motivational tools of Lord Nelson looked pretty attractive. But out of life-and-death necessity, the modern military has developed a set of role expectations that can provide guidance to both project managers and team members.

First, military officers are taught that it is not only their *right* but also their solemn *duty* to tactfully share their true opinions with their leaders *up to—and this is the key—the point at which the leader makes the final decision*. Then the subordinates' duties shift: They must stifle their personal views and support the leader's choice, so long as personal conscience will allow.

This approach isn't perfect, but it is vastly superior to the sort of intramural warfare that someone like Henry can trigger. Project cultures change, but slowly. However, project managers can set the right tone for their efforts by clarifying expectations about dissent: When is it expected? When is it encouraged? When is it unwelcome? Such clarification would have gone a long way toward channeling Henry's behavior in a more productive direction.

The Misused Project Manager

David Perkins, PMP

PM Network 88 (September 2000)

Are you being asked to perform a significant number of tasks outside of your project manager role? Are you expected to execute many of your own project's tasks? Are you performing activities that require little intellectual or managerial stimulation? Do you feel a lack of organizational sponsorship in pursuit of additional project management skills? If you answered yes to any of these questions, you may be a misused project manager. Good project managers have a reputation for getting things done, whatever it takes. However, even project managers have limits. Abusing their skills or not providing them training to enhance their skills can have detrimental effects on project managers, on organizations, and even on others' perceptions of the project management profession.

How does one define a misused project manager? A general definition could be a project manager whose skills are improperly utilized or misapplied by functional departments, senior management, or both. Mistreatment of skills primarily occurs because organizations lack an understanding of and respect for the project management profession. When misuse is prevalent, a misuse life cycle is initiated, as shown in Figure 1.

Ultimately, misuse results in consequences to the project manager, the organization, and the project management profession. The project manager or the organization may pursue solutions to eradicate the misuse. If the solutions are accepted by the organization—project managers, senior management, executive management—and are realistically achievable, the benefits include retained project managers and more efficient organizational utilization of these managers. If the solutions are not accepted or even attainable, the same consequences could be amplified, or more negative consequences could result. An unfortunate consequence is that misused project managers may leave the company, while proper corrective actions could have prevented this from happening.

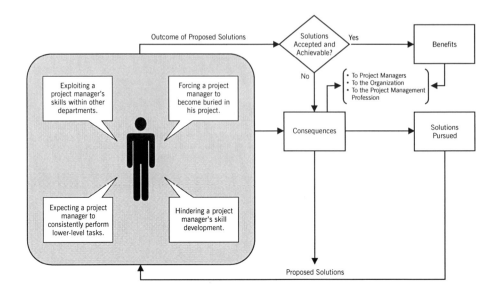

Figure 1. The Misuse Life Cycle

Elements of Misuse

Too Many Skills

The first element of misuse is *exploiting a project manager's skills within other departments*. A successful project manager is a seasoned, knowledgeable worker and has a superb suite of skill offerings. In fact, demonstrated proficiency in prior positions most likely leads to one's promotion to a project manager position. However, a project manager's skills may be so exceptional that organizations could be enticed to leverage those skills in other areas, often to the disadvantage of the project manager.

A popular example is requiring a project manager to be a resident technical expert outside of normal project activities. In general, being a technical "jack of all trades" and an effective project manager combines the best of both worlds—an especially successful combination in highly technical or specialized environments. Unfortunately, when the organization knows that a project manager is a technical expert, there is a temptation to lure him away from normal project management responsibilities. This can be a trap for some former engineers who have the reputation for "being technical." Moreover, this type of project manager may be suffering from technical skills exploitation and not even realize it! Whether the exploitation is forced or voluntary, the distressing result is that the project manager may become so entangled in the technical cobwebs of the organization that he could lose sight of the specific projects being managed.

Other examples of skills exploitation abound. This area of misuse generated much feedback (or venting) from correspondence with selected project managers. One project manager for a computer manufacturer is expected to create bill-of-materials orders, request part numbers, and even pull stock from the warehouse! A project manager at a distribution company is at risk of being relegated to line-management roles because of her abilities and prior experience in this type of work. If trapped in these roles, the number of projects she would be allowed to manage would diminish over time. Another project manager, a former technical trainer, is still expected to conduct training classes, provide technical support to clients, assist with writing or updating training materials, and support product demonstrations at trade shows. These situations illustrate that it can be difficult for a project manager to shake off previous roles, especially if considerable expertise has been demonstrated. The result is the organization's tendency to misapply a project manager's skills to these former roles.

Taking the Plunge

A second element of misuse is *forcing a project manager to become buried in his project*. How many times have you as a project manager been required to "dive into" your project in order to save it? One project manager at a small, family-owned company was required to write a 150-page user's manual in support of a project that he was managing. The result was seventy-hour workweeks for nearly a month! Another example is in product development, where project managers are sometimes required to write product test specifications and conduct validation tests for projects they are managing.

I do not want to imply that project managers are conceited or that they want to avoid specialized work. Many project managers enjoy immersing themselves in a project—perhaps longing for the days of previous occupations such as writing software or designing circuits. Also, it is good for the project team to occasionally see the project manager in the trenches with them, especially after normal hours, as this can help create team unity and mutual respect.

However, if a project manager is consistently mired in the details of his project and is expected to perform project-related tasks that would normally be assigned to functional departments, general oversight of the project could be lost; the result can be a failed project. Good project managers do not want to fail and will do whatever it takes to save a project. If project managers are subjected to this type of misuse over a long period of time, the unfortunate result could be increased stress and, ultimately, burnout.

Those Basic Tasks

As a project manager, how many times have you grumbled under your breath as the copier jams after the 200th copy? Or how about the transparencies that you have to run out and purchase because the presentation to your customer is to be delivered in one hour? I believe it can be safely assumed that most project managers have suffered from another element of misuse: *expecting a project manager to consistently perform basic tasks*. This appears to be a common Achilles' heel in most project management careers.

Professionals at almost every level have to perform basic tasks on occasion—make their own copies, send faxes, and so forth; with the proliferation of electronic devices, this is expected. However, where is the line drawn for project managers? When does the project manager stop being a gofer and start being a manager? A project manager will make the 200 copies and send the fifty-page fax, but the issue is that the professional project manager generally doesn't have the time to perform these tasks. These jobs can take the project manager away from managerial responsibilities. The result can be neglected projects. Efficient assistants are worth their weight in gold—project managers need their support in executing these basic tasks so that managers can devote more time to managing projects.

Not Enough Skills

Thus far, I have presented elements of misuse that relate to a project manager's existing skill set. But, what about the situation in which a project manager is not supported or encouraged to attain the proper project management skills in the first place? This leads to the final element of misuse: *hindering a project manager's skill development*. This element can be separated into two subelements: absence of company-sponsored project management training and lack of a defined project management career path within a company.

One of the most disheartening aspects of any position is when an organization does not value an individual's position, especially when the organization is unwilling to sponsor training to enhance that individual's professional skills in that position. The project manager position is no exception. Since the profession is only recently becoming part of the mainstream, many organizations simply do not see a need to improve their project managers' skills.

Lack of organization-sponsored training exists when other elements of misuse aleady are present. If an organization does not respect the role of project management, why would it want to improve the skills of its project managers? One project manager at an information technology company is expected to perform project management tasks, but the company is unwilling to sponsor any related skill-enhancement training. Out of necessity, she is required to purchase most of her own books and autonomously seek training courses. It's not surprising that this same project manager mentioned being subjected to areas of misuse previously discussed!

How about the situation where an organization is willing to enhance its project managers' skills, yet not provide a logical career path for these same project managers? Project managers need a predefined and logical (from a project management profession perspective) career path so that they are motivated to enhance their project management skills on behalf of the organization. It may be difficult for smaller companies to provide a realistic path, but larger companies that have many project managers on staff have no excuse. One project manager recently was offered a promotion from senior project manager to director of operations for a product assembly area. He rejected the offer because it did not represent a logical progression within the project management profession. Not surprisingly, the company did not have an established career path for its project managers.

Consequences of Misuse

The consequences to the project manager are obvious. Most likely a project manager will develop a sense of inequity if it is perceived that her peers are not as severely misused. If the project manager cannot tolerate the misuse, and if management is unwilling to rectify the situation, the obvious result could be apathy, high stress, or, ultimately, separation from the organization. If separation occurs, both sides lose—although the project manager may gain if a better position is found at another company.

Also, when prevalent over time, the element of expecting a project manager to consistently perform basic tasks could severely taint the image of a project manager. As an example, consider a functional manager that you know (perhaps your boss) and imagine her consistently performing basic tasks. Over a period of time, wouldn't this manager lose some of your respect and the respect of other subordinates? Project managers are managers and deserve the chance to gain the organization s esteem. Performing basic tasks on a consistent basis prevents this from happening. Table 1 lists the primary consequences to the project manager for each element of misuse.

The organization suffers when project managers are misused. If the pattern of misuse permeates the organization, a continual exodus of project managers could occur, resulting in a clearly negative organizational impact. Even the attitudes of those project managers who remain in the organization may suffer, resulting in lower team morale, possible team dysfunction, and overall project team disarray. Another way the organization suffers is that project managers as

Element of Misuse	Primary Consequences to the Project Manager
Exploiting a project manager's skills within other departments.	• Repercussions related to the neglect of direct project responsibilities. • Entrapment into formal roles. • Minimized cohesiveness in the project management department if many project managers are exploited.
Forcing a project manager to become buried in his project.	• Hindered ability to oversee a project(s) from a management perspective. • Increased stress from higher workload, possibly leading to burnout. • Project manager may become embittered.
Expecting a project manager to consistently perform lower-level tasks.	• Lack of respect from the organization. • Improper skills enhancement. • Increased apathy.
Hindering a project manager's skill development.	• Ill-equipped to perform job functions. • Inhibited project management skills enhancement. • Lack of direction regarding career path within the organization.

Table 1. Primary Consequences to the Project Manager for Each Element of Misuse

resources are inefficiently applied. The organization does not get the "bang for its buck!" Table 2 lists primary consequences to the organization for each element of misuse; note that some consequences can apply to multiple elements of misuse.

The overall perception of the project management profession also suffers when project managers are misused. This is especially true for those entering the profession. When new project managers observe their peers doing a significant amount of work outside of the department, being inundated with detailed project tasks, consistently performing basic tasks, or not being trained properly, an inaccurate first impression could develop. This could cause newcomers to doubt their project management career choice and pursue other careers. If misuse is widespread, even members within the organization who interact with project managers on a daily basis will develop a negative perception of the project management profession.

Element of Misuse	Primary Consequences to the Organization
Exploiting a project manager's skills within other departments.	• Other departments may develop false expectations. • Project management responsibilities may get neglected.
Forcing a project manager to become buried in his project.	• Potential discontinuity within the project team. • Project management support for the project threatened.
Expecting a project manager to consistently perform lower-level tasks.	• Organizations develop false perceptions of what project managers can really do. • Overcompensation for lower-level work.
Hindering a project manager's skill development.	• Project managers are not as effective as they could be. • Misguided project management career paths.

Table 2. Primary Consequences to the Organization for Each Element of Misuse

Breaking the Pattern of Misuse

Breaking the pattern of misuse can be a daunting task for the project manager, and it largely depends upon the characteristics of organizational culture, politics, and so forth. One approach is to educate your immediate supervisor and your immediate supervisor's supervisor about the true benefits of project management. This can be easier said than done, particularly if your management is unwilling to learn about project management practices. Another strategy is to identify someone in senior management who may be open to implementing project management practices, request confidentiality, and submit a business plan showing the return on investment as a result of implementing such practices. Since executive management will be concerned with the value added to the company, showing ROI is critical. An unfortunate last resort is to realize that there is no hope for change, and leave the company. Table 3 makes recommendations for breaking patterns of misuse.

Warning Signs When Pursuing a New Position

When seeking a new position, avoid being placed in a misuse situation by looking for warning signs, as outlined in Table 4.

Element of Misuse	Breaking the Pattern of Misuse
Exploiting a project manager's skills within other departments.	• Require your services to be fee based. • Set expectations for duration of your services at least a month in advance.
Forcing a project manager to become buried in his project.	• Log how may hours you spend each day doing functional area work, compare against your managerial activities, and communicate data to senior management. • Provide creative incentives to your project team to pick up the slack.
Expecting a project manager to consistently perform lower-level tasks.	• Document how may hours you spend each day on these tasks, show the loss of productive project management work, and communicate data to senior management. • Attempt to outsource these tasks to another person (if allowed, be open to compensating him from your budget).
Hindering a project manager's skill development.	• Obtain training autonomously and then prove to the organization that it makes a difference. • Develop and communicate a proposed career plan for you to grow within the organization, highlighting benefits to the company.

Table 3. Breaking the Pattern of Misuse for Each Element

At the individual level, the job interview provides a good opportunity to look for warning signs. Notice if the interviewer is asking you detailed questions about your professional project management skills. Also observe whether the interviewer is focusing more on your specialized experience and less on your project management experience. If so, this could imply that you would be drawn into more specialized work as opposed to managing it. Attempt to ascertain if the interviewer (to whom you would be reporting) is demonstrating a lack of project management knowledge.

At the organizational level, investigate prospective companies, and try to determine if they have documented and implemented business practices specifically related to project management. If so, attempt to determine if the practices have been institutionalized, and for how long. If not institutionalized, this could indicate a lack of formal project management structure—a major red alert! Determine if the organization has (or is obtaining) formal certifications (for

Setting	Warning Signs
At the Individual Level (Job Interview)	• Interviewer not asking you detailed questions about your professional project management skills. • Interviewer focusing more on your specialized (e.g., technical, training, etc.) experience and less on your project management experience. • Interviewer (to whom you would be reporting) demonstrating a lack of project management knowledge.
At the Organizational Level (Facts)	• Organization does not have documented, implemented, and institutionalized project management practices. • Organizations project management practices are not consistent with industry-recognized standards. • Organizational structure does not grant formal authority to project managers.

Table 4. Warning Signs When Pursuing a New Position

example, ISO 9000 or Software Capability Maturity Model Level 2) and then relate these certifications to accepted project management practices. Finally, ascertain if the company's organizational structure formally empowers its project managers.

Organizations need sound project management practices! Eliminating the elements of misuse will allow companies to retain project management professionals, minimize adverse effects to their departments, and create a climate that draws others to the profession. As the project management profession continues to gain prominence, the likely (and hopeful) result will be a continued downward trend in the misuse of project managers.

Section 7

Closeout and Evaluation

The Forgotten Phase

Paula K. Martin and Karen Tate, PMP

PM Network 29 (February 2000)

Whether you use a four- or five-phase project management model, the last phase is always closeout, the phase that most project teams forget.

After the final deliverable is delivered to the customer, most project teams think that they're done—that the project is over. But they're wrong. They still need to complete the last phase of the project management process—closeout.

Very few project teams take the time to complete closeout, thus condemning themselves to making the same mistakes over and over, because it's during closeout that we capture our lessons learned and transmit what we have learned to others.

The closeout phase can be broken down into three broad categories of activities: evaluation, lessons learned, and sponsor review. After the customer has accepted the final deliverable, it's time to have the customer evaluate the project. Is the customer satisfied with the final deliverable? Did it meet his needs and expectations? How would he rate the project process? Was he kept informed? Did he have the level of input or participation he desired? What would he have you do differently next time?

You'll also want to get similar feedback from the sponsor and any other key stakeholders. Have them complete a simple evaluation form, or sit down with them and interview them. What went well? What would they change? You'll want your team members to complete a similar evaluation of the project. In addition, you'll want them to assess the team process—how well did the team members work together? Did the team achieve the performing stage of team development and if not, why not? Were the team meetings productive? How could they be improved? And so forth.

Next, you need to complete the final status report, which should include the customer's rating of the final deliverable, final status of deadlines, budgets, and changes to the plan. Now you're ready to have the lessons-learned meeting with the project team.

One way to develop the lessons learned with the team is to do an affinity diagram. Ask each person to write on Post-it Notes their ideas of what went well and what they would do differently next time. Then place the Post-it Notes on two pieces of banner paper—one for each topic. After all the Post-it Notes are on the wall, ask the team to group them within each topic. This should be done silently. After all the topics have been organized, ask the team to write a lessons-learned statement that captures each grouping. This provides a semi-anonymous way to capture everyone's ideas and process these into the group's lessons learned. Go through the final status report and evaluate each section. "How did we do in this area?" "What could we have done better?" Add any new lessons learned to the list. This process will help team members internalize the lessons learned and capture the group's consensus for inclusion in the closeout report.

Next, discuss how the team's lessons learned might be turned into recommendations for improving the overall project management system in the organization. Include these recommendations in the closeout report. This report should include an executive summary, the final status report, lessons learned, and recommendations for improvement. Set up a sponsor review meeting to go over the closeout report before it's issued.

After you issue the report, you're still not done. What's left? Celebration! Take a minute to pat yourself on the back for the good work you've done. And don't forget to recognize individual team member's contributions, as well as those of the whole team.

Closeout is a critical part of the project management process. It's how we learn to do better next time. Skip it at your own and your organization's risk.

How to Prepare and Conduct a Project Review

Joan Knutson

PM Network 6 (October 1996)

At the end of ninety days plus one month, a program manager conducts a project review. Why ninety days plus one month? Well, the project has been under way for three months (one quarter) and it takes one month to prepare the briefing. The program manager makes his report at the project review meeting and one or more of the following occurs: a new schedule is distributed; a new design/technical approach is recommended; the status of the first deliverables has been changed from complete to "preliminary" or has a to-do list attached; and/or it is announced that the first milestone has already been missed.

Sound familiar? With a complex project, aggressively bid, it isn't a matter of *whether* you'll get into trouble; it's a matter of how soon you'll get into trouble—and how fast you can get out of it. Typical pitfalls that portend trouble for a project are:

- Excessive optimism (or pessimism) when estimating the job.
- Ignoring early danger signals (a project does not into get into trouble in one day).
- Hoping things will "work themselves out"—the ostrich approach.
- Suppressing bad news/problems.
- Submitting to organizational politics rather than doing the correct thing.
- Relying upon secondhand inputs rather than digging in yourself where there are major problems.
- Not asking for help.
- Fear of hurting peoples' feelings or becoming unpopular (project management is not the place to make a bid for the congeniality award).

Don't Lose It

Don't wait for trouble to surface. At the end of the first week, conduct a project review meeting. At this meeting, the key question should be, *"Were the milestones met?"* If the answer is "Yes," review the deliverables in detail. Have they been quality controlled? Of prime importance is whether or not the people/functional areas that will use these deliverables find them acceptable.

Slippage can create disastrous delays and backlogs. Assume the project has ten milestones that have to be met each week, and on week one you have missed five of them. Consequently, the next week fifteen milestones must be completed, the ten required for the second week in addition to the five that were not completed the first week. Run this scenario out, and you will have a pyramid of delayed milestones. It does not take an advanced degree in math to figure out that this project is in deep trouble.

Preparing for a Review

When milestones are not being met, the program manager should be focusing upon why it is not done; the impact of it not being done; when it will be done; if a work-around is needed; and the earliest date to get the project back on schedule. These problems should be resolved at the project review meeting.

Clearly Define the Objective of the Meeting

Each project review briefing cannot cover in detail each issue and every aspect of the project—schedule, budget, resource utilization, quality, and technical and design considerations. The participants who will attend should determine the objective.

As an illustration, if the attendees are the management committee and/or the customer, they will want to concentrate on problem isolation and resolution. They will want to know about what has gone wrong, what you have done to fix it, and what, if any, support you need from them. If the audience is the project team, you will be concerned about the fundamental nitty-gritty areas. You/they will want to know what has been accomplished, what slipped, what impact the slippage had on the project, what is being done about it, and what is coming up in the near future. With these issues in perspective, you have the basis for a renewed recommitment to completion.

Prepare a Well-Thought-Out Agenda

Allocate your agenda time wisely. Cover the most important topics early, when people are alert and will address them with vigor. Later in the meeting people may get tired and preoccupied and make commitments that are not well-thought-out. Future problems and misunderstandings may result. On your copy of the agenda, insert the scheduled time for each topic in the margin. Allow some buffer time in case the topic takes longer than expected. Preview the agenda with the appropriate people to ensure that you have not omitted anything, included anything extraneous, or neglected to clarify the objective of each topic.

Invite the Essential People

It serves no purpose to have all team members attend every meeting. Of course, a "core team" should always be present. Beyond that, the balance of the team members should be encouraged to attend only when they have something to contribute or have a need to be kept informed. A project review meeting on the first Monday of each month could become tedious if the agenda has no relevance to the current activities of the attendees.

Dry Run "High Risk" Speakers

The program manager should not always make the entire presentation. For example, an engineer may report on a technical design, a marketing representative on a sales strategy, or a computer programmer on a new automated system. Before the presentation request that your speakers walk through (talk through) their presentation, both for their benefit and for yours. It is too late to make modifications when they are in front of the audience presenting erroneous or inappropriate data.

Organize the Meeting to Your Best Advantage

As the first speaker, you will present an overview of the meeting, the objective to be reached, and a quick preview of the agenda. With this effective form of introduction, you both set the tone and alert the participants to your major concerns.

Conducting the Review

Once the agenda is set, follow it! It is essential to follow the logical sequence of topics and not to stray from the format. If an attendee attempts to circumvent your game plan, use the agenda to bring the subject back into focus.

Don't overrun your agenda. Since most schedules are tight, people allocate just so much time to your review meeting. Since there is a prevailing feeling that too much time is spent in meetings, make the briefing concise and stay on target. Record time allotment on the margin of your working agenda. Maintain your pace and move on when you need to. When appropriate, carry the discussion over to the next meeting. Assign to team members the responsibility of investigating subjects and reviewing the results before the next meeting. Remember the rule of thumb: People can be productive in a meeting environment for approximately one to one-and-a-half hours. After that, it's all downhill.

Don't lose control of your meeting. If you can't manage a project review meeting, what does that tell your boss, customer, or your project team members?

Typical Agenda

An agenda for a project review briefing might include:

- Major accomplishments since the last review.
- Schedule status (actual versus plan).
- Financial status (actual versus plan)—including a clear explanation of variances from the plan.
- Major issues (problems) and action plans. Indicate specific assistance required from management or the customer, as well as from any of the functional areas within the matrix. These action plans must include deliverables and deadlines.
- Plans for the next period.
- Special topics (just the ones with a sense of urgency).
- Review of action items generated from this meeting and a time and place for the next meeting.

Questions to Ask

A list of questions, beyond the obvious ones on time and budget, to ask the project team members at the briefing could include the following: Do you foresee any future problems? Is your labor force in jeopardy, i.e., people being pulled off projects? Is there dissatisfaction among your people? What's bothering them? How are you dealing with recurrent problems? What sources of input are you lacking to do your job? Have you made preparation for long-lead deliveries? Are you accepting substantive changes that should be addressed in a change control (change of scope) process?

Reviewing Specialists

Nearly 200 years ago, French statesman Charles Maurice de Talleyrand-Perigord noted, "War is much too serious a matter to be entrusted to the generals." Today's project management corollary is: "The success of your project is too serious a matter to be entrusted solely to specialists." You can't afford to lose control of your project by permitting the experts to function beyond their area of expertise and beyond that which makes common sense to you. No matter how competent the specialist, many lack your breadth and perspective to envision how all the pieces fit together. However, you must endure the pain and invest the time to gain an insight into specialized areas of expertise.

If you are a program manager for the engineering group and have never been on the manufacturing plant floor, or if you are in the construction world and rarely go to the site, or if you are in the information services area and haven't recently visited either the computer room or the user's location, you are making a big mistake.

You have two means of survival when reviewing specialists who possess an expertise in a highly specialized area. 1) Do your homework so that you have a working knowledge of their area, and make them aware of your efforts to familiarize yourself with their world. 2) Break the work packages into small segments, with short time frames, and clearly defined deliverables so that you will then be in a position to ensure quality and maintain overall control.

Focusing on Yesterday, Today, and Tomorrow

The program manager must monitor and control the project from the outset—the first day would not be too soon. Your sense of urgency and commitment will set the pace from the beginning. As a means of establishing control, arrange for a formal project review briefing at the end of the first week. Prepare thoroughly for every briefing. This means more than just creating beautiful overheads or flip charts. Think through the objectives of the meeting and the strategies that you will use to reach those objectives. Some obvious issues must be addressed: Is the project meeting the baselines? If not, what factors are involved? What is the future impact? How will we get back on track? But there may be other, more subtle issues; you must flush out the underlying people and/or political conflicts or small, unresolved problems could grow in magnitude. Direct your attention to the future through your concern with projection/trend analysis, forecasts, as well as the current environment—your focus should simultaneously be on yesterday, today, and tomorrow.

Direct special attention to the review of those people on the team with a special expertise. Projects have been adversely impacted by the well-meaning optimism of a technocrat who did not understand the effect of their slippage on the balance of the project.

For you, the program manager, a well-run project review is the forum in which you can accomplish many of your key objectives: improve communications, motivate the project team, maintain control, evaluate status, isolate problems, institute action plans. Use this opportunity well!

Employee Evaluation and Appraisal

Cornelius Flynn

PM Network 37 (August 1997)

Just as managers are judged on the success or failure of the projects to which they are assigned, nonmanagement staff—rightly or wrongly—is rated in the same way. Most organizations recognize this, and have in place some system by which all employees, including managers, are assessed on a regular basis by a system generally referred to as the "performance appraisal system."

An organization's performance appraisal system generates valid information about employee work effectiveness for the purpose of making informed human resource decisions. A systematic assessment of how effectively each job is being performed, appraisal also tries to identify the reasons for a particular level of performance and seeks ways to improve future performance.

Organizations must evaluate employee performance for a number of reasons. Employees must behave in a desired manner on the job and their work must be evaluated for its contributions to organizational goals. But also, employees should clearly understand what the organization expects in terms of performance, and they need to know that valid information about their performance is used to make decisions about salary increases, promotions, bonuses, and training. With a good performance appraisal system in place, employees' motivation to do a good job should be increased because they know that salient rewards are linked to measured performance.

Organizations realize that a good appraisal system also makes managers more effective. Managers can use the performance appraisal system as a motivational tool. An effective appraisal system creates many opportunities for providing formal and informal feedback about performance. If there is no formal, objective performance appraisal system, employees often believe that the organization is uninterested in treating them fairly.

The Appraisal Process

A key feature of an appraisal system is to separate personal from organizational determinants of job performance. Our natural tendency for dealing with ineffectiveness is to emphasize the individuals' inadequacies while ignoring the organization's contribution to providing conditions to make effective performance possible. But there are subtle, crucial distinctions that must be drawn between individual determinants and the organizational determinants of job performance.

Individual differences in the workplace fall into three categories: core characteristics, skills, and motivation. In seeking to understand the reasons for an individual's level of performance, all three are important. However, in terms of the practical objective of improving job performance to the benefit of both the individual and the organization, core characteristics are of much less relevance. There is no gain from highlighting a perceived inadequacy in an individual unless there is some possibility of remedying the situation. Skills and motivation, on the other hand, can be modified through training and incentives, and are therefore of greater relevance for appraisal systems.

The starting point for deciding what should be appraised is a systematic job analysis, with special emphasis on skills and motivation rather than on core abilities. As far as collecting and recording the data is concerned, a number of different performance rating systems have been developed and are commercially available.

As far as the personal determinants of job performance are concerned, the first stage in any appraisal system is to determine the individual's level of effectiveness by identifying how his abilities, skills, and motivations interact with the various responsibilities and tasks identified by the job analysis. The next stage is to provide feedback to the individual about his performance. Since a key objective of any appraisal system is to find mutually agreed-upon ways of improving performance, it is vital that the appraiser and employee agree not only on current performance, but also on what needs to be done to improve it. Following on from this is the identification of the employee's training and development needs. The training and development aspect should not concentrate solely on skill requirements for the individual's current job but should also focus, where appropriate, on the development of the individual for a more important position in the future. Once all of these steps have been completed, the appraiser and the individual being appraised should agree on realistic performance objectives to be achieved by the next review period. In this context, the appraiser should also be in a position to indicate the organizational resources that will be provided to help achieve these objectives.

Appraisal data can also be used as additional information to aid various personnel decisions, such as promotions, transfers, and determination of financial rewards. A good appraisal system has to strike a delicate balance between being used as an aid to personnel decisions and being used to determine training and development needs.

While appraisal concentrates on the individual, the appraiser may also identify shortcomings at the organizational level, leading to changes in job design or resource allocation. Once the organization identifies the appraisers, it must give them the tools to do the job, including the influence or authority needed to support or implement organizational changes leading to better performance. A key factor here is appropriate training for the appraisers themselves. Such training should encompass what aspects of performance should be appraised and how the information is to be collected and recorded.

The Interview

The customary vehicle for discussing appraisal data with individuals is the appraisal interview. Such interviews are understandably delicate since the agenda highlights perceived shortcomings and inadequacies, as well as strengths, between people with whom good working relationships are expected to be maintained in the future. Consequently, the success of any appraisal system depends on the skills of the appraisal interviewers. While no prescriptive set of rules can be given for such interviews because of the complex human interactions involved, some basic guidelines can be suggested.

First, apparent deficiencies in the core skills should not be the subject of discussion since the employee is unable to modify them. The focus should always be on modifiable behaviors. The word *behavior* should be emphasized here because the more the interviewer and the employee can identify concrete behavioral events of the past, the more readily they can agree about past performance and changes for the future.

For the system to work, interviewers must give authentic feedback about both positive and negative aspects of performance. Interviews that focus exclusively on the positive, while ignoring needs for improvement, cannot achieve their purpose. Conversely, those that focus only on the negative can be demotivating for the employee.

The provision of training opportunities is a key aspect of appraisal. Interviewers must be willing and able to commit resources not just for training individuals for their current job but also to develop those who have the potential for more responsible jobs in the future. If resources are not available due to reasons outside the control of the manager, then the manager is obliged to inform the employee that the absence of further development opportunities is not a reflection on performance. Naturally, if a manager does not offer resources based solely on performance, the employee should be made aware of this.

Upward communication is encouraged in the interview; otherwise, the employee may perceive the whole procedure as dictatorial. It is also critical that mutually agreed-upon, realistic targets are set for the future. It is well documented that individuals given realistic targets that they accept are more motivated to reach such targets. This can be difficult for both manager and employee if the goal of the employee is to assume the manager's position. In this type of situation, the employee may not express a goal or the manager deliberately may not make resources available for the development of the employee. It is advisable that the organization assign a different appraiser for this appraisal, particularly if a review of previous appraisals presents the potential for uneasiness at the interview or uncertainty with the classification of the employee.

Appraisals should never be an exercise where all instances of inefficiency are blamed on the shortcomings of the employee. Jobs are often performed ineffectively because organizations have failed to resource them properly and no amount of training, goal-setting, or exhortation to do better will overcome such organizational sources of inefficiency.

Follow-Up

A common complaint regarding the appraisal system is that employees perceive the process as an annual affair that's ignored during the intervening times. For the system to be successful for both the organization and the employee, it is essential that the system be continually monitored as it tracks the employee's path. This continuous assessment applies both between appraisals and to the overall career development of the employee. This is particularly true if an employee has experienced a constant change of managers, for reasons outside of performance. If resources are requested and not subsequently used, or an agreed-upon career plan is not followed, then management has reason to have concern. Remember, the growth of employees is for the mutual benefit of both the employee and the organization; of course, goals can be changed over time by both parties. Thus, it is essential that both the manager and the employee continually assess the forward-looking aspects of appraisals.

Pitfalls

Few managers would question the organization's need to assess the performance behavior of its employees or that the process of assessment must produce results that are both fair and accurate. However, errors can enter the process when the manager fails to observe performance accurately or provide timely feedback to employees on their performance and goals. Errors also seep into the process if the organization does not train new managers in the proper techniques of appraisal.

The errors that occur in performance appraisal work are usually errors resulting from variation problems concerning the validity of the performance appraisal system. Validity refers to the quality of the measuring components in a performance appraisal system. It should be confirmed that the components actually measure what they are supposed to measure. The most common errors are:

- Personal bias—a stereotype or bias that influences a rating upward or downward.
- Halo effect—rating an employee the same on all performance dimensions because of a general impression.
- Recency error—the emphasis of recent performance examples in making performance assessments.
- Central tendency error—assigning average ratings to all employees, causing little variation among ratings.
- Strictness or leniency errors—supervisor ratings based on the belief that no employees measure up to standard, or that all employees measure up to standard.
- Similarity error—supervisor has a personal performance quality that she looks for in subordinates.
- Forcing the rating—deciding an overall rating first and then going back to adjust ratings on individual dimensions to justify the overall rating.

It is paramount to the success of an appraisal system that all parties are keenly aware of the role of the system and the duties of all involved. Although training for the supervisors is highly recommended, it is widely felt that those lower-level employees being evaluated also be given at least some informal training in the process. This will allow employees to recognize any errors made during the process, and such knowledge will allow an informed appeal to be lodged if necessary. The more the system is understood, the greater the probability of it being a success within an organization.

Finally, a Way to Completely Measure Project Manager Performance

Dick Cochran

PM Network 75 (September 2000)

Each project manager has tools to assess the performance of a project, including timelines, deliverables, budgets, and quality standards. But how can you measure the achievements of the project managers? Specifically, what tool gives you such detail that both those who hire, assign, and promote project managers, and project managers themselves, get meaningful feedback?

Project management evaluation is typically looked at as "on time, on budget, on purpose." But how competently a project manager completes a project is also critically important. Because each of the project manager skills can significantly impact the quality of any project, this conventional approach to measuring success just isn't enough.

The managers of project managers—those ultimately responsible for a project's success—need to know how to assess every aspect of the project manager's performance. And project managers themselves have high stakes in getting a complete and fair review when it comes to knowing their own strengths and weaknesses.

Why Measure Competencies?

Measuring competencies answers the following questions and more: What is the project manager's impact on the people of the organization? Did someone quit because of poor management and direction? Not being respected or feeling out of the loop, underused, or undervalued? Indeed, measuring a competency such as interpersonal and communication skills could prevent problems that result in people walking away from the project. Certainly, a deficit in a competency such as personal values might antagonize certain groups whose support is needed for future projects. And poor marks in the competency of customer focus could discourage stakeholders from all areas. When competencies are weak, therefore, the quality of any project is substantially lowered.

Using quantitative measurements from a variety of key people, not just the boss, gives a much more complete picture of a project manager's performance. In fact, this feedback is even more critical for a project manager whose team members do not report directly to him. Instead of having the clout of being the boss, the manager's power comes from honing communication and leadership skills to a fine point. Measuring competencies in a meaningful way reveals the true value of work.

360-Degree Feedback Tool

In the October 1999 issue of *PM Network*, Judith Olney wrote, "It's important to measure the ability of all project managers to apply project management skills and capabilities *effectively*." The only way to obtain this type of data is through 360-degree assessments or behavior event interviewing.

The term *360-degree feedback* refers to getting a well-rounded (360-degree) view of what's going on. Input is gathered from a variety of people surrounding the project manager whose skills are being measured. Thus, the best input comes from the boss, peers, team members, direct reports, stakeholders, and others in project support positions that work closely with the project manager.

Customized Competencies

One company I work with found the 360-degree feedback tool very helpful in measuring the comparative performances of a group of project managers. The manager in charge of the evaluation started by identifying the competencies critical to customer success and then created a customized set with them. This set is specifically related to each project manager's responsibilities in this company. Being able to customize the competencies made the measurement much more relevant than having fixed categories—a strong advantage of the 360-degree feedback tool.

Your organization might choose different ones than those selected by my client, which were project planning, project management, leadership, people management, business management, interpersonal and communications skills, personal characteristics and values, and client focus.

Behaviors and Measures

Practically speaking, competencies themselves are too broad for accurate assessment. It's difficult to answer a vague question like, "How are the interper-

```
1 = Unacceptable/Failing
2 = Below Standard/Poor
3 = Fair/Lower End of Average Range
4 = Meets Standard/Average
5 = Good/Higher End of Average Range
6 = Exceeds Standard/Excellent
7 = Outstanding
N = Does Not Apply
```

Table 1. Assigned Value Scale

sonal and communication skills?" So, for each competency, my client identified several behaviors, which include specific activities that define the competency. For example, the interpersonal and communications skills competency would have these behaviors: keeps people informed, writes effectively, is a good listener, and develops productive one-on-one relationships.

Those individuals who interacted with the project manager whose performance was being measured rated each of these behaviors. Based on seeing that person in action at work, the raters gave a quantitative score to each behavior on the survey.

To increase the validity of the raters' observations and make sure they all use the same scorecard, measures, which are agreed upon and observable indicators of a particular behavior further define the behaviors. Under interpersonal and communications skills, for example, the observable behavior of keeps people informed was broken into three measures that indicate behavior: seeks information from others, provides timely information, and is respected by others as a source.

Assign Values

Then the raters (peers, direct reports, team members, bosses, stakeholders, suppliers, support people, other managers, and so forth) assigned a value from 1 to 7 or N for each behavior (see Table 1).

The assigned value scale is designed from 1 to 7 or N for many reasons. Using an odd number allows an observed behavior to be rated right in the middle. When they have a greater choice than 1, 2, or 3, raters feel that they can be fairer and differentiate more carefully in their ratings. In addition, having an N choice for "does not apply" or "no response" is important in order to get an honest "I don't know" response. Giving this as a choice, rather than forcing an uncertain one, also makes the data more valid.

Here's how three groups rated the project manager's behavior under the interpersonal and communications skills competency of keeps people informed: score from managers, 6.1; score from team members, 4.9; score from peers, 5.5. The assigned numbers show an average of the values that the three categories of raters gave for one behavior. The overall rating for keeps people informed was 5.5.

Best Respondents

The best respondents include those who have the most interaction with the project manager: supervisors, team members, direct reports, and so on. In fact, each respondent can provide a different perspective on the project manager's performance. The better the selection of respondents who rate the project manager's activities, the more valuable the feedback. This is where the value of the 360-degree feedback tool really shines. From here, you can build a complete picture of the performance based on each of the agreed-upon competencies and behaviors.

Confidential Input and Reporting

Doing a traditional performance evaluation for anyone can be a time consuming process. That's why companies don't conduct them frequently and often leave them incomplete.

Today's advanced communications and computing power, though, help smooth the process and improve the quality of feedback. How? By putting a 360-degree feedback survey on a floppy disk or, even better, using the Internet. Using this tool, each survey takes a rater or respondent only fifteen minutes to complete and the data from all respondents can be sent to an automated collection area where it is compiled into a comprehensive forty-page report.

This process assures confidentiality—that, in turn, assures more thorough and honest feedback from respondents. It also puts the information in control of a disinterested party outside the company, never in the hands of an individual who could abuse the confidentiality requirement.

The report generated allows people to mine the data for useful information that can be viewed from a variety of perspectives. In the example shown in Figure 1, a project manager's performance is compared against the average performance of all project managers in the company. Notice that the project manager is rated higher than the group in the leadership competency, but lower in product management and business management. This feedback suggests important areas in which the project manager can improve during the next review cycle.

Information can also be viewed according to the category of respondents, as shown in Figure 2. The top line on this graph shows the project manager's self-score. It looks as if the project manager in Figure 2 has a consistently high opinion of himself. The point of concern comes from seeing where the project manager's boss rated him on the bottom line on the graph. Note that the team

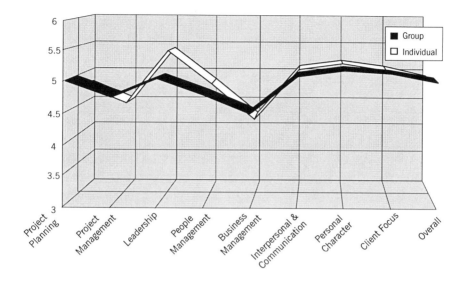

Figure 1. Individual Compared to Group

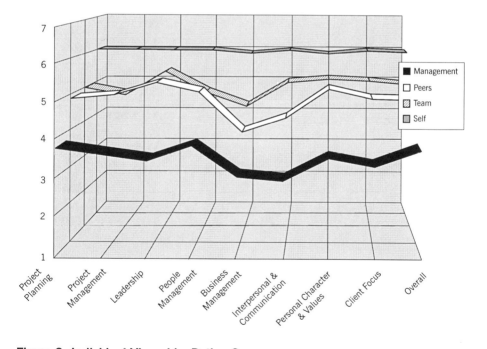

Figure 2. Individual Viewed by Rating Group

rating of the project manager's performance is in the middle of the two. This shows a significant discrepancy, so it should be discussed and resolved, taking into account all points of view.

As these examples show, the 360-degree feedback report helps understand how well project managers perform, in their own eyes and in the eyes of those with whom they work, measured against the key competencies and behaviors necessary to be successful in the job.

Successful Implementation

Satisfied users have found the key to using this 360-degree feedback tool well is to take time initially to build people's confidence in the process. That involves communicating its purpose clearly to all participants. Exactly for what will the information be used? Will project managers agree to use the feedback as a way to start improving their people skills on the job? Will the organization use it to set salaries and grant future projects? Determining these issues upfront will garner the right kind of support needed for the always-sensitive evaluation process.

I recommend that you look at the first 360-degree feedback conducted for each project manager as a development tool only. It becomes a benchmark for an ongoing evaluation program. It also can help verify the clarity and selection of the competencies themselves.

References

Olney, Judith. 1999. Executive Notebook: Measuring Project Manager Competence. *PM Network* (October): 21–22.

Section 8

Worldwide Teams and Cultural Issues

The Virtual Project: Managing Tomorrow's Team Today

John R. Adams and Laura L. Adams

PM Network 37 (January 1997)

Extraordinary demands are placed on project personnel—demands that require extraordinary commitments in order to accomplish the task at hand. Generating this commitment through the process of team building is a primary responsibility of any project manager. The processes of team building have been studied extensively by both academics and practitioners for decades, but until recently nearly all of these studies were conducted within the bureaucratic setting—that is, the team members shared a common workplace, saw each other frequently, knew each other well, and expected to continue working together for an extended period of time. The team-building concepts developed within such an environment naturally reflect these working conditions as either stated or implied assumptions, and the concepts derived from these studies can be assumed to hold only as long as these assumptions hold.

These concepts still hold for projects intended to support and improve bureaucratic organizations. In the vast majority of cases, however, the working conditions experienced by modern projects differ greatly from those surrounding traditional bureaucratic work. Nevertheless, the basic definitions of team building continue to emphasize the assumption of typical bureaucratic working conditions. For example, one leading textbook in the field states that "actual teamwork involves small groups of three to fifteen people that meet face-to-face to carry out their assignments" (Kast and Rosenzweig 1985). Even in the Project Management Institute's *A Guide to the Project Management Body of Knowledge* (*PMBOK® Guide*), one of the five basic "tools and techniques" of team development is called "collocation," which "involves placing all, or almost all, of the most active project team members in the same physical location to enhance their ability to perform as a team" (2000, 115). In both of these publications, the concept of the "virtual project" is clearly ignored.

In the new, virtual-project environment, team members seldom share a common workplace, may rarely see each other, may never have worked together before, and may never work together again after the project is complete. For an ever-increasing number of organizations, the world is represented by an environment of rapid technological advancement, particularly in the area of communications; complex organizational structures needed to deal with tough global competition; and dynamic markets that demand short production runs of unique products. Downsizing, outsourcing, and employee empowerment have become facts of life in the climate of many organizations, while job security is rapidly becoming a thing of the past. The survival of many organizations depends on the ability of the organization to rapidly change its structure, culture, and products to match the changing demands of the environment. Let's explore the conditions faced by the modern project manager in developing an effective and productive project team within a virtual project.

The Virtual Project

The virtual project, also known as a "distributed team," is one in which the participants are geographically distributed to an extent that they may seldom, if ever, meet face to face as a team. The geographical distances involved do not have to be great; individuals who work in the same industrial complex may be functioning in a virtual project if their schedules do not allow them to meet face to face. As distances increase, however, the difficulties of communicating and building teams increase significantly. When team members are spread across several time zones, opportunity for direct communication is severely limited, and the associated costs of both face-to-face and electronic communications increase dramatically. Electronic communication takes on much more importance in virtual projects because electronic systems must assume the burden of making the development of effective project teams possible.

Jaclyn Kostner has written extensively on the virtual project. In *Knights of the Tele-Round Table* (1994), she documents the unique issues faced by project managers who must manage such a virtual or distributed project. The issues she defines are shown in Table 1.

Developing trust is the greatest challenge to the remote project manager. It's difficult for distant team members to get to know each other well; consequently, they tend to communicate poorly because they often are less than comfortable with each other. Both of these situations destroy the trust that is so essential to creating good teamwork. Developing a group identity across distances is also difficult because people normally associate with events that occur at their local levels. Teams tend to have problems effectively sharing information across distances.

Issues	Problems	Suggestions
Developing Trust	Irregular, inconsistent communication; lower level of comfort and familiarity among team members; "us versus them" attitude.	Provide and use a variety of communication alternatives. Communicate electronically except when signatures are required. Make project management software available to all team members.
Developing Group Identity	Fewer shared experiences; lack of cohesion; little understanding of other members roles and responsibilities.	Conduct regular teleconference meetings when the need warrants. Manage the agenda to include a variety of participants and ensure that everyone is involved in the discussion. Use logos, mottoes, and creative humor. Stay in contact when meetings are not required. Note: Do not exclude anyone from group discussions.
Sharing Information	Difficulty sharing adequate levels of information across distances, lack of formal opportunities to discuss work-related issues; lack of a common system to transmit information across distances.	Use technology to develop additional information-sharing opportunities: cellular phones, pagers, faxes, telephones, email, Internet, and computer to computer. Distribute all key reports to all team members. Put information at one central access point, e.g., a project web page, a LAN account.
Developing Clear Structures	Uncertain roles and responsibilities of team members; clashing cultures create different expectations, few clearly defined processes for decision-making.	Use standard formats for meetings. Define goals, objectives, problems, and concerns at the kickoff meeting, and reiterate them frequently. Have participants describe and define potential problems and concerns, and evaluate risks as a group.
Formation of "Cliques" or Informal Subgroups	Cliques tend to create antagonism and competition between the team and the project manager, between team members, or among the cliques themselves.	The project manager can't prevent them from forming but can manage these subgroups. Identify and keep track of them. Create subcommittees for dealing with problems, drawing members from the different cliques. Look for opportunities to mix participants from the different cliques, and initiate or create these opportunities when necessary.
Understanding Information	Each team member has different information (inconsistent); each member has varying levels of information (incomplete); each member has a different perspective of the information. All = inequities of information.	Ask members to explain their viewpoints. Ask members to describe the actions they plan to take, and solicit possible impacts to other involved parties. Use different levels of information for different participants, as appropriate.

Table 1. Virtual Project Management Suggestions

One reason for this may be the lack of informal opportunities for discussion at lunches or during coffee breaks. Developing clear structures is an issue for the virtual project manager because distant work groups need more than the traditional vision, mission, and goals that are important for all project groups. Members of virtual teams tend to develop relationships with those who are located with them rather than with those who are at distant sites. The formation of such "cliques" can create competition or antagonism between the project manager and/or team members located elsewhere. Lastly, each distributed team member tends to have information that is somewhat different from that held by others. More importantly, each team member views information from a different perspective. Such inequities of information frequently increase the opportunity for miscommunication among team members.

If issues such as these are not dealt with, the virtual project experiences management difficulties far in excess of the more "typical" project with higher levels of collocation. Fortunately, the technology that has made virtual projects both possible and necessary also provides opportunities for dealing progressively with these problems.

Implementing Virtual Project Teams

Table 1 includes suggestions created by virtual project managers for using the advantages of project management team building to overcome virtual team difficulties. Generally these suggestions encourage project managers to make creative use of modern communication technologies to bring the team together and encourage the participation and sense of ownership that generates commitment to the project and team objectives.

Since it's seldom possible in the virtual project to meet face to face, experienced project managers recommend using a variety of electronic communications. Trust seems to develop as the individual team member learns more about the project manager, other team members, and the project. It's therefore essential that team members be encouraged to communicate with each other frequently, as well as with the project manager and the team as a whole. Virtual project managers use all forms of electronic communication—cellular phones, pagers, faxes, email, web pages, and computer-to-computer transmissions across local area and wide area networks—to distribute everything from key reports to jokes, logos, and mottoes. These communications are specifically intended to increase the common experiences shared by the team members and thus increase the bonds among them. Regularly scheduled video and telephone conference calls increase team members' exposure to project information, as well as to each other.

When cliques form as subgroups of the project team, these subgroups are managed, not ignored. Subcommittees are created to resolve project problems, specifically drawing members from different cliques together so that they learn more about each other. Team members are frequently asked to explain their viewpoints and to discuss their plans with the team at large to improve the common understanding of information about the project, its progress, and its prospects.

Four specific types of electronic communication, which didn't even exist just a few years ago, are being used extensively by managers of virtual projects to help overcome the lack of formal and informal personal contact among the team members.

The Internet

As technology creates conditions that demand faster reactions, team building over extensive distances, and more extensive communications, that same technology provides new approaches with which to deal with these issues. The Internet provides a means for communicating quickly and inexpensively throughout the world. It is essential for all participants in virtual project teams to have access to the Internet and to email. The virtual project manager relies on email to exchange project data with the dispersed team, especially when team members or clients are internationally located. Email is a particularly good tool for exchanging the detailed information necessary to update the status of project activities. This task is difficult to accomplish verbally via telephone or videoconference because of the detail involved and the difference in time zones. Transmitting such data by facsimile can be expensive due to the volume of data involved, the frequency of needed updates, and the requirement for consistent information flows.

With email as the primary mode of communication, information flows easier and faster, and the difference in time zones is less likely to be a critical failure factor. The ease of communication encourages the team to communicate more often and in more detail. Team members get to know each other more personally, and therefore develop more cohesive working relationships. One word of caution, however: many companies, in a misguided attempt to economize, are limiting the use of email to "official" business and eliminating personal comments, jokes, and other "non-essential" communications. It is precisely these "informal" transmissions that can at least partially make up for the lack of personal contact. Informal email communications can replace some face-to-face contact and help generate the close working relationships, commitments, and friendships that are traditionally considered to be characteristic of successful project teams.

The Pager

A byproduct of today's business environment is that technical specialists (team members) frequently are working on multiple projects and are considered "highly valuable resources." The time of these highly valuable resources may be quite limited. Though regularly scheduled project meetings are critical throughout the project life cycle, these valuable resources may often be required elsewhere, and the project manager may need to help conserve their time. One way to make the best use of a team member's time is to use a paging system. Each team member carries a pager, and the pager numbers are published with the team roster. When agenda topics don't directly relate to a particular team member or function, that person can be released from attendance, freeing up time that can then be used more productively. If an issue surfaces that requires that person's attention, she can be "paged" into the teleconference call. This allows for quick responses to problems and issues and limits the number of "open action items" on meeting minutes. This procedure must be established at the project's kickoff meeting, when the project manager discusses team roles, responsibilities, and expectations. A culture must be developed within the project where each team member is expected to respond quickly to paging, especially when a 911 code, meaning an emergency needing immediate response, is attached to the pager number.

Teleconferencing

Teleconferencing is not as new as some of the previously mentioned techniques, but its use has expanded dramatically in recent years, along with the increase of virtual projects. Everyone thinks that they understand teleconferencing, but few are able to use it effectively. The lack of visual communication means that only the spoken word is available for the transfer of information, so that individual speakers must identify themselves when contributing to the discussion. The medium was originally designed to provide communications between two people. When more people are added to the conference, managing the conversation flow rapidly becomes a complex issue. The goal is to assure that everyone has an opportunity to contribute and that all issues are dealt with in a reasonable period of time.

Using telephony technology for communicating among several people requires careful management and control of the communication process. The project manager cannot manage the results of the communications but must manage the process of getting to those results. The conference needs to be well organized and structured. A detailed agenda is essential to a productive conference call. The project manager should schedule the call in advance so that an agenda can be published and distributed at least two to three days prior to the meeting. The agenda should always include specific items of information: purpose of the teleconference, day-date-time of the call, call-in number, expected duration of the call, chair of the meeting (the project manager), a detailed listing of items to be discussed, and the key participants for each item noted. The project manager can then facilitate discussion among these key players, solicit input from other team members, and maintain a solution-oriented attitude. This structure allows all essential persons to share in the conversation and present their viewpoints while keeping the team focused on the critical issues at hand. The structure also prevents side conversations and keeps the team from straying from the intended topic until a solution has been achieved.

Videoconferencing

With a geographically dispersed team, the cost of travel, including the cost of team members' time during travel, is too high to justify having the team involved in periodic face-to-face status meetings. However, current issues may be too critical to rely on email, teleconferencing, and one-on-one voice contact. This is a time when videoconferencing is the most appropriate form of communication.

A capability not present in other forms of electronic communication, videoconferencing allows participants to feel more involved with each other because they can communicate on many different levels. Body language and facial expressions can be observed and interpreted—in many cases, transferring more meaning than the actual words. Full team participation in developing the initial work breakdown structure and the project plan, both of which occur in the kick-off meeting, is crucial to developing the commitment to the virtual project team. It is particularly appropriate to have the kick-off meeting in a site that is video-conference accessible, if possible, so that if some people can't attend, they can still be involved.

Despite all its good points, there is a downside to videoconferencing. Some of the common problems and barriers are logistical. For example, all participants must be located at prearranged receiving and transmitting sites. Also, although the cost has been decreasing slowly, videoconferencing is still quite expensive, especially when numerous sites and satellite-based communications are involved, and some sites may not be readily accessible.

Also, even though technology is gradually moving forward and the signal transmission speed is increasing, videoconferencing uses a wide bandwidth, which translates into a significant delay in viewing the movements and expressions of participants. This delay, as well as an individual's tendency to be uncomfortable in front of a camera frequently combine to make the whole process somewhat stiff and stilted. This seems to be a particular problem in systems where the participants can see themselves and worry about how they look to others.

Since the purpose of this extraordinary use of electronic communications is to increase the stability of the virtual project, it is particularly important that all team members be able to work with the detailed project plan. All team members should have access to whatever software is being used to plan and control project activities. They should also have easy access to the project files. The liberal distribution of project documentation provides enhanced communication as well as an exposure to the project cultural structure.

A basic knowledge of team building is essential to the effective management of any project. With the virtual project, however, the methods and techniques necessary for implementing the project team-building process have changed. Face-to-face communications are obviously desirable, but they may no longer be possible because of time or cost constraints. Fortunately, the same technologies that have made the virtual project a possibility also provide the methods for developing effective teams comprised of dispersed project participants.

Virtual project managers must be both knowledgeable and creative in using the modern communication technologies available to them for the purpose of enhancing the common experiences of their project team members, and hence the commitment that can be generated for projects' objectives and goals. Perhaps more important, however, is to recognize that the ability to effectively use all of the current electronic communication techniques available to the project manager is rapidly becoming a mandatory skill for anyone likely to be involved in virtual projects.

Referneces

Kast and Rosenzweig. 1985. *Organization and Management: A Systems and Contingency Approach*. McGraw-Hill.

Kostner, Jaclyn. 1994. *Knights of the Tele-Round Table*. Warner Books.

Project Management Institute. 2000. *A Guide to the Project Management Body of Knowledge (PMBOK® Guide)* – 2000 Edition. Newtown Square, PA: Project Management Institute.

Cohesive, Productive Distance Teams

Joan Knutson

PM Network 14 (October 1998)

"This is Jane speaking. I just found out that PMI is having a singing contest at the conference this October. I think it would be a great idea if we, as a group, competed. We here in San Francisco think it is a great plan. Beauregard, in Atlanta, and Pierre, in Paris, I hope you think it is a great idea, too.

"What was that, Pierre? I can't quite hear you. Must be the static over this teleconference phone. Anyway, since the PMI conference is in Long Beach, I thought that one of the Surfer Boys' hit songs would be just right. I'll take over as project manager and send out a project plan and a rehearsal schedule by the end of next week.

"We're hanging up here in San Francisco. Talk to you all soon."

The moral of this story: *Teams aren't cohesive just because you say they are. You have to work at it, especially in the case of distance teams.*

"Cohesive project team" almost sounds like an oxymoron, especially when you add the word "distance." As executives, your project managers may be so preoccupied with the project schedule and the production of a quality deliverable that they forget the nuances required to manage a remote team. The topic of "cohesive, productive distance teams" may be a good candidate for a coaching session with your project managers. Let's look at the difficulties of managing remote teams and some ways to enhance their cohesiveness and productivity.

Difficulties in Managing a Remote Team

Distance teams are legitimately named because one or more people have significant geographic space between where they work and where others on the team work. We most often think of this geographic space as being between one country and another. However, a distance team's members could be located at different points in one country, or even at different campuses in the same town.

The distance between the project players begets the problem. This distance can mean time spent shuttling back and forth to different buildings, or it can mean distance equating to time zones where face-to-face meetings are not an option. And difference in time zones brings not only difficulties in scheduling conversations during everyone's normal workday but also issues concerning the different cultures of which people are a part.

Let's discuss the eight rules for mitigating difficulties in managing cohesive and productive remote or distance teams.

The Rules

1. Be Sensitive to Culture

Culture is the acceptable protocol for how one behaves and communicates. These protocols differ depending on where or how one was raised. There is no one correct or incorrect protocol. What one person may perceive as incorrect may be absolutely the most appropriate behavior for someone else.

When we speak of culture, we often assume that we mean cultures based on borders separating one country from another. That can certainly be the case. In our scenario, Pierre was probably aghast at the brazen approach Jane took when announcing that everyone was going to compete in the PMI singing contest. But Beauregard from Atlanta probably was also put off by the announcement for different reasons.

Sensitivity is most important in addressing the issue of cultural differences. Think before you speak, and ask if what you have said or done is acceptable. Build a trust level where each "culture" can be open and honest when situations are confusing or annoying.

If a culture is across countries, it is worth researching the likes, dislikes, conventions, and protocols of foreign countries. While you're at it, don't forget to send team members in other countries some good books about the American culture.

2. Orchestrate Face-to-Face Meeting(s)

No amount of money is too much. Having the entire team meet each other at least once face to face is critical. Knowing what a person looks like, how she holds her head when she talks, what makes her laugh, and seeing pictures of her kids and pets brings people closer together.

You may be talking to someone over the phone and find her brusque, officious-sounding, and curt in her responses. Over the phone, you can't see her expression or the environment in which she is trying to carry on the conversation. When you meet her in person, though, you may find that she is actually very shy, and you begin to understand that the pressures of her job don't allow time for long conversations.

Face-to-face meetings scheduled periodically establish relationships that can resist the test of distance for long periods of time.

3. Provide Consistency

When our project team members are all down the hall from one another and someone gets tied up in a meeting and calls to say, "Let's postpone the meeting for fifteen minutes," no one gets very upset. But when one or more team members are several time zones away and have orchestrated their days (and sometimes their nights) to be available for a conference call meeting, fifteen minutes can become a major inconvenience.

What a distance team needs most is stability. Meetings set for a certain time of the day should be held *on time*. Agendas should remain the same (with minor changes). And status reports should hold to the format established at the beginning of the project.

The team as a whole can attain such a level of consistency by creating a communication protocol at the beginning of the project. This communication protocol is strictly adhered to unless the team as a whole agrees to change it.

4. Establish Roles and Responsibilities (Both Team and Task)

Who are you; who am I? What do I do; what do you do? Where does my project territory begin and end, and where does yours begin and end?

Firmly establishing roles and responsibilities is crucial to the success of all teams, but even more so when teams are at remote locations. When we are all in one place and someone steps on my toes, I can go into his office, or we can go out to lunch, and talk it over. I can't do that when that someone is miles and miles away.

Therefore, setting clear roles within the context of the team and specific responsibilities relative to each of the tasks within the work breakdown structure can prevent misunderstandings from festering into rifts between team members and ultimately between the different geographic locations as wholes.

5. Isolate a Single Point of Contact

This is a delicate issue. Should everyone at every location be encouraged to talk to everyone at every other location? Imagine the phone calls, interruptions, and emails. According to time-management theory, every interruption results in ten minutes of productive time lost.

Having a single person serve as a point of contact in each location is more productive. Her job is to filter what questions and issues she can handle, then funnel the remainder in a batch method to the appropriate people for response.

That said, there is no need to take this rule too literally. If there is an immediate need for communication, exceptions can be made.

6. Initiate "Inclusive" Celebrations

One of the intangible things that make a cohesive team is planned celebrations. Yet we often forget to include those folks at remote locations. And what is worse, on the next conference call, those of us at the celebration make all kinds of references to the fun that was had and the inside stories about what went on. How thoughtless!

There are ways to include the folks at various locations. At a preset time, have everyone hook up through a teleconference or a videoconference so that all cut a cake at the same time or drink a champagne toast together. The rest of the celebration can go on independently, but those few minutes of connection make a difference.

Also the trinkets that often become part of the project milieu should be sent to everyone. These trinkets may include the embroidered shirt, the embossed cup, or the engraved paperweight. Make sure that everybody gets one. Have pictures taken of all the subteams at different locations and find a central bulletin board on which to hang them. Be creative!

7. Educate on Teleconferencing and Email Skills

The modes by which groups at various locations can communicate are limited so that it is important for management to provide remote teams with the best technology available and that people using the technology be well informed on how to make each unique type of communication the most productive.

And, for that matter, why be limited to just those two media? How about videoconferencing, even if it means renting a location on an infrequent basis? And why not set up a chat room on specific topics, or a bulletin board?

8. Add Time and Budget into the Plan That Addresses Distance Teams

As you can tell from reading rules 1 though 7, managing a cohesive and productive distance team takes additional time, effort, and money. It takes time and effort on the part of the project manager to set up the necessary protocols to bind and hold the team together. It takes the time and effort of the team members to invest in the team relationship. And it takes money to pay for the trips, technology, and creative gimmicks to build the synergy inherent in a successful team.

The consistent theme here seems to be working hard at creating and maintaining the entity we call a "cohesive and productive distance team." Excellent books and articles already exist on the subject. As an executive, I would ask that you peruse some of this material and/or that you require your project managers to do so.

Each organization is different and each configuration of a remote team is different, with its own issues and problems. Don't hope that these problems will go away or think that they aren't important enough to address. A dysfunctional team with various locations out of control can bring down an entire project enterprise, no matter how brilliant the concept of the deliverable or how perfect the project plan.

The variable of a cohesive and productive project team is crucial. Don't take it lightly. *Teams aren't cohesive just because you say they are.* You have to work at it, especially distance teams!

Global Work Teams: A Cultural Perspective

Larraine Segil

PM Network 25 (March 1999)

As business becomes increasingly cross cultural, business management is playing an instrumental role in this process. Contemporary managers talk about going global, internationalizing activities, and relocating facilities abroad. This type of organizational restructuring means that more employees are required to work with counterparts in different countries. The result is the growing use of a combination of work teams and international internal alliances: global work teams.

The global work team is an emerging type of internal alliance. As the workforce is going global, such a team concept is quickly following suit. And with good reason: global work teams can have a dramatic impact on an organization's bottom line because they capitalize on the expertise of a variety of people and offer companies a better understanding of the needs of international customers.

Yet, global internal alliances are not easy to implement. In fact, they are often as difficult to manage as cross-border partnerships between companies. A number of obstacles can impede their progress, which makes proper planning and management crucial to their success. In addition to the expected logistical problems, organizations now must learn to deal with and overcome differences in cultural behavior and expectations. These differences must be explored up-front and a plan for dealing with them must be developed. Otherwise, companies will be ill prepared to cope with the resulting cultural and business mistakes.

Among the 1,400 companies that have participated in my programs on alliances, a vast majority of the larger ones are now in cross-border, team-based alliance relationships. The most challenging, many executives agree, are those within their own organizations.

According to Tony Barnes, director of human resources development at the Japan Center in England, global work teams are reaching the next stage: "I think corporations as we've known them have actually run their course and are beginning to break into autonomous business units. Global teams are one way of cross-pollinating—they move people who are successful in one branch of the organization to work with people in another country and another branch of the organization." To foster the creation of a cohesive team, cultural issues need to take center stage. If not, their incompatibility can lead to the demise of an otherwise solid, strategic internal alliance.

Understand Cultural Differences

The first, and perhaps most critical, element in creating profitable international work teams is fostering an understanding of the various cultures. Team members must understand and appreciate the expectations and business practices of other peoples before they can join to create a unified team. They must acknowledge cultural incompatibilities and differences, and must be willing to listen to others and learn about their ways in order to find acceptance and common ground. Strong alliances—whether internal or external—are not deals; they are relationships. They are built on certain levels of trust and understanding. Without creating this foundation, the alliance's chances for success are slim.

The concept I drive home to senior managers of global organizations is "transculturalization"—namely, adapting management processes to the differing beliefs of the countries and cultures with which they interact. This requires a proactive effort to adapt—not a reactive response. It also involves damage control for the fracturing of trust, which is difficult to achieve.

Organizations need to create opportunities for teams to talk about cultural differences and provide opportunities for team members to learn about them. Intel Corp., based in Santa Clara, Calif., uses a number of cross-cultural internal alliance teams. Sharon Richards, training program manager, points out that "for the team to be effective, the members have to really identify and harness the different cultural strengths and what contributions each member can make to the team."

Select the Right Team Leader and Team Members

To create effective teams, organizations must select team leaders who possess certain qualities. Leaders must be flexible and willing to support the team. They must want to help team members work together, understand their cultural differences, and facilitate communication. They must also possess a global mindset that will prompt them to respond quickly, thoughtfully, and creatively to challenges that arise.

Once the team leader is chosen, organizations must select the optimal cross-cultural team members. Minimizing the importance of this step will affect the team's performance. Sylvia Chevrier, a lecturer at the University of Quebec, conducted a study of three European teams of engineers working in the telecommunications industry. She found that joining a cross-cultural team is often a matter of choice. Most of the interviewed team members were interested in international careers. And, more than 50 percent had previous international experience.

However, not all members had chosen to get involved in an international work team. For instance, some members were selected only because they had appropriate skills and knowledge of the organization. This is not enough. Skills are important, but they are not everything. You can teach technical skills more easily than you can change a personality or develop a good communicator. Interpersonal and communication skills, flexibility, and the willingness to learn about other cultures are just as important as technical skills.

When participants agree to work on an international work team, they sign a sort of psychological contract implying that the benefits of learning from other cultures should outweigh the difficulties. Team members agree to tolerate differences and adjust to diversity. On international teams, it is not always possible to instill one way of doing things—participants need to accept the coexistence of different behaviors in ways of communicating and conducting business.

In Chevrier's study, the interviewed engineers noted several different approaches to conducting business. For example, German participants are extensively prepared for meetings and stick strictly to the agenda, while Latin participants are ready to improvise and feel free to start on unexpected topics. Latin people also easily speak their minds, while Scandinavians feel they need to express themselves only if they have objections or if they disagree with a decision.

One engineer was quick to point out, "In our country [Portugal], you get consensus when everybody agrees. Here consensus is reached when nobody speaks. It took time to adjust."

To be effective, the team members had to be comfortable working with these varying approaches to business. Employees who cannot be flexible should not be on the team.

Create a Shared, Common Goal

The formation of the internal alliance must be based upon a common, shared goal. When a team is composed of people from different functional backgrounds and across countries and cultures, the complexities of interaction become challenging to manage. Having a focused approach creates an overall umbrella under which the team will operate and is critical if it is going to move forward. Clear goals need to be set and reinforced throughout the life of the alliance. One of the important elements that I observed in my research into more than 235 companies at the California Institute of Technology, as well as with many of the existing alliances on which The Lared Group advises, was that the definition of success differs greatly, depending on cultural expectations.

I presented a program in Singapore, which involved multinational companies as well as local organizations. The cultural expectations were apparent in the discussion on creating value in alliances: Asian managers were more relationship focused; Western (United States and European) managers focused more on revenues. These issues became particularly difficult when internal alliances were discussed between the local area executives and their United States or European headquarters' counterparts. "We have a major education problem on our hands. We cannot be driven by quarterly results in an environment where relationships and *guanxi* (networked contacts) are everything," said the Asia managing director. The company is installing cross-cultural education programs at the highest level of management in order to integrate the "relationship" message companywide.

Balance Commitment and Priority

The process of cross-cultural adjustment suggests the frailty of arrangements in cross-cultural teams. As the roles and responsibilities are delineated, team members must accept their assignments and understand their contributions to the ultimate goal—and each team member must place the same level of priority on achieving that goal. The balance of the interests of team members can be questioned at any time, and any imbalance puts a strain on working together to achieve a common goal. As a result, cross-cultural teams are often on the verge of disintegrating. If, for any reason, common stakeholders feel their interests are damaged, the whole team might be pulled down.

Enhance Communication

Enhanced communication—including face-to-face meetings—will keep the team focused on the goal at hand and will help maintain a high level of commitment. Personal meetings early in the creation of the team build trust from the outset and assure clarity of the team's vision and objectives. They also help make future meetings—conducted via teleconferencing, videoconferencing, email, and the like—run more smoothly.

It is important that the right people attend the meetings—involving both those who will implement and key players whose input is valued. During the meetings, be sure to get everyone involved in creating a plan for implementing and managing the internal alliance.

After assessing the similarities and differences of the team members, developing the plan helps bring all the pieces back together by highlighting how best to carry out the various tasks of the team. The plan should focus on staffing, resource allocation, monitoring of the project, expectations, and financial considerations. The underlying message of the plan should be fostering mutual problem-solving skills, encouraging the use of candid discussion, and negotiating compromises among members to address the problems that are destined to arise. An implementation plan should address who will do what, how contributions will be made, what communications mechanisms will be in place for approvals, how the information will flow, what incentive programs are appropriate, and how the team will fit into the existing organization.

Distributing written minutes of the meetings immediately afterward will help ensure that all team members and key company personnel understand the tasks that were assigned and the agreements that were made. These initial meetings lay the groundwork for the global team's formation and direction. Addressing these issues up-front and planning for trouble spots minimizes the frustrations when cultural differences and language barriers begin to surface.

I have found that communication issues become far more important over time. I recommend an approach called the "points of interface" methodology, which addresses a protocol and format for multiple opportunities for communication, but has a streamlining effect of refining information transfer so that information is only given, verbally and nonverbally, in culturally appropriate ways. Of course, this requires planning and resource allocation to the process of the internal alliance, not just its substance.

Global internal alliances are here. International companies must embrace them and create strategies for implementing them effectively. By planning for and managing cultural differences, organizations can create effective global work teams that provide team members with the challenges and rewards they seek, and provide companies with the innovation and competitiveness they need.

Section 9

Managing Change

The Team-Friendly Organizational Structure: A Paradigm Shift

Sherryl G. Wilkins, PMP

PM Network 39 (August 1999)

Globalization, along with the change in the United States to a service economy, has prompted organizations to transform themselves in order to maintain and achieve leadership and enterprise agility. The structure of an organization is the formal means by which it coordinates the activities of its workforce to accomplish its goals and objectives. Periodically, organizations must restructure in order to stay competitive and efficient. The new environment requires a fresh look at the strategic visions and assumptions that have historically driven the organization. The organizational structure should take its form from a firm's chosen strategy. This transformation requires new roles and responsibilities, with a new set of management practices. The challenge of organizations will be to prevail over inertia and people's fear of change, along with establishing new measures of success.

Twentieth Century Organizations: A Historical Perspective

At the beginning of the twentieth century, the American industrial workforce, having recently shifted focus from its agrarian origins, saw the rise of trade associations made up of craftsmen. Consumer products were made by the singular endeavors of individuals. The entire development and delivery process of product design, production, testing, measurement of quality standards, delivery, and follow-up support was provided by a single individual. Along with great individual skill and pride of workmanship, there were hidden costs in this means of production, as later techniques would show.

The vision of early twentieth century industrialists, most notably Henry Ford, ushered in the idea of specialization of labor, and a new organizational structure was born. The assembly line brought about an organizational structure in which many highly specialized functions performed their specific tasks in a sequential and repetitive fashion, allowing quick delivery of the product to the consumer for the lowest possible cost. In the evolution from the one-person project team, where one person did everything, we progressed to the division of labor structure where there were many functional specialists, each performing a highly skilled, yet very narrow, serial task.

Over time these specialist areas grew more self-serving, and limited parochial interests began to create artificial barriers between the functions. The ambition concerns of departmental functions became the primary focus, many times taking precedence over the needs of the consumer. As each specialized function gained in autonomy, it devised and worked to its own standards. Only when a function became sufficiently satisfied with its work did the end product get passed to the next serial function.

Surprisingly, the process that had originally cut production time significantly was now responsible for significantly increasing product-to-market time. What eventually became clear is that if the highly specialized and extensive functional knowledge silos could be tapped and utilized in a synergistic and simultaneous fashion, then new products might be more innovative while being brought to market more quickly.

Project teams are designed to work in this way. In a project-based organization, teams are formed by members from various functional areas to work in a complementary way toward a common objective. Many large firms have restructured operations such that work is defined as a portfolio of projects linked to the overall business strategy. Enterprisewide projects are prioritized according to key business drivers. Here cross-functional project team members share mutual accountability. They form, disperse, and reform, bringing the right talents, resources, and focus to get the job done in a compressed schedule for delivery (Fleming and Koppelman 1997).

The Impact of Change on Organizational Behavior

A key challenge is maintaining a delicate balance between forces that encourage or demand change and forces within organizations that resist it. A look at the behavioral impact of the change is filled with both pitfalls and opportunities. The transition impacts human behavior in two major ways: fear and resistance to change. Fear in an organization precipitated by environmental change can be assessed in four dimensions.

Uncertainty

Uncertainty, always present in organizational life, can be debilitating for a workforce when there is a lack of clear information on the personal impact of the change. Staff should also be made known of any necessary responses to the change. The scheduling of the communication feedback loop between upper management directives and management's workforce needs to be frequent and responsive to allay unnecessary fear.

Instability

In this rapidly changing environment, organizations must be willing to adapt, change, and remain flexible. While organizational strategies and business processes are adapting, the new way of responding to the environment must be communicated throughout the organization. Old ways must be unlearned and the new, fleet responsiveness to the marketplace made a part of the organizational culture. Continual organizational learning is paramount.

Complexity

Today we are dealing with an environment that is highly complex. According to Peter Senge, author of *The Fifth Discipline* (1990), we're dealing with two types of complexity. Detail complexity is the traditional domain of most business analysis. Here we see the use of forecasting tools, strategic plans, and the like, to handle the many variables affecting business outcomes. Though the variables are prolific, the cause-and-effect relationships of detail complexity are somewhat predictable (especially when confined to functional knowledge stores) and manifest rather quickly.

The tougher challenge is what Senge (1990) calls dynamic complexity. In contrast, conventional business management tools are stymied by dynamic complexity. In situations that are dynamically complex, cause and effect are very subtle and the effects manifest over much longer time periods, and differ depending on time frame, location, populations, and so forth. Many times, doing the obvious thing does not produce the obvious, desired outcome. Cross-functional management exponentially increases variables like population, location, and even time frames in our current global workplace. In gaining a competitive edge, the organization's most potent leverage comes from mastery of dynamic complexity. The key here is to see not only the linear cause-and-effect links, but to see the interrelationships of the variables and the processes as a whole. The project-based organization will facilitate seeing the interrelationships more quickly as the cross-functional teams gain prominence. Critical to the success of this environment is the ability of team members to understand the value and be able to employ the holistic systems thinking required for handling the growing dynamic complexity of our global environment.

Beneficence

The level of beneficence, generosity, or helpfulness of the organization with regard to resources for its workforce during the period of transition bears a direct relationship on the level of fear that prevails and the learning that does or does not occur.

Many times, to an outside observer, an individual or an organization's stubborn resistance to change seems incomprehensible, and downright self-defeating. Signals for change are ignored, or even though plans are made, they never get translated into the correct actions. Three sources for resistance to change are habit, resource limitations, and threats to power and influence.

Habit. Inertia is a natural physical law. So it is not surprising that people and organizations tend to resist change. Group rules or norms for behavior many times represent accumulated organizational experience and learning. The comfort in employing these behaviors, along with their high payoff in the past, is not easily replaced. Most importantly, the workforce is smart enough to know that the change is not going to be cost free. It will require considerable new learning on its part, along with the discomfort of giving up the familiar, comfortable, and workable—though inefficient. Be aware that functional areas, as well as external suppliers and distributors not a part of the organizational change, may be uncooperative and push back. A strategy to gain their buy-in is critical to success.

Resource limitations. The resource costs to functional managers in the short term are not insignificant. Retraining department personnel, in conjunction with making sure that the current work gets done, can place an enormous drain on resources. Even if the long-term benefits look good, the long term is only potential. Resistance to change may be traced to a short-term need to survive.

Threats to power and influence. While changes in structural relationships and resource responsibilities may affect the formal power structure, informal power is still very much attached to individuals, based on their personal assets of knowledge, credibility, and expertise.

Change often undermines power arising from expertise. The transition from a manufacturing economy to a service economy—a product provider to a solution provider—calls for different skills and demands new expertise. The threat of rearrangement of power relationships can create barriers, even sabotage, to protect self-interest and the status quo.

Organizational structure can be more durable and powerful than market strategies and much more difficult to change and refocus. Psychologist Kurt Lewin developed a model of organizational change that provides a framework for understanding the change process:

1. Diagnosis—finding the problem and selecting a solution.
2. Unfreezing—preparing for change and generating ownership.
3. Movement—making the changes.
4. Refreezing—institutionalizing the changes (Neal and Northcraft 1990).

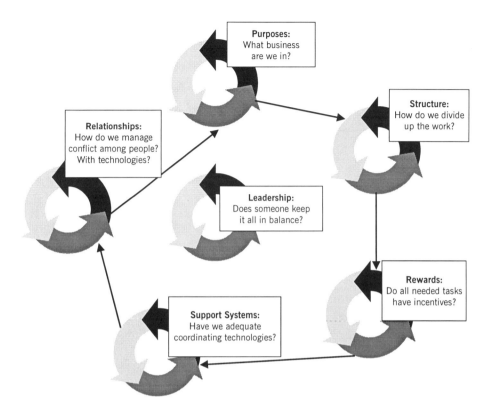

Figure 1. Interpretation of Weisbord Theory

Problem diagnosis and recognition of the need for change is critical to the evolution of the organizational structure. M. R. Weisbord (1976) expanded on the Lewin model's diagnosis phase. Weisbord's model provides a means for isolating problems, finding the root causes, and defining an effective solution, as shown in Figure 1.

The changes required to transition from responding to a manufacturing economy to a service economy will involve some alteration in a company's purpose or mission. As the organization moves from being simply a provider of products to a business solutions provider, the organization must ask itself, "What business are we in?"—and communicate the answer to its workforce.

Leadership throughout the management ranks is of primary importance in recognizing the necessary changes in knowledge, skills, and attitudes of the organization at large. Management must understand and buy into the fact that:

■ It requires substantial commitments in education and training to successfully implement these changes. Leaders must positively challenge people by making them aware that team success will require a continuous journey of self-improvement on everyone's part.

- Education, both formal and informal, must derive from the new paradigm in order to support the new strategic vision.
- The new strategy must be communicated again and again to keep everyone focused on the message, and to eventually help the message become internalized by everyone.
- During the transition period, performance progress must be monitored and feedback given with respect to successful implementation of the new strategy.
- Individual performance must serve the team performance. Development of a team culture will facilitate this change in attitude. A sound set of reward plans must support the business strategy and culture change. In the case of a project-based organization, rewards must be focused on both team and individual contribution. Team awards/rewards must do more than just give lip service to the team approach. Behaviors that get rewarded are the behaviors that are repeated.
- To minimize confusion and uncertainty among employees, there must be clear distinctions concerning individual and collective roles. Distribution of work and performance standards should be clear and aligned with the business strategies.
- Rather than managers, empowered teams need leaders to motivate, coach, facilitate, teach, and create the vision for how the team will produce the outcomes necessary for success.

Lewin's model for organizational change—diagnosis, unfreezing, movement, and refreezing—encompasses a need for change, a vision, preparation for change, change, and the institutionalization of change. If we simplify successful change into its most basic components, we might find the basic building blocks of change, shown in Figure 2.

What happens when any of the key ingredients for a successful transition are missing? Without *pressure for change*, there is a tendency to procrastinate and push requirements to the bottom of the inbox. Without a commonly understood *shared vision*, there's a lack of momentum, and a fast start fizzles. Without the necessary resources (*capacity for change*), the inability to properly execute the requirements results in anxiety and frustration. Without a *clear plan of action*, haphazard efforts and false starts leave you at the starting block. Without *sustained reinforcement (follow through) and continued learning* incorporated into the change process, there is erosion of results and a lack of momentum.

Clearly, the omission of any of the critical building blocks to change will derail your strategy.

Thus far, we have looked at organizational behavior and change from the top down. Even more important is the assimilation of the change from the bottom up. Everyone must recognize the individual demands this organizational change

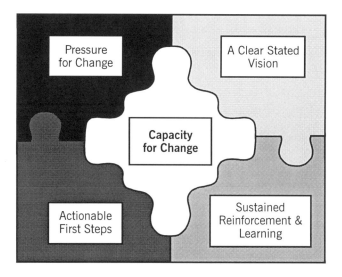

Figure 2. Building Blocks for Change

imposes. Workers need to establish a new orientation toward leadership. This leadership is not hierarchical, but refers to the span of influence an individual commands. We—not someone else—are in control of our creations. The danger is that workers may suddenly find themselves thrown into highly autonomous situations without the self-leadership skills to cope. The team environment demands self-leadership on the part of every team member. Individuals must recognize the tremendous personal stake they have in taking responsibility for their personal growth and development. The need to constantly sell yourself for the next project requires an entrepreneurial view of your skills, competencies, and talents.

Without a doubt, it is more difficult to change people than processes. However, when all is said and done, the business is its people. People are the primary change agents that will determine the successful outcome of our business strategies and mission.

References

Fleming and Koppelman. 1997. Project Teams: The Role of the Project Office. *Transactions of AACE* Int. 1: 157.

Senge, Peter. 1990. *The Fifth Discipline*. New York: Doubleday.

Neal and Northcraft. 1990. *Organizational Behavior: A Management Challenge*. Dryden Press.

Weisbord, M. R. 1976. Organizational Diagnosis: Six Places to Look with or without a Theory. *Group and Organization Studies* 1: 430–47.

Project Management in an Era of Increasingly Rapid Change

Jean McWeeney, PMP

Proceedings of the 28th Annual Project Management Institute
1997 Seminars & Symposium

Fundamental technology changes take place approximately once every eighteen months—and this pace of change is increasing. Fundamental change is no longer an unusual circumstance during a project's life; change is a constant. Project managers must learn to factor this into their planning. Additionally, they need to more effectively utilize their general management skills—including leading, communicating, negotiating, problem solving, and influencing the organization—in order to lead their projects through both internal and external changes.

The pace of change today—in technology, in the global marketplace, and in organizational flux—is unprecedented. Successful project managers are the ones who accept this fact of business life and learn how to lead their teams through change. Their greatest tests, as well as their greatest accomplishments, occur during times of change.

In this article, we discuss the effect of change on project teams and how effective project managers extend their skills to guide those teams through change.

Four Phases of Change

The first step toward effective project management is to understand the phases of change (see Figure 1). A project team and each team member's productivity levels go through predictable cycles during each of these phases. Understanding the phases and recognizing the predictable symptoms enables you, the project manager, to model appropriate behavior and to assist those team members who become stuck in an early phase.

The first phase of change is resistance. Do you remember your first reactions to the announcement that your project was being canceled? It was probably something like, "No, that's a ridiculous idea!" Denial is common at this stage. What was your reaction to the news that your organization was merging with another? Very negative, *resistant* reactions are to be expected when people first learn of an impending change. That is what you should expect from the team members on your project. During this resistant phase, productivity drops precipitously.

The second phase of change is characterized by low productivity. During this phase, team members are facing a great deal of anxiety and many unknowns. There is ample opportunity for rumor. What will happen? During this phase team members have not yet bought into whatever the change is; perhaps they do not yet know what their next project will be or how their current project is to change. If they do know the nature of the change, they have not yet accepted it.

The third phase of change is acceptance. At this stage, team members have figured out that the change is really going to happen, and they have figured out how they can fit into the new direction of the project.

The fourth phase of change is the recognition of new opportunities. The project manager is frequently at this phase when the team is still in the first resistance phase. At this point it is important to explain how you went through the same emotions, too. Empathize and validate the team members' feelings. Did the project on which your team worked so hard get canceled? Then have a wake, ritual, or ceremony to "celebrate" the end and put some closure to it. Explain to the team members the four phases of change and how they are going to feel. Show them the phases of change productivity graph.

Do not expect that because you have explained these phases to the team that things will change overnight. The team or individual may attempt to get out of whatever phase they are stuck in several times before it finally works. Recognition of this will help you deal more effectively with your team members.

General Management Skills

Resisting change is useless; it's coming whether you like it or not. Therefore, a second step toward effective project management is to expand your general management skills to be attentive to change. These skills include leading, communicating, negotiating, problem solving/decision-making, and influencing.

Leading

Leading during times of change requires the project manager to be attentive to external issues. You must be one step ahead of technology, legal, and regulatory shifts. You must know how these external issues affect the project. For example, should the platform of choice be client/server or the Internet? Will your organization be facing deregulation in the near future? Will the project result in a product that is already out of date if it is completed according to schedule and with the current specifications?

Once you become aware of any external issues affecting the project, you need to convey this information to the project team. Let them know the alternatives. If you feel that a change in plan is needed because of external issues, get the team on board. Remember, you are an *agent* of change and you must help lead the organization toward appropriate solutions. Various leadership skills are needed in order to be an effective change agent. They include good listening skills, the ability to synthesize information from disparate sources, and effective communication and influencing skills.

Besides leading the organization through external issues, internal issues must be attended to. You need to "look up, look down, look all around." That is, be attentive to changes within your own project team, and be attentive to what is happening within other parallel project teams or organizations. Look for what direction the organization is taking with regard to products or mergers. What does it mean for the future of your project? For example, would a merger with a company with similar projects affect your project? The same leadership skills and attentiveness to change possibilities is needed to deal with these internal issues.

Communication

In times of change, your skills at communicating will need to expand to recognize that change can be difficult or even threatening for people. You should keep team members well informed on issues of change but focus on the relevant information. If you have a message of change, remember to focus on the clarity of your message. Three things will help organize your message for clarity: 1) know what you want to communicate; 2) drop what is unimportant; and, 3) structure it for effectiveness (have a beginning and an end) (Daly 1996).

Understand that information will be filtered, possibly inadvertently, and a message of change may become distorted. The rumor mill may heat up. Have you ever experienced a reorganization that resulted in the rumor that a nemesis was getting reassigned? You and your team may jump for joy; you may even feel free to say what you really feel to your nemesis only to find out that your nemesis has become your new boss. Be prepared for a lot of misinformation as well as surprises during times of change.

Negotiating

A Guide to the Project Management Body of Knowledge (PMBOK® Guide) defines negotiation as conferring with others in order to come to terms or reach an agreement (2000). Project management frequently involves constant negotiation, especially in times of rapid change. There are a few methods that you, as the project manager, can use to ensure that your negotiations are successful.

First, understand both parties' interests. Do you know why the other party is insisting on something? Secondly, you should understand both parties' alternatives when presenting your case. Alternatives help define the lower bounds of negotiation. Knowing your alternatives is an important part of successful negotiating.

Negotiation requires creativity. Learn to think outside the project manager box. Engage your team and any other resources at your disposal in finding alternatives. This can be the fun part of negotiating!

Problem Solving/Decision-Making

A project manager dealing with change may be called upon to utilize more creative problem-solving skills. How can this project be delivered in time to meet the users' needs and yet be adapted to changing technology? Or, how can a team meet the changing requirements from the customer? The *PMBOK® Guide* defines problem solving as including problem definition and decision-making (2000). Causes and symptoms of a problem must be distinguished. Decision-making includes identifying potential solutions and making a choice among them.

Influencing

Why is being able to influence important during times of rapid change? During a time of flux, a lot of issues get reevaluated and decisions get made. Therefore, there are lots of opportunities for the project manager to positively influence the organization's direction.

In order to be successful at influencing you need to recognize who are the decision-makers in the organization and understand how to work with them. There are oftentimes two types of decision-makers within the organization: rational ones and ambitious, deceitful ones. You will need to deal with each in a different manner. A prerequisite for ensuring your success with either is: *be trustworthy*.

To successfully influence the rational decision-makers, first, understand their goals or agenda. Find out what drives them. If the decision-makers have a hard time articulating their goals, try the "what-if string" method. "What if we tried this approach?" Each question should lead you and the decision-makers closer to an articulation of what their goals are. To get the rational decision-maker to accept your ideas, you must be articulate and enthusiastic. You need to tie your goals to your decision-maker's and provide solutions. Remember to be flexible in adapting your goals to others'.

Unfortunately, there are oftentimes ambitious, deceitful decision-makers within the organization. You will need to learn to recognize who they are, for they can oftentimes be saboteurs. Do not attempt to understand their motives or agendas; their goal is usually personal ambition. To get them to accept your ideas, tie your solution to their success. Again, be flexible. One risk you assume in dealing with this type of decision-maker is being perceived as selling out. You should be willing to assume this risk if it will help you accomplish your goals.

Success

These tactics should help you remain successful as a project manager in an era of increasingly rapid change. Oftentimes change allows for growth and the opportunity to stretch your abilities. Remember the four phases of dealing with change and the general management skills outlined. They should help ensure your success on any given project.

References

Daly, John. 1996. Bolstering Your Communication Effectiveness. Presentation, The Institute for Managerial Leadership: The University of Texas at Austin.

Project Management Institute. 2000. *A Guide to the Project Management Body of Knowledge (PMBOK® Guide)* – 2000 Edition. Newtown Square, PA: Project Management Institute.

Project Recovery: Short- and Long-Term Solutions

Thomas R. Block, PMP

Proceedings of the 29th Annual Project Management Institute
1998 Seminars & Symposium

Traditionally, corporate interest in project management has focused mainly on training professionals and managers and purchasing software. However, there seems to be an increasing interest in project recovery. This interest has been generated by the high stakes involved in projects, competitive pressures, and senior management's frustrations with its inability to receive timely project data despite technological advancements. This article focuses on the reasons for project failures and what can and should be done to prevent them. Simply stated, in the short term the problem has to be fixed quickly to avoid serious consequences, and in the long term senior management must enforce practices that will prevent further recurrences of project failures.

Why Projects Get into Trouble

Projects get into trouble for a number of reasons. Lack of planning or poor planning is a major contributor. We have all heard the saying: "We didn't have time to do it right the first time, but we always have time to do it over again." Everyone involved in a project has to share the blame for poor or no planning. The pressures put on a project manager to get started often lead to disaster. Other factors that lead to project problems are: speculative technology, incomplete specifications, scope creep, project drifting, cost overruns, lack of skilled resources, date-driven schedules, no-risk assessments, optimism of project team, and projects that are too big and complex.

Some common warning signs of runaway projects are as follows:

- Inadequate project planning—Simple to-do lists replace detailed, long-term planning assignments.
- Faulty task management—Tasks are gauged by how long they will take rather than by the actual resources (staff hours) required to get the job done.
- Poor reporting and communications—No one seems to have a good handle on all aspects of a project.
- Insufficient documentation—The records don't clearly indicate which phases of a project have been completed and which tasks have yet to begin.
- Abrupt scheduling changes—If a project's time to completion varies by more than 10 to 15 percent without a clearly documented explanation, you probably have a runaway on your hands.
- Project disorganization—The project is hampered by organizational changes. No one is clearly accountable for various aspects of the project. Lines of reporting are not clear.
- Muddled business objectives—The reasons for undertaking the project in the first place are vague.
- Extreme complexity—As the project goes along, it becomes more complicated, not less.

Senior Management's Interest

Unfortunately, project recovery often receives high-level attention at the eleventh hour when the situation is desperate. It is an intense time. The customer is often ready to terminate the project, and senior management is busy trying to rebuild relationships that were neglected. Senior management has little patience and tolerance, and it wants immediate results. If they have not already done so, senior management members are ready to relieve the project manager and any other managers associated with the project. The corporation's reputation is in danger of being tarnished, and lawyers from both sides seem to be running the project. Most of the professionals assigned to the project want out or have already left. This is the situation that faces senior management as it ponders how to "save" the project, its reputation, and the corporate reputation.

How Is Project Recovery Accomplished?

Since the project situation is so grave, senior management has to take action, but it is often difficult to know what action to take. The paradox of project recovery is that several options, such as the use of a "tiger team"—composed of senior professionals—or bringing in consultants, will in turn prove counterproductive. The project progress will be slowed or halted as the project improvement recommendations are implemented. The project intervention and recovery actions taken by senior management, with the best intention to improve the project, will initially produce the opposite results.

At this point it appears that the project is hemorrhaging, and it is hard to tell what needs to be done first or whether the project can even be saved. The Department of Defense uses a rule of thumb for troubled projects. If the project is 15 percent complete, or if 15 percent of the resources are consumed, and the project is behind schedule and over budget, there is no way that the project will get back on schedule and within budget. This rule of thumb was derived after a review of 800 software development projects.

Before project recovery can begin, the person given the task needs two important pieces of information. First, what are senior management's expectations? In other words, how does it define a "recovered or saved" project? Secondly, what is the real situation on the project? It is normally difficult to get senior management to completely articulate its expectations and to define what it means by a *saved* project. Here are typical senior management statements:

- We want the project completed to the customer's satisfaction.
- We want the customer to understand the value that we bring to this business arrangement.
- We need this customer as a reference for future business deals.
- We want to preserve our corporate reputation in the industry.
- We want the project to make money.
- We want to renegotiate a deal we can live with.
- We need to assign a project manager that can get along with the customer.
- We need to get the best people in the company assigned to this project.

Seven-Step Project Recovery Program

Armed with whatever guidance can be gained from senior management and a Seven-Step Project Recovery Program, the daunting task of project recovery begins. Here are the steps to follow: 1) assessment, 2) action plan, 3) commitment, 4) project standards, 5) coaching and mentoring, 6) knowledge transfer, and 7) reinforcement reviews.

Assessment

Since you won't have the luxury to conduct a thorough, time-consuming analysis, an assessment questionnaire is helpful. Whatever assessment tool is used, the questionnaire should be consistent, measurable, and easy to complete by the project team. If completing the questionnaire is perceived as additional work, it will not be completed accurately and could provide misleading information. Keep in mind that most of the project members are completely stressed from working fourteen-hour days, seven days a week. They are tired, defensive of any questioning of their efforts, and will not appreciate any additional work.

This cursory assessment gives initial clues on what may be wrong with the project and the competency of the individuals involved. However, more information is needed. More information is gained through follow-up interviews conducted with key project members. These interviews have to be coordinated and scheduled with the project manager so that requisite project members are available. The interview has to be well organized for two reasons. First, the project member's time is critical. This interview session cannot be perceived as a time waster. Second, a well-organized, precisely conducted interview will impress the project members and add credibility to your contribution to the project. The results of the interviews and the questionnaire are analyzed, and then findings, recommendations, and an action plan are developed.

Action Plan

The findings, recommendations, and action plan are then briefed to the project manager and key project members to gain their final input and commitment before briefing senior management and the customer. The primary purpose of briefing the project personnel is twofold: to avoid surprises and to clarify any misunderstanding or conclusions from the data collected. The placing of a positive spin on the facts collected should never be the intent of the project personnel briefing. Often your integrity and ethics can be challenged at this briefing since some project members may feel threatened.

Commitment

Commitment from senior management, the project team, the customer, and all other stakeholders to comply with the recovery action plan is crucial to project recovery. If senior management approves the recommendations and is committed to the project recovery plan, continue with the seven-step project recovery program.

Project Standards

Normally, the project lacks procedures and standards. These are developed rapidly along with a project communications plan. The project procedures and standards are kept in a project workbook. The project communications plan and the project workbook are key to project recovery. They must be developed rapidly and communicated and enforced vigorously.

Coaching and Mentoring

The coaching and mentoring focuses on the procedures and standards and continues throughout your stay in the project. Often you must set the example by actually doing some of the project management work. This will help you gain acceptance and credibility by pitching in and helping.

Knowledge Transfer

Knowledge is normally transferred through coaching and mentoring. However, at times it may be necessary to conduct informal project management training for the project members. It's also difficult to judge whether the project team has absorbed enough project management knowledge to handle the daily tasks, thereby allowing you to leave. Customer confidence and feedback certainly help to make the proper decision. The decision to leave is a tricky judgment call, since often the project members are not convinced that project management helps.

Reinforcement Reviews

For this reason, reinforcement reviews are scheduled for after you leave the project. These reviews are conducted monthly or quarterly, depending on the severity of the project problems. The purpose of the review is to ensure that the procedures and standards are being carried out and to determine whether further consulting and coaching is necessary. Senior management must be cautioned that the project can be back in trouble quickly if help is pulled too soon or if the reinforcement reviews are not conducted.

How to Avoid Project Recovery

The short-term approach of project recovery is necessary to preserve the corporate image and to survive, but it will not enable corporate growth in a competitive marketplace unless senior management is committed to a long-term, holistic project management approach. Without the long-term approach, senior management will be continually addressing the symptoms of project problems and never address the root causes.

Some ideas to help avoid getting into the project recovery in the first place follow:

- Start the project plan development in the sales cycle.
- Train salespersons in the value of project management.
- Reengineer the sales process to include project management.
- Assign project managers earlier.
- Conduct appropriate reviews of all project proposals.
- Prioritize all projects in the portfolio.
- Adequately fund project planning.
- Fully support and aggressively monitor project startups.
- Invest in project start-up assistance teams.
- Require all projects to have baselines.
- Include project management plans and tools in proposals.
- Require project managers to manage to the plan.
- Invest in a long-term solution to remain competitive.

Summary

Successful corporations must address the short-term problems and also pour a project management foundation for the future that will allow for continued growth and a reduction in 911 calls for project recovery. The long-term approach should consist of ideas and plans that will help your projects avoid getting into trouble in the first place—a project management methodology, a full-service project office, appropriate project management software to support the business and project-office needs, progressive project management training and development, and mentoring and consulting. This holistic approach will not work unless senior management support is present and communicated.

Risk Management in a Downsized Environment

David F. Connors, PMP

PM Network 41 (June 2001)

Think about managing a project in a recently downsized environment. The normal reaction is to register concern that key individuals have been eliminated or have left voluntarily ... they were, of course, the ones with the most options and greatest mobility. After the fact, we resize to validate our baseline and key assumptions. How can we perform all the creative tasks that we have committed to the stakeholders? Will we be able to recover from the losses and maintain our commitments? Do we still have a core group of design and development personnel that can complete the project on schedule and within budget? Where are our exposures? What adjustments must we make? We call team meetings and review all commitments and determine if a bottom-up or a top-down plan review is appropriate. We ultimately recommit, possibly using a new or revised schedule, and move forward confidently, only to miss our schedule by a significant margin. "Where did we go wrong?" the stakeholders demand to know. "We looked at all of your concerns; we made staffing adjustments, giving you our best people, and even made adjustments to the schedule. How, where, and when did we fail?"

The Problem May Be Inherent in the System

Management, intent on preserving its schedules and commitments, and subsequently its revenue and profitability, consciously makes the decision to eliminate "non-critical skills" and protect its "creative core of key personnel." To that end, management members eliminated administrative and support personnel, hiring temporary personnel as replacements, and thought that they were covered. What project manager threatens to quit because an administrative release coordinator rather than a design engineer is eliminated? What project manager, for that matter, is even aware of or tracks staffing in those administrative support areas? Hierarchically, some of these people and their tasks may be so far removed from the center of activity that the project manager is not even aware that they exist, let alone what and how they do their jobs. Within the management chain, the higher you go within the organization, the administrative personnel surrounding that manager are more senior. As such, management is protected from the upheaval by the natural order of things and therefore, it sees little or no direct impact from its decisions.

Hidden Costs

Recently many of our largest and fastest-growing companies have been eliminating support positions. As an example, secretarial staff has been cut repeatedly. If there are no secretaries that must mean that there is no expense associated with memos, and all memos are now free—right? Of course, this doesn't make logical sense. Here's how it works. Management presumes that the technical people will assume an additional burden and do their own memos—after all, they all have very costly workstations with all the latest tools. If the technical and middle-management staff needs secretarial support, it can be hired from a temporary agency at a much lower cost than the cost of retaining a permanent hire.

What's the net result here? Prior to the job cuts, let's assume that a word-processing professional could type a one-page letter at a cost of $1. Now the managers and technical people type their own memos. Of course, they don't type very well, and they take five times as long. They are also being paid four times as much. That $1 memo now costs $20 in this cost-savings environment! Additionally, people already overworked because of an additional workload, brought about by earlier personnel cuts, are not doing their primary job while typing that letter. Schedule and reschedule a meeting a few times, and the hidden costs begin to come out. Management isn't cost cutting; it is cost hiding!

A few years ago people could typically scan their mail at varying depths, depending upon the subject matter, and forward that mail to the proper person. This task took about an hour a day. With the advent of email, the volume of paper and copy time is no longer a consideration, and people are all buried with "e-carbon copies" and can spend four to five hours *after* the workday attempting to catch up on their mail so that they don't miss some critical missive. These same people, in all probability, are also spending several hours a month maintaining their workstations and resolving problems that the recently eliminated workstation support personnel formerly did—again in lieu of doing, or in addition to doing, their primary job. Toss in an "exception condition," such as the need to expedite a delivery to maintain schedule, and the fabric of work begins to unravel. We risk missing our schedule when much of our technical and management time evaporates into the mists of administrative and support housekeeping.

What are exception conditions? Picture a restaurant filled with customers. Two waitresses bring out meals to their respective tables. Each hears from one of their patrons that "this isn't what I ordered." Two exception conditions have occurred. Fixing the problem or the "recovery action" depends on many factors. If the meal orders were switched by mistake, the plates can be exchanged in the kitchen, and the problems are solved. However, if each patron has cut into his meal and taken a bite, we have a much bigger exception, and the recovery must be quite different. In the meantime, each patron might be seated at a table as part of a group so that now one person is not eating, and the others are feeling self-conscious. A domino effect takes place: as new meals are prepared for the "offended party," desserts are delayed at both tables, which delays the end of the meal and closing out the checks, which prevents later parties from being seated on time. If you have ever been to a new restaurant and experienced "opening night," you understand this domino effect. Now relate these exception conditions and recovery actions to your finely drawn project schedule.

In most corporate administrative support areas, after a short training period, temporary administrative and support personnel do very well with the normal day-to-day activities of their jobs. What is commonly forgotten is that the more experienced support people really earn their pay when *exceptions* occur. Typically, over time, temporary personnel cycle from job to job or company to company—they are, after all, *temporary* help. Their experience is often capped at an "entry" level. And over time, core experienced, full-time help may leave to assume new duties or opportunities. When this occurs the greatest risk is that there is no one left in the support organization with experience in handling a majority of the possible process failures or exceptional conditions.

Who Do We Turn to for Help?

What happens when there is no one left who understands how to move the administrative processes along? A department may see little direct impact from the *first* downsizing; we still have the depth of organization to be able to find a person who has the experience to solve a support problem. Eventually, however, the result is that administrative and support tasks fall back on the key technical people that we have so carefully protected from support problems. While they are busy with support efforts, their critical creative work grinds to a halt.

This type of situation normally occurs at the worst possible time: when a failure of one sort or another has occurred, and we enter recovery mode. This is a situation where a timely response is critical in order to prevent a hiccup from becoming a heart attack! A frantic call is made to the administrative department to invoke an exception process, and the person answering the phone has no idea what to do or how to begin. When questioned, this person can respond only in mechanical terms: "I get a J-2 form via email and forward it XYZ with the material I get from you."

Who sends you that email? "I don't know. It comes from a user—ID JJPN0382." Who knows how to do this? "I don't know. Bill always did those things, but he's gone now."

As we trace the process back through our organization, we get several variations of the same answer. The temporary people don't have the experience, or authority, to circumvent the established process, and those who were so empowered are no longer around.

The end result is that the exception process that used to take an extra few hours now takes the active involvement of key technical and support management personnel for perhaps several days to recover. During this time period, they are inefficient, frustrated, and not doing *their* primary jobs. Accomplishing the recovery takes an unacceptable amount of time, slows down the entire process, halts all other dependent processes, and impacts overall morale. The schedule is missed, and the risk management process has failed.

For years we have been unconsciously dependent on what has been an overnight recovery process that required a few hours of overtime by "someone" in one of our support groups. Now invoking that process can require more than a week's effort by our most critical people, who are forced to understand and reinvent a process they only knew by name a few days ago. This risk exposure also becomes more likely in areas with projects having long cycle times. There is also a greater probability of having less frequently used skills disappear over time in large project areas where there are large organizations supporting them. These skills may simply fade away, unnoticed until they are gone.

A Whole New Area of Risk

It was insidious, but over time an ever-increasing percentage of our normal workday has become consumed by recovery actions. These aren't exciting or even particularly unique activities; these are situations when someone gets ill or a machine needs scheduled or unscheduled maintenance. We unconsciously rely on and become dependent upon our support personnel to perform recovery actions for us. We do this so often that we typically consider their actions a part of the norm! "That's not a failure, not even an exception," we cry. "It was merely a hiccup!" We don't plan for these events, but somehow we take them into account when we schedule our workload. Not knowing what will go wrong, we unconsciously build the time into our schedule—but not enough that we have to justify the time or put that time into the manageable float. We usually aren't even aware of these exceptions. We expect a certain number of errors and build them and their recovery into our schedule. There has historically been no need to highlight them.

Until now! The support personnel who also handled these exceptions as a "normal" part of their workday may no longer be available, thereby creating a new exception category. The entire project is at risk due to inexperience, not by the key technical or planning personnel, but by the cornerstones of our process—the ever-reliable, dependable, helpful, frequently invisible, and therefore forgotten administrative and support personnel.

In trying to save us by downsizing to cut costs, management may have eroded our base of support personnel and created a stealth risk. We are suddenly at risk of having a whole new group of tasks and personnel on the critical path. We must recognize that fact and ask a whole new series of questions when creating our project plan in this new environment with its new challenges and risks.

In a downsized environment, project managers must now pay particular attention to support functions and not take them for granted. We must investigate and question what happens in the event of a process failure. We must ask what can go wrong and who will correct the problem. The cost to add these new investigations to the planning process is minimal, but the cost of ignoring them can be disastrous.

Alternatives to Downsizing

Rick Maurer

PM Network 41 (June 1999)

Market pressures force organizations to change rapidly. Given this unrelenting pace, leaders find they can no longer mull over decisions before taking action. Organizations must be nimble in considering and acting on changing needs in staffing. Leaders must ask:

- What mix of skills do we need today?
- What skills are we likely to need in the future?
- Do we have the right number of people employed today?
- How will these numbers change in the future?
- How do our staffing costs compare to others in our type of business?

These are difficult, but essential, questions. Those who fail to address them will be forced to react quickly when crises occur. Shoot-from-the-hip responses almost always result in a reduction in force. Research shows us that downsizing is a risky gamble, with less than half seeing improvements in productivity or revenue. And there are alternatives to consider.

Many of the alternatives rest on two important pillars:

1. *Share the Pain*. This seems to be a significant factor in the success of alternatives, according to researcher Wayne Cascio (1995). Sharing the pain means that no one—from executive to maintenance worker—is immune from the strategies for saving money.

2. *Strong Human Resource Initiatives*. The human resource department must be proactive in developing career assessment, training, placement opportunities, and creative wage and benefit packages.

Listed are thirteen alternatives to downsizing that either address long-term staffing needs or provide short-term expense reduction. Option 14—downsizing—is considered as another possible choice. Although I believe it is a bad choice for people and organizations, it is so much a part of corporate thinking these days that it must be considered along with the other options. Now, let's discuss the alternatives.

Long-Term Staffing Alternatives

1. Hiring Linked to Vision
The institution identifies what skills it will need in order to meet its vision and goals. During job interviews, human resources and department managers need to ask questions specifically related to the skills it will need now and in the future. This strategy helps assure the recruiting and hiring of people who can meet future challenges.

2. Cross-Training
By understanding the skill mix of staff today and linking it to the skills needed in the future, the organization allows individual employees to determine what they need to do in order to remain gainfully employed. It also gives the training department a clear mandate regarding the type of skills training they need to make available to staff.

In their excellent book, *Competing for the Future*, Prahalad and Hamel (1994) suggest that businesses identify their core competencies and build strategies based on these fundamental building blocks. This provides a foundation for the organization and employees to build a career-development process that matches what the organization needs.

3. Succession Planning
The institution needs to identify the types of management and technical skills it needs in various positions. Human resource should work with line managers to identify likely candidates so that they can begin preparing them for positions once they become vacant. Often, succession planning is left to chance. Baseball provides a good analogy for effective succession planning. With its arm systems, players move up from A to Double A to Triple A as their skills increase and as openings occur.

4. Redeployment Within the Organization
Redeployment can be linked to "alternative placement," but it seems to be used most often within the organization. Successful redeployment requires:
- A sophisticated career management process so that managers and employees are aware of open positions.

■ Career assessment and development activities that allow people to get ready for positions. One company linked individual career planning to corporate objectives so that people could see how their plans fit into overall direction. It allowed individuals who wished to remain within the company to make career development and placement decisions that increased their chances of succeeding.

5. Creating Value-Added and Revenue-Enhancing Opportunities

This is an employee buyout within the organization. A group of employees create a new business or line of service that the company can market. (3M is a leader in this form of entrepreneurship.) Of course, the company does not enter this agreement lightly. When Ford was about to sell the name, Mustang, to a foreign automaker, engineers asked Ford leadership for a chance to reintroduce a Ford version of the car. Leaders said that they would agree if the engineers could demonstrate that the car could be built to certain stringent quality specifications with a manufacturing time that rivaled their most efficient operations. On their own time, the engineers developed plans that met these requirements.

Cost-Saving Strategies

6. A Comprehensive Model

Automakers, as well as other industries in Japan, have adopted a series of steps they use as an alternative to downsizing. If the first step doesn't get the needed savings, they move to the next.

■ Compensation—Fifty percent of compensation is set, the other 50 percent is determined by profit or productivity measures.
■ Hours—Cut the number of hours.
■ Wages—Cut salaries.
■ Placement—Make arrangements with other employers who will agree to take displaced workers.

7. Reduced Hours

A policy is established that either places everyone in a particular job category on a flexible working arrangement or creates a flex-pool made up of volunteers from the department. The goal is to reduce the number of hours worked by each employee.

Job sharing is a variation of flextime and has been used successfully in many organizations. People divide a job between them, with each person receiving proportionate benefits.

8. Lower Wages

Wages are lowered in order to save money. Wage-reduction programs differ, but here are some typical elements:

- Everyone in the institution is part of the wage-reduction program.
- Executive compensation is reduced by the highest percentage, followed by middle management, with non-management staff suffering the smallest percentage of loss.
- This is usually a temporary program instituted to get through a downturn or until other reductions, such as attrition, can take place.

9. Attrition

Attrition, waiting for people to retire or leave on their own, can work in two ways: 1) Use natural attrition. Don't fill positions when people leave. This can work in an organization where turnover is sufficiently high to gain the savings quickly. 2) Offer voluntary early retirement or other packages to people within a certain category, such as a particular position for years of service. If this offer does not result in enough savings, it is extended to a broader pool.

10. Alternative Placement

Offer early retirement incentives to pension-eligible employees in a specific area. If that doesn't get a sufficient response, expand the pool, and so on. None of these options includes downsizing.

The organization makes arrangements with similar institutions or suppliers for placement. A variation of this occurred at AT&T: After the company said it would downsize, it ran ads letting other technology companies know that there were many talented men and women available for positions. Although AT&T was accused of using this as a public-relations gimmick, the tactic resulted in a significant number of requests for more information about potential candidates.

11. Leave of Absence

People are offered a leave of absence with full benefits for a specified period of time to help an organization weather a downturn. Although people are promised a job upon completion of the leave, it may not be the same job or at the same pay level. This alternative must be used as a temporary measure to help an organization through a crisis.

12. Employee Buyout

Some organizations have allowed employees to buy the operation that was slated for closing and set up their own business.

13. Shared Ownership

An alternative to wage cuts is concessions for equity—in other words, trading pay increases for pay cuts in return for company stock. This requires a high degree of employee participation in decision-making. Employee ownership seems to alter when people are owners in name only but are shut out of the decision-making process.

14. Downsizing

Downsizing means that the organization makes a decision to terminate people against their will. Although sometimes described as getting rid of dead wood, the sweep of downsizing is much broader. (If an organization really has so much dead wood, shouldn't those who allowed this condition to persist be the ones to go?)

There appears to be no good way to downsize. Studies indicate that in over half the cases, it does not meet its intended goals. And many companies find that they must rehire staff within a year. Morale and productivity often plummet. Among employees who remain after downsizing, more than half report increased stress. And the risk of violent behavior of people laid off is six times that of their employed counterparts. In a study of 531 large corporations, three-quarters reported having cut payrolls. Of the 85 percent that sought higher profits, only 46 percent saw any measurable increase; 58 percent sought higher productivity, but only 34 percent saw even a slight increase; 61 percent wanted an increase in customer service, but only 31 percent achieved it.

Considering the Alternatives

A series of questions must be considered when thinking about staffing. Answering them will require knowledge of the current situation, clear assumptions regarding the likely possible futures that face the organization, and an ability to speak candidly and listen carefully to the knowledge, thoughts, and opinions of other key decision-makers. These questions are divided into two parts: anticipating the future and exploring options. In anticipating the future, we need to ask:

- What's our vision for where we would like to be? Although conditions will certainly change and unexpected challenges will arise, leaders must have a clear picture of where they want to go.
- Do we have the skills to meet the vision? Often organizations find that they need to change dramatically in order to meet their visions. This requires an examination of the core competencies and skills as they relate to the vision.

Each of the alternatives should be considered separately, using the following questions. Asking these questions should help determine which mix of options is most suitable for the organization.

- Will this option help us move toward our vision? Some options are a quick fix; others are longer range. It is important to examine each as it relates to reaching the vision. The vision may suggest that you will need fewer staff, a different set of skills, or perhaps to even increase staff in some critical areas.

- Is this option consistent with our corporate values? Many organizations have developed a set of core values. When these are taken seriously, they influence all decision-making. Johnson & Johnson's handling of the Tylenol scare—removing all products until the cause of the contamination was discovered—is an example of how values influence decision-making.

- What are the short- and long-term financial costs of applying this option? Some options provide immediate short-term gain (such as downsizing), but studies indicate that for many the long-term benefits are never realized. It is important to look at both the short- and long-term implications of all alternatives.

- Will this option help us make a smooth transition from the current state to our vision? Change is never easy, but it is important to use options that provide clear steps for making the transition toward the vision.

- What impact will this option have on the people who must support us? An organization's reputation may be critical to its future success. For example, a healthcare institution's relationship with the community is based on trust. Staffing options that erode the belief that the institution is a part of the community may have an impact on the public's belief that it can receive good care. A hospital's reputation comes from quality of care and from the word on the street regarding the institution. Public perception may be important to your organization as well.

- What impact will this option have on morale, quality, and productivity? In order to realize the vision, most employees will need to support this option. When morale is low people lie low, unwilling to stick their necks out and take chances. Most organizations cannot afford to have a risk-averse group of employees.

- How will corporate headquarters react to this option? If your organization is one part of a larger corporate entity, then the values and practices of that parent company must be taken into account when considering staffing options. If your preferred staffing option runs counter to corporate practice, the leaders within your organization must determine if they are willing to attempt to influence headquarters to change their policy.

The final three questions are the most important. Now that you have looked at an option closely, ask:

- What are the major benefits of taking this approach?
- What are the major costs or risks in taking this approach?
- If my career were at stake, how would I react to this option? (Often this question is neglected, but addressing it can add a much-needed human dimension to the discussion. For example, while downsizing might sound fine for those folks over there, it may take on a very different flavor when we are the targets.)

Ideas for Getting Started

- Do your homework. The human resource department should explore organizations in your industry that have used the fourteen approaches/staffing options listed earlier. Find out what worked and what didn't. Human resources should prepare its findings in easy-to-skim documents so that executives can grasp the essence of these approaches quickly.
- Convene a meeting of senior management. Explain why this issue is critical. (Words like *survival* and *profitability* come to mind.) Go over the alternatives, and then ask executives to apply the questions listed earlier to the alternatives that hold the most appeal. Encourage them to consider each alternative as an ingredient in an omelet—one approach might be okay, but blending a few together might make a more appetizing meal.
- Get the staff involved. People want to be part of shaping their own futures. People are more committed to decisions they had a hand in making.

Members of a human resource department at Corning were asked to cut 30 percent of their costs and then finally to eliminate their entire unit. Everyone was involved in considering alternatives that affected their lives. Some chose to take severance packages, others asked for career training, and so forth. It was stressful and contentious at times, but everyone seemed to be adjusting well to the changes.

There are many ways of getting an entire organization excited and involved in changes. If you have an internal organization development professional, she should be able to design effective ways to meet this goal.

Experiment. If the organization is reluctant to try cross-training, for instance, try it out before you make it the law of the land. Pilot tests allow you to experiment, work out the glitches, and bail out if the idea doesn't work.

These are suggestions, but you know what works in your organization. Develop a strategy for engaging senior management (and then the rest of the organization) that fits your unique culture. But act now. Unless you are hidden away in some corner of the world that hasn't heard about global competition and the need for rapid change, you have no time to lose.

References

Cascio, Wayne. 1995. *Guide to Responsible Restructuring.* The U.S. Department of Labor.
Prahalad and Hamel. 1994. *Competing for the Future.* Harvard Business School Press.

Index

H

hiring   25, 107, 141–42, 291, 297

human resource(s)   xiii, 29, 70, 87–88, 132–33, 137, 139, 140–41, 199, 240, 267, 296–97, 302

I

IDPT   *See* Integrated Product Development Team(s)

influence   23, 34, 46, 50–51, 85, 100, 110, 124, 127–28, 138, 143, 162, 165, 242, 276, 279, 283, 301

influencing   49–50, 138, 165, 280–83

Integrated Product Development Team(s) (IPDT)   *See* team(s), Integrated Product Development

international   xiii, 16, 131, 133–34, 266–68, 270
   project manager   130–31
   team(s)   *See* team(s), international

K

kickoff   92, 149
   meeting   *See* meeting, kickoff

L

leadership   15, 18, 33, 35–37, 49, 60–61, 73, 80, 87, 92, 101, 161, 169, 173, 175, 182, 200, 246, 248, 273, 277, 279, 282, 298
   attributes   5
   project   *See* project, leadership
   qualities   xiii, 186

learning style   182–83, 187

M

meeting, kick-off   91–92, 149–50, 258–59

meeting, pre-kickoff   91–93

mentor   4, 185, 187–194

mentoring   xiii, 3–4, 17–18, 25, 184–88, 190–91, 194, 287–90

mentorship program   190–194

misuse   221–27, 229
   elements of misuse   224, 226, 229

motivation   19, 45, 63, 110, 112, 121, 140, 162–66, 212, 240–41

N

negotiation(s)   38–39, 41–48, 65, 73, 81–83, 96–97, 282–83

networking   63, 100

P

partnership(s)   23, 25, 68, 80, 101, 266

practice   8, 12, 29, 42, 46, 92, 117–18, 120–21, 127, 134, 172, 176, 185, 188–89, 195, 202–03, 301

pre-kickoff meeting   *See* meeting, pre-kickoff

project
   leadership   3–4, 18, 21–22, 30, 32, 63, 171, 179–80
   quality   208
   recovery   285–90
   review   68, 235–39
   schedule   82, 84, 127, 145, 147, 209, 261, 293
   scope   94–95, 106–07, 124, 126
   virtual   *See* virtual, project

Q

QFD   *See* quality function deployment (QFD)

quality   24, 35–36, 61–62, 64, 75, 78, 81, 89, 94–95, 97–98, 101, 112, 133–34, 147, 162, 174, 186, 199, 207–10, 239, 244–46, 273, 301
   control   83–84, 236
   project   *See* project, quality
   quality function deployment (QFD)   96, 122–128

R

real-time   165

recovery   286, 293–94
   project   *See* project, recovery

relationship   25, 38, 43, 47, 49, 52, 59–62, 67–68, 77–78, 82–86, 88–89, 95, 133–34, 154, 162, 164, 197, 216, 218, 255, 257, 263, 267, 269, 276, 301
   building   x, 64–65, 215
   client   90
   contractor   ix, 29
   customer   ix, 141
   interpersonal   53, 69, 112
   long-term   187, 209
   professional   43
   short-term   47, 184
   team   75, 220, 264

Upgrade Your Project Management Knowledge

with First-Class Publications from PMI

A Guide to the Project Management Body of Knowledge (PMBOK® Guide) – 2000 Edition

PMI's *PMBOK® Guide* has become *the* essential sourcebook for the project management profession and its de facto global standard, with over 700,000 copies in circulation worldwide. This new edition incorporates numerous recommendations and changes to the 1996 edition, including: progressive elaboration is given more emphasis; the role of the project office is acknowledged; the treatment of earned value is expanded in three chapters; the linkage between organizational strategy and project management is strengthened throughout; and the chapter on risk management has been rewritten with six processes instead of four. Newly added processes, tools, and techniques are aligned with the five project management processes and nine knowledge areas. For example, reserve time, variance analysis, and activity attributes are added to Chapter 6 (Project Time Management); estimating publications and earned value measurement are added to Chapter 7 (Project Cost Management); and project reports, project presentations, and project closure are added to Chapter 10 (Project Communications Management). This is one publication you'll want to have for quick reference both at work and at home.

ISBN: 1-880410-23-0 (paperback);
ISBN: 1-880410-22-2 (hardcover);
ISBN: 1-880410-25-7 (CD-ROM)

PMI Project Management Salary Survey – 2000 Edition

This 2000 Edition updates information first published in 1996 and expands coverage to over forty industry affiliations in nearly fifty countries in seven major geographic regions around the world. Its purpose is to establish normative compensation and ben-efits data for the project management profession on a global basis. The study provides salary, bonus/over-time, and deferred compensation information for specific job titles/positions within the project management profession. It also contains normative data for a comprehensive list of benefits and an array of other relevant parameters. *The PMI Project Management Salary Survey* – 2000 Edition is a vital new research tool for managers and HR professionals looking to retain or recruit employees, current members of the profession or those interested in joining it, researchers, and academics.

ISBN: 1-880410-26-5 (paperback)

Project Management for the Technical Professional

Michael Singer Dobson

Dobson, project management expert, popular seminar leader, and personality theorist, understands "promotion grief." He counsels those who prefer logical relationships to people skills and shows technical professionals how to successfully make the transition into management. This is a witty, supportive management primer for any "techie" invited to hop on the first rung of the corporate ladder. It includes self-assessment exercises; a skillful translation of general management theory and practice into tools, techniques, and systems that technical professionals will understand and accept; helpful "how to do it" sidebars; and action plans. It's also an insightful guide for those who manage technical professionals.

"The exercises and case studies featured here, along with the hands-on advice, hammer home fundamental principles. An intriguing complement to more traditional IT management guides, this is suitable for all libraries." —*Library Journal*

ISBN: 1-880410-76-1 (paperback)

The Project Surgeon: A Troubleshooter's Guide To Business Crisis Management

Boris Hornjak

A veteran of business recovery, project turnarounds and crisis prevention, Hornjak shares his "lessons learned" in this best practice primer for operational managers. He writes with a dual purpose—first for the practical manager thrust into a crisis situation with a mission to turn things around, make tough decisions under fire, address problems when they occur, and prevent them from happening again. Then his emphasis turns to crisis *prevention*, so you can free your best and brightest to focus on opportunities, instead of on troubleshooting problems, and ultimately break the failure/recovery cycle.

ISBN: 1-880410-75-3 (paperback)

Risk And Decision Analysis in Projects
Second Edition

John R. Schuyler

Schuyler, a consultant in project risk and economic decision analysis, helps project management professionals improve their decision-making skills and integrate them into daily problem solving. In this heavily illustrated second edition, he explains and demystifies key concepts and techniques, including expected value, optimal decision policy, decision trees, the value of information, Monte Carlo simulation, probabilistic techniques, modeling techniques, judgments and biases, utility and multi-criteria decisions, and stochastic variance.

ISBN: 1-880410-28-1 (paperback)

Earned Value Project Management
Second Edition

Quentin W. Fleming and Joel M. Koppelman

Now a classic treatment of the subject, this second edition updates this straightforward presentation of earned value as a useful method to measure actual project performance against planned costs and schedules throughout a project's life cycle. The authors describe the earned value concept in a simple manner so that it can be applied to any project, of any size, and in any industry. *Earned Value Project Management, Second Edition* may be the best-written, most easily understood project management book on the market today. Project managers will welcome this fresh translation of jargon into ordinary English. The authors have mastered a unique "early-warning" signal of impending cost problems in time for the project manager to react.

ISBN: 1880410-27-3 (paperback)

Project Management Experience and Knowledge Self-Assessment Manual

In 1999, PMI® completed a role delineation study for the Project Management Professional (PMP®) Certification Examination. A role delineation study identifies a profession's major performance domains (e.g., initiating the project or planning the project). It describes the tasks that are performed in each domain, and identifies the knowledge and skills that are required to complete the task. The role delineation task statements are presented in this manual in a format that enables you to assess how your project management experiences and training/education knowledge levels prepare you to complete each of the task statements. Individuals may use all of these tools to enhance understanding and application of PM knowledge to satisfy personal and professional career objectives. The self-assessment rating should not be used to predict, guarantee, or infer success or failure by individuals in their project management career, examinations, or related activities.

ISBN: 1-880410-24-9, (paperback)

Project Management Professional (PMP)
Role Delineation Study

In 1999, PMI® completed a role delineation study for the Project Management Professional (PMP®) Certification Examination. In addition to being used to establish the test specifications for the examination, the study describes the tasks (competencies) PMPs perform and the project management knowledge and skills PMPs use to complete each task. Each of the study's tasks is linked to a performance domain (e.g., planning the project). Each task has three components to it: what the task is, why the task is performed, and how the task is completed. The *Role Delineation Study* is an excellent resource for educators, trainers, administrators, practitioners, and individuals interested in pursuing PMP certification.

ISBN: 1-880410-29-X, (paperback)

PM 101 According to the Olde Curmudgeon

Francis M. Webster Jr.

Former editor-in-chief for PMI®, Francis M. Webster Jr. refers to himself as "the olde curmudgeon." The author, who has spent thirty years practicing, consulting on, writing about, and teaching project management, dispenses insider information to novice project managers with a friendly, arm-around-the-shoulder approach. He provides a history and description of all the components of modern project management; discusses the technical, administrative, and leadership skills needed by project managers; and details the basic knowledge and processes of project management, from scope management to work breakdown structure to project network diagrams. An excellent introduction for those interested in the profession themselves or in training others who are.

ISBN: 1-880410-55-9, (paperback)

The Project Sponsor Guide

Neil Love and Joan Brant-Love

This to-the-point and quick reading for today's busy executives and managers is a one-of-a-kind source that describes the unique and challenging support that executives and managers must provide to be effective sponsors of project teams. *The Project Sponsor Guide* is intended for executives and middle managers who will be, or are, sponsors of a project, particularly cross-functional projects. It is also helpful reading for facilitators and project leaders.

ISBN: 1-880410-15-X (paperback)

Don't Park Your Brain Outside: A Practical Guide to Improving Shareholder Value with SMART Management

Francis T. Hartman

Don't Park Your Brain Outside is the thinking person's guide to extraordinary project performance. Hartman has assembled a cohesive and balanced approach to highly effective project management. It is deceptively simple. Called SMART™, this new approach is Strategically Managed, Aligned, Regenerative, and Transitional. It is based on research and best practices, tempered by hard-won experience. SMART has saved significant time and money on the hundreds of large and small, simple and complex projects on which it has been tested. Are your projects SMART? Find out by reading this people-oriented project management book with an attitude!

ISBN: 1-880410-48-6 (hardcover)

The Enter*Prize* Organization: Organizing Software Projects for Accountability and Success

Neal Whitten

Neal Whitten is a twenty-three-year veteran of IBM and now president of his own consulting firm. Here he provides a practical guide to addressing a serious problem that has plagued the software industry since its beginning: how to effectively organize software projects to significantly increase their success rate. He proposes the "Enterprize Organization" as a model that takes advantage of the strengths of the functional organization, projectized organization, and matrix organization, while reducing or eliminating their weaknesses. The book collects the experiences and wisdom of thousands

of people and hundreds of projects, and reduces *lessons learned* to a simple format that can be applied immediately to your projects.

ISBN: 1-880410-79-6 (paperback)

Teaming for Quality

H. David Shuster

Shuster believes most attempts at corporate cultural change die because people fail to realize how addicted they are to the way things are, the root causes of their resistance to change, and the degree to which their willingness to change depends on the moral philosophy of management. His new book offers a stimulating synthesis of classical philosophy, metaphysics, behavioral science, management theory and processes, and two decades of personal teaming experience to explain how individuals can choose change for themselves. Its philosophy-to-practice approach will help people team in ways that promote exceptionally high levels of bonding, individual creative expression (innovation), and collective agreement (consensus). Shuster shows how personal work fulfillment and corporate goals *can* work in alignment.

ISBN: 1-880410-63-X (paperback)

Project Management Software Survey

The PMI® *Project Management Software Survey* offers an efficient way to compare and contrast the capabilities of a wide variety of project management tools. More than two hundred software tools are listed with comprehensive information on systems features; how they perform time analysis, resource analysis, cost analysis, performance analysis, and cost reporting; and how they handle multiple projects, project tracking, charting, and much more. The survey is a valuable tool to help narrow the field when selecting the best project management tools.

ISBN: 1-880410-52-4 (paperback)
ISBN: 1-880410-59-1 (CD-ROM)

The Juggler's Guide to Managing Multiple Projects

Michael S. Dobson

This comprehensive book introduces and explains task-oriented, independent, and interdependent levels of project portfolios. It says that you must first have a strong foundation in time management and priority setting, then introduces the concept of Portfolio Management to timeline multiple projects, determine their resource requirements, and handle emergencies, putting you in charge for possibly the first time in your life!

ISBN: 1-880410-65-6 (paperback)

Recipes for Project Success

Al DeLucia and Jackie DeLucia

This book is destined to become "the" reference book for beginning project managers, particularly those who like to cook! Practical, logically developed project management concepts are offered in easily understood terms in a lighthearted manner. They are applied to the everyday task of cooking—from simple, single dishes, such as homemade tomato sauce for pasta, made from the bottom up, to increasingly complex dishes or meals for groups that in turn require an understanding of more complex project management terms and techniques. The transition between cooking and project management discussions is smooth, and tidbits of information provided with the recipes are interesting and humorous.

ISBN: 1-880410-58-3 (paperback)

Tools and Tips for Today's Project Manager

Ralph L. Kliem and Irwin S. Ludin

This guidebook is valuable for understanding project management and performing to quality standards. Includes project management concepts and terms—old and new—that are not only defined but also are explained in much greater detail than you would find in a typical glossary. Also included are tips on handling such seemingly simple everyday tasks as how to say "No" and how to avoid telephone tag. It's a reference you'll want to keep close at hand.

ISBN: 1-880410-61-3 (paperback)

The Future of Project Management

Developed by the 1998 PMI® Research Program Team and the futurist consultant firm of Coates and Jarratt, Inc., this guide to the future describes one hundred national and global trends and their implications for project management, both as a recognized profession and as a general management tool. It covers everything from knowbots, nanotechnology, and disintermediation to changing demography, information technology, social values, design, and markets.

ISBN: 1-880410-71-0 (paperback)

New Resources for PMP® Candidates

The following publications are resources that certification candidates can use to gain information on project management theory, principles, techniques, and procedures.

PMP Resource Package

Doing Business Internationally: The Guide to Cross-Cultural Success
by Terence Brake, Danielle Walker, and Thomas Walker

Earned Value Project Management, Second Edition
by Quentin W. Fleming and Joel M. Koppelman

Effective Project Management: How to Plan, Manage, and Deliver Projects on Time and Within Budget
by Robert K. Wysocki, et al.

A Guide to the Project Management Body of Knowledge (PMBOK® Guide) – 2000 Edition
by the Project Management Institute

Global Literacies: Lessons on Business Leadership and National Cultures
by Robert Rosen (Editor), Patricia Digh, and Carl Phillips

Human Resource Skills for the Project Manager
by Vijay K. Verma

The New Project Management
by J. Davidson Frame

Principles of Project Management
by John Adams, et al.

Project & Program Risk Management
by R. Max Wideman, Editor

Project Management Experience and Knowledge Self-Assessment Manual
by Project Management Institute

Project Management: A Managerial Approach, Fourth Edition
by Jack R. Meredith and Samuel J. Mantel Jr.

Project Management: A Systems Approach to Planning, Scheduling, and Controlling, Seventh Edition
by Harold Kerzner

A Guide to the Project Management Body of Knowledge (PMBOK® Guide) – 1996 Edition

The basic reference for everyone who works in project management. Serves as a tool for learning about the generally accepted knowledge and practices of the profession. As "management by projects" becomes more and more a recommended business practice worldwide, the *PMBOK® Guide* becomes an essential source of information that should be on every manager's bookshelf. The *PMBOK® Guide* is an official standards document of the Project Management Institute and will continue to serve as one of the reference documents for the Project Management Professional (PMP®) Certification Examination through 2001, after which the 2000 Edition will be used.

ISBN: 1-880410-12-5 (paperback),
ISBN: 1-880410-13-3 (hardcover)

PMBOK Q&A

Use this handy pocket-sized, question-and-answer study guide to learn more about the key themes and concepts presented in PMI's international standard, *PMBOK® Guide*. More than 160 multiple-choice questions with answers (referenced to the *PMBOK® Guide*—1996 Edition) help you with the breadth of knowledge needed to understand key project management concepts.

ISBN: 1-880410-21-4 (paperback)

Also Available From PMI

Project Management for Managers
Mihály Görög, Nigel J. Smith
ISBN: 1-880410-54-0 (paperback)

Project Leadership: From Theory to Practice
Jeffery K. Pinto, Peg Thoms, Jeffrey Trailer, Todd Palmer,
Michele Govekar
ISBN: 1-880410-10-9 (paperback)

Annotated Bibliography of Project and Team Management
David I. Cleland, Gary Rafe, Jeffrey Mosher
ISBN: 1-880410-47-8 (paperback) ISBN: 1-880410-57-5
(CD-ROM)

How to Turn Computer Problems into Competitive Advantage
Tom Ingram
ISBN: 1-880410-08-7 (paperback)

Achieving the Promise of Information Technology
Ralph B. Sackman
ISBN: 1-880410-03-6 (paperback)

Leadership Skills for Project Managers, Editors'
Choice Series
Edited by Jeffrey K. Pinto, Jeffrey W. Trailer
ISBN: 1-880410-49-4 (paperback)

The Virtual Edge
Margery Mayer
ISBN: 1-880410-16-8 (paperback)

The ABCs of DPC
Edited by PMI's Design-Procurement-Construction Specific
Interest Group
ISBN: 1-880410-07-9 (paperback)

Project Management Casebook
Edited by David I. Cleland, Karen M. Bursic, Richard Puerzer,
A. Yaroslav Vlasak
ISBN: 1-880410-45-1 (paperback)

Project Management Casebook, Instructor's Manual
Edited by David I. Cleland, Karen M. Bursic, Richard Puerzer,
A. Yaroslav Vlasak
ISBN: 1-880410-18-4 (paperback)

The PMI Book of Project Management Forms
ISBN: 1-880410-31-1 (paperback)
ISBN: 1-880410-50-8 (diskette)

Principles of Project Management
John Adams et al.
ISBN: 1-880410-30-3 (paperback)

Organizing Projects for Success
Human Aspects of Project Management Series, Volume One
Vijay K. Verma
ISBN: 1-880410-40-0 (paperback)

Human Resource Skills for the Project Manager
Human Aspects of Project Management Series, Volume Two
Vijay K. Verma
ISBN: 1-880410-41-9 (paperback)

Managing the Project Team
Human Aspects of Project Management Series, Volume Three
Vijay K. Verma
ISBN: 1-880410-42-7 (paperback)

Value Management Practice
Michel Thiry
ISBN: 1-880410-14-1 (paperback)

The World's Greatest Project
Russell W. Darnall
ISBN: 1-880410-46-X (paperback)

Power & Politics in Project Management
Jeffrey K. Pinto
ISBN: 1-880410-43-5 (paperback)

Best Practices of Project Management Groups in Large Functional Organizations
Frank Toney, Ray Powers
ISBN: 1 880410 05 2 (papcrback)

Project Management in Russia
Vladimir I. Voropajev
ISBN: 1-880410-02-8 (paperback)

A Framework for Project and Program Management Integration
R. Max Wideman
ISBN: 1-880410-01-X (paperback)

Quality Management for Projects & Programs
Lewis R. Ireland
ISBN: 1-880410-11-7 (paperback)

Project & Program Risk Management
Edited by R. Max Wideman
ISBN: 1-880410-06-0 (paperback)

The PMI Project Management Fact Book
ISBN: 1-880410-62-1 (paperback)

A Framework for Project Management
ISBN: 1-880410-82-6, Facilitator's Manual Set (3-ring binder)
ISBN: 1-880410-80-X, Participants' Manual Set, (paperback)

Order online at www.pmibookstore.org

Book Ordering Information
Phone: +412.741.6206
Fax: +412.741.0609
Email: pmiorders@abdintl.com

Mail: PMI Publications Fulfillment Center, PO Box 1020, Sewickley, Pennsylvania 15143-1020 USA